POWER
in
World Politics

POWER
in
World Politics

edited by
Richard J. Stoll
Michael D. Ward

Lynne Rienner Publishers • Boulder & London

Published in the United States of America in 1989 by
Lynne Rienner Publishers, Inc.
1800 30th Street, Boulder, Colorado 80301

Published in the United Kingdom by
Lynne Rienner Publishers, Inc.
3 Henrietta Street, Covent Garden, London WC2E 8LU

Library of Congress Cataloging-in-Publication Data

Power in world politics/edited by Richard J. Stoll and Michael D.
  Ward.
   Bibliography: p.
   Includes index.
   ISBN 1-55587-125-9 (alk. paper)
   1. Balance of power. 2. International relations. 3. World
politics—1945– I. Stoll, Richard J. II. Ward, Michael Don, 1948–

JX1318.P685 1989   88–28337
327.1'1—dc19   CIP

British Library Cataloguing in Publication Data
A Cataloguing in Publication record for this book
is available from the British Library.

Printed and bound in the United States of America

The paper used in this publication meets the requirements of
the American National Standard for Permanence of Paper for
Printed Library Materials Z39.48–1984.

Contents

Acknowledgments

Wanda Jean Umbriet of the Institute of Behavioral Science has been especially helpful in providing support as this project moved from conception to fruition, as has the staff of Lynne Rienner Publishers.

We would also like to thank "BITNET" for providing an excellent low-cost way of facilitating long-distance collaboration.

Richard J. Stoll
Michael D. Ward

Contributors

Marina Arbetman
Department of Political Science
Vanderbilt University
Box 40, Station B
Nashville, TN 37235

Bruce Bueno de Mesquita
Hoover Institution
Stanford University
Stanford, CA 94305–6010

James A. Caporaso
Department of Political Science
University of Washington
Seattle, WA 98195

Thomas R. Cusack
IIVG/GE
Steinplatz 2
D-1000 Berlin
West Germany

William K. Domke
Lawrence Livermore National
    Laboratory
University of California
P.O. Box 808
Livermore, California 94550

Stephan Haggard
Center for International Affairs
Harvard University
Cambridge, MA 02138

Gretchen Hower
Merriam Laboratory
Department of Political Science
University of Illinois at Urbana
512 East Chalmers Street
Champaign, IL 61820

Jacek Kugler
Department of Political Science
Vanderbilt University
Box 40, Station B
Nashville, TN 37235

David Lalman
Department of Government and
    Politics
University of Maryland
College Park, MD

Richard L. Merritt
Merriam Laboratory
Department of Political Science
University of Illinois at Urbana
512 East Chalmers Street
Champaign, IL 61820

T. Clifton Morgan
Department of Political Science
Rice University
Box 1892
Houston, TX 77251

Paul R. Pudaite
Merriam Laboratory
Department of Political Science
University of Illinois at Urbana
512 East Chalmers Street
Champaign, IL 61820

James Lee Ray
Department of Political Science
Florida State University
Tallahassee, FL 32306

Richard J. Stoll
Department of Political Science
Rice University
Box 1892
Houston, TX 77251

Charles S. Taber
Merriam Laboratory
Department of Political Science
University of Illinois at Urbana
512 East Chalmers Street
Champaign, IL 61820

Michael D. Ward
Institute of Behavioral Science
University of Colorado, Boulder
Box 487
Boulder, CO 80309-0487

Dina A. Zinnes
Merriam Laboratory
Department of Political Science
University of Illinois at Urbana
512 East Chalmers Street
Champaign, IL 61820

1

Grist for the Mill

Richard J. Stoll and Michael D. Ward

The Concepts of Power

Although some may disagree, we believe that the majority of the field would support the assertion that power is the most central concept in world politics. The study of power is never far away; at times the field may move off and award another concept "pride of place," but we are always drawn back to placing power in the center of our research. This book is not an exception. As historical and scholarly concerns shift once again toward an assertion of the centrality of power in world politics, it seemed important to update our scholarly assessments of this concept. After approximately two decades, both the popular press and the scholarly one are recentering their evaluations of world politics toward assessments of the relative power that contemporary nations hold vis-à-vis one another. Not only is the "balance" being reintroduced into international affairs, but also the "rise and decline" of the superpowers, primarily in economic and political terms, has captivated observers of both "high" and "low" politics. Whether founded on the economic reforms of the Chinese, the economic prowess of the "four dragons" (Japan, Taiwan, Singapore, and South Korea), the decline of so-called U.S. hegemony in the world system, or the maturation of society in the Soviet Union, it is clear to many that trusted ways of thinking about power relations on the globe may no longer be adequate.

While many world politics scholars can agree that power is an important concept, there is less unity as to the definition of the term. Disagreements about its meaning have undoubtedly contributed to the difficulty of achieving a generally recognized measurement; what satisfied one researcher as a gauge of power is considered inadequate by another. To begin our discussion on power, we offer a taxonomy used by K.J. Holsti (1983, p. 164–168). He breaks the concept of power into three elements: capabilities, acts, and responses.

1

Capabilities are resources (human, material, etc.) that can be used by one to influence another. Acts are the processes and relationships with which an actor intends to influence another. Responses are the actions of the target of the influence attempt. Thus, to say a state is powerful may mean that (1) the state has a large amount of resources for use in influence attempts; (2) the state is undertaking a large number of actions to influence other actors; (3) targets respond in a manner consistent with desires of the state making the influence attempt.

The early 1970s brought with it an awakening to the realization that military power and dominance were no longer the most accurate yardsticks with which to judge how nations were able to effect beneficial outcomes in foreign affairs. The dependency and interdependence approaches both underscored this fact of modern life, a fact that has been rediscovered many times in the course of history. As the interdependencies among the major players in world politics grew more dense and more complex, those players learned how to use these interdependencies to benefit. And as the so-called Third World emerged as more politically and economically shrewd and productive than even the most optimistic "development theorists" might have envisioned, the international reorganizations that followed the economic and political crises in the 1970s, primarily the oil *crises* engineered by OPEC, led to a vastly changed distribution of power resources around the world. So too did the rapid growth of the four dragons (and others), as well as the steady progress made by the Soviet economy. In short, not only was the global distribution of resources and material capabilities altered, but so too were the acts and responses that comprise the ebb and flow of international politics.

Given the changing global political environment in which the differential power of nations is undergoing marked change, and given the changing nature of our conceptions of the importance of *military*, *economic*, and *political* power, we believe a volume elaborating and highlighting these concerns has considerable scholarly value. Thus, our purpose has been to present a variety of chapters which focus on this complex of ideas about world politics. Despite their diversity, the chapters of this volume share two common elements. The first is substantive: all the chapters focus on power in world politics. The second is methodological: each uses a scientific approach to study power. We believe that, both separately and collectively, these contributions push forward our understanding of power in world politics.

Power and World Views: Who's on First?

There is a long history of power measurement in world politics, both from the academic and policymaking perspective. In the post-World War II era, power measurement is most closely associated with the realist school (Morganthau, various editions), which views politics as a "struggle for power." But the concept of power (and therefore the need to measure it) is important in other world views as well.

In the early 1970s, in the wake of the OPEC oil embargo, a number of scholars turned to the concept of interdependence to examine the key relationships between states (Keohane and Nye, 1977). But while theorists of interdependence argue against viewing power as unidimensional and force oriented, it is still an important concept in their world. However, they argue that in an interdependent world, there are a number of issue arenas in which states (and other actors) compete, and that the resources necessary to exercise power change with the issue. But power is still the key to influence.

Power also figures prominently in the work of dependency theorists. Their view of the world contains centers and peripheries, with the centers exercising a tremendous amount of influence over the periphery. But it is the power of the centers which allows them to achieve their dominance over the peripheries.

In short, the concept of power plays a central and necessary role, not only in the theorizing of the realists, but also of those who see the world through the lens of interdependence and of dependency. While this does not mean that a single approach to power (or measurement of it) has universal applicability—far from it—it does mean that power is of great importance to scholars using a wide variety of approaches to the study of world politics.

The Scientific Study of Power in World Politics

Power has also been central to the scientific study of world politics, and the problems of its study have created tremendous difficulties for scholars using this approach. The measurement of power was especially difficult for early generations of scientific scholars of world politics. Since there was no universally shared world view, the definitional debates of the traditional scholars carried over into this new method in inquiry. But the nature of the scientific approach itself posed additional difficulties.

A commitment to the scientific approach is a commitment to concrete conceptualization. It is not acceptable to say that power is complicated, or illusive, or incapable of precise definition. A scientific researcher can acknowledge difficulties because of these factors but must nevertheless proceed ahead. In the mid-1960s, with few explicit guideposts, pushing forward was not only arduous but destined to create additional disagreements, as different scholars followed different routes to meet the criteria of good scientific scholarship.

Empirical scientific studies faced an additional set of difficulties. Testing theories, models, and hypotheses required data, and to use the words of a first generation scientific scholar, these data had to be made (Singer, 1966). Even when dealing with the measurement of capabilities, and starting with available information from governments, organizations, and some private publications, much work had to be done. Developing a data set covering a set of countries over a span of time could (and did) take years.

The results of these early efforts may seem crude by today's standards. Studies that went beyond conceptualization or datamaking often moved only to conduct some simple tests of basic propositions—"brush clearing" as it was often called. But through these efforts, the scientific study of world politics advanced, and the works in this volume owe a debt to those early scholars.

The Contributions

We have divided the contributions to this book into three categories.

The first part addresses *the state of the art*. It includes four chapters in which one or more capability-based measures of power are assessed. In some cases, authors have used indicators they have developed, and in others, a measures developed by another author is presented.

The second part contains chapters that undertake a more conceptual analysis of power. These contributions shift from a focus on specific indicators, to placing power in a theoretical context, and toward evaluating what is needed in that context.

The third part contains chapters describing a theoretical or empirical investigation in which power plays a key role. Thus, both the concept and indicators of power are taken as givens, and the focus of these chapters is using power as a central part of an investigation.

Assessing Measures of Power

The first chapter in part 1 is by Richard L. Merritt and Dina A. Zinnes. They compare a series of power measures developed by others. These measures span the gamut from indicators based on a few components combined in a simple fashion, to those that contain a number of components, combined in a complicated fashion. The thrust of their inquiry is the degree of difference in state rankings across the variety of indicators.

Charles S. Taber penned the second contribution. It is a logical follow-up to Merritt and Zinnes. Using basically the same set of indicators, Taber's concern is the measurement of power of the so-called less developed countries (LDCs). In particular, he investigates whether the set of indicators rank LDCs with the same degree of precision as developed countries.

Jacek Kugler and Martina Arbetman offer a chapter that also discusses several measures of power. Relying primarily on the major powers from 1850 to 1980, they compare the Correlates of War Project capability measure, with GNP, and GNP adjusted for relative political capacity (a measure Kugler developed previously with Organski). Their concern is not only the evaluation of these indicators, but also whether military capability and nuclear weapons play a key role in differentiating measures of power. These factors are very relevant to the nature of power in the post-World War II era and have consequences for the degree of difference between today's world and that of the prenuclear era.

The final chapter in the first part is by Paul R. Pudaite and Gretchen Hower. The primary purpose of their effort is to introduce a more rigorous method of indicator construction, which allows for the development of an explicit interpretive model for a theory. To illustrate the benefits of their approach, they rework a portion of Bueno de Mesquita's work on expected utility theory and international conflict.

Reconceptualizing Power in World Politics

James A. Caporaso and Stephan Haggard provide a chapter that carefully and critically examines the role of power in the international political economy nexus. This focuses on the role of agency and structure in power relations.

Michael D. Ward's chapter extends his previous work (with Lewis L. House) using behavioral power. Here, he introduces the concept of net power, a combination of behavior power and national capabilities. Using both the superpower dyad and Egypt–Israel, he compares net power to the COW Project power capability measure. As with Kugler and Arbetman, the main concern of Ward is the nature of power in the modern world and the continuities and discontinuities of the concept of power in the earlier era.

The next chapter in the part is by Richard J. Stoll. His focus is on the major powers. Using several measures of power capability, he asks several questions from the perspective of several world views. First, with these measures, is power unidimensional or multidimensional at specific points in time from 1850 to 1980? Second, do states designated as major powers appear at the top of the power rankings? As you can see, the theme of the continuity of the concept and measurement of power across different historical eras is very prominent in this section.

William Domke's chapter, like several others in this volume, is concerned with developing a valid measure of power. His methodology is the same as that used by Kugler and Arbetman. But Domke's focus is on the

19th century. Specifically, he first evaluates a set of individual power indicators for twenty-eight states in the year 1890. He then goes on to measure the political capacity of these states, and to use this measure to weight GNP data for a more valid indicator of national power.

Assessing the Role

The first chapter in this part is by Bruce Bueno de Mesquita and David Lalman. Building on their previous work, they investigate the escalation of disputes to war among European states from 1816 to 1965. They compare predictions from expected utility theory, balance of power theory, and hegemony theory. Power is a central concept in each of these theories.

The chapter by T. Clifton Morgan and James Lee Ray, also uses formal theory to develop and test a model concerned in part with power. Employing a bargaining framework, they investigate the effect of possession of nuclear weapons on the escalation of disputes to war. Their study sheds light on whether we must consider the possession of nuclear weapons as a separate and distinct element of a state's power, or whether these weapons merely duplicate other aspects of power (this is also part of Kugler's contribution to this volume).

Thomas R. Cusack's piece is a theoretical investigation. Using a computer simulation, he investigates three sets of rules for power management by states. He studies the impact of these rules on the survival of states and of the system in a multistate form. This serves to draw our attention to the long-term consequences of commonly made assumptions about decisionmaking by states.

Conclusion

What will the reader learn from these chapters? Perhaps most importantly that the study of power is alive and well in the study of world politics. To reiterate a point made earlier, the study of world politics does not stray far from the study of power. All the contributors to this book place power at the center of their inquiry. But beyond this, there are several more specific lessons to be learned from this collection.

First, despite very different views in world politics of how states interact, and how to measure power, there are more communalities across these perspectives than one would think. States commonly considered to be major powers emerge at the top of power capability rankings. Nuclear weapons may have less of an impact on state behavior than is commonly assumed. Even more intriguing, there are strong similarities in rankings of contemporary and historical nations across different capability-based measures of power.

Second, as the study of world politics turns more to the study of the less developed countries, strong cautions are in order. The problems of power measurement and indicator construction are far greater for these states than for developed states.

Third, creative procedures for indicator construction can aid our research. These procedures can allow us to integrate aspects of power that are usually considered to be intangible. They can also improve the rigor of our tests. We can even find ways to deduce the long-term consequences of a set of assumptions in a careful and thorough fashion.

Importantly, the essays in this volume point to the complexities of understanding power relations in the contemporary world and suggest that it is not necessary to give ground in face of those complexities. Systematic, theoretically oriented study of power in world politics is not only possible, but it exists and is informative as well.

Finally, when we turn to the empirical evaluation of models, we should compare substantive models to each other, rather than pick one model and compare it against a null model. Such composite tests shed more light than the traditional single-model tests.

Whither Power?

Beyond asserting that power has not withered in its centrality in world politics, we hope the reader will entertain here some brief comments on where we think the study of power in world politics should go in the near future.

1. Despite the impressive progress that has been made, we need to devote more effort to power measurement. This measurement must be based on an underlying theory of what power is and how it affects world politics. Particular attention should be given to the difficult problems of LDC power measurement. These theories will not be singular, nor should we expect that our measurement efforts will be monolithic.

2. We foresee work that places power in more sophisticated frameworks. For example, consider the recent work of Kennedy (1987). Although his work was predated by political scientists such as Charles Doran and Wes Parsons (1980), A.F.K. Organski and J. Kugler (1980), and Karen A. Rasler and William R. Thompson (1983), it should still serve as a stimulus for additional work, retaining state power as an important factor but exercising its impact in a complex environment.

3. Despite Holsti's tripartite conceptualization of power, much more work is needed to elaborate and unfold the action and response categories. We have pretty firm and robust ideas, as a discipline, about what the resources of power in world politics are. In addition, we are beginning to discover how some of those resources are extracted. But we are just beginning to scratch the surface of how they are utilized to produce beneficent outcomes. How is power applied to *get one's way?* William H. Riker's (1986) essays may point to some answers to this kind of question, and certain aspects of strategic (meta) game theory might offer clues, but as yet we are unable to provide an answer to this perplexing and important question.

To conclude, the study of power has always been central to the study of world politics. The selections in this volume indicate that this will remain true for the foreseeable future. This is apparent not only because we have come so far but also because so much remains to be done.

1

Assessing Measures of Power

2

Alternative Indexes of National Power

Richard L. Merritt and Dina A. Zinnes

In 1513, when Niccolo Machiavelli penned his chapter in *The Prince* entitled "How the Power of Every Principality Should Be Measured," he concerned himself, much as his predecessors and contemporaries did, with military personnel, resources, leadership, strategy, and popular as well as military morale. This makes sense. After all, if a state wishes to influence its neighbors or is about to become embroiled in war, its leaders want to know what the enemy's capabilities are and to compare the latter with their own. Implicit in such calculations is the assumption that the balance of capabilities between two states is a good predictor of their relative influence. The analytic task then is to develop appropriate measures of capabilities.

From such calculations it is tempting to seek indicators of power status in the overall comity of nation-states, to generalize about national power. The concern shifts from the specific question of how state X might fare in a confrontation with state Y to the broader question of rank ordering nation-states with respect to all applications of power, peaceful as well as warlike.

The search for the key variables underlying "power" together with their appropriate indicators can be traced as far back as the 1700s, when a veritable industry arose to gather and publish "statistics" on the characteristics and capabilities of nation-states. Beginning with a concern for the balance of military forces, the factors taken into account expanded to include other elements. A leading international relations textbook of the postwar era by Hans Morgenthau (1948) considered the "elements of national power" to include geography, natural resources (food, raw materials), industrial capacity, military preparedness (technology, leadership, quantity and quality of armed forces), population (distribution, trends), national character, national morale (including the quality of society and government as decisive factors), and quality of diplomacy; a half-dozen years later Morgenthau (1954) added quality of government (with its attendant problems of balance between resources and policy, balance among resources, and popular support).

As the concern for power in specific confrontations widened to a concern for power more generally, the set of potentially relevant variables increased. And with the increase in variables came the problem of index construction. Even leaving aside the problem of reducing variables to common scales, the question of how appropriately to combine variables became a troublesome, not easily solvable, problem. The validity issue underlying the assessment of a nation-state's power became double-barreled: What variables should be included and how should those variables be combined?

In the decades following World War II a number of different answers were posed about the question of appropriate indexes of power. Since the face validity of each index is well documented by its creator, the general analyst is left with a confounding embarrassment of riches. Which index is "best"? In part the answer to such a question requires a further specification: Best for what? This is a rather deep theoretical question, one that raises important issues concerning the match between theory and concept measurement.[1]

Another approach is to ignore the question of which index is "best" and to ask instead: Is there any difference among the results found by various indexes? This is the central concern of this chapter. Our task is threefold: first, to summarize the more prominent indexes of power that researchers have proposed, highlighting both similarities and differences; second, to compare the empirical consequences of these alternative approaches; and third, to explore the implications of these findings. In this chapter we intend neither to explicate the various definitions given to the term power nor to argue for any particular definition. For our purposes we are comfortable with the notion of power suggested by such classic writers as Robert A. Dahl (1957), John C. Harsanyi (1962), or Karl W. Deutsch (1963): how probable it is that X can exert d amount of influence over Y with respect to issue g.

From National Capabilities to National Power

How have analysts used data-based approaches to determine the relative power of nation-states? In the following pages we review some of the indexes that have captured the attention of international relations scholars.

Most systematic efforts to compare the capabilities of two or more nation-states rely on aggregate data. Such data describe the characteristics of an entire population or aggregate of individuals: the size of the population, ratio of men to women, their racial or ethnic composition, military and social expenditures, size of the armed forces, and so on. Generally speaking, such data are of two kinds. Sometimes aggregate data are *summational*. They add up the total of individual events or behaviors, for example, the numbers of babies born in a country, people who marry, or those who die constitute, respectively, that country's birth, marriage, and death rates.

In other circumstances, however, the whole is not the sum of its parts, but rather more or less than the sum. "To count the percentage of authoritarian persons, or to ascertain the proportion of individuals who come close to a particular notion of a 'democratic, civic culture' in their opinions" does not necessarily say whether or not the society as a whole is democratic (Scheuch, 1966, p. 159). It is quite possible to imagine a society democratic in its orientation that contains large numbers of people whose personalities have a bent toward authoritarianism, or a democratic population that accepts or has accommodated itself to a dictatorial regime. This second category of aggregate data consists of what Raymond B. Cattell and his associates (Cattell et al., 1951, p. 408) call *syntality* variables, that is, "characteristics of the group when acting as a group, e.g., its aggressiveness, its support of artistic productions."

Most of the indexes that have been developed to measure power are summational. Although several major indexes combine summational and syntality variables, there are to our knowledge no power indexes based solely on Cattell's syntality variables. This is undoubtedly due to measurement difficulties: aggregate measures pose significant reliability problems, but the reliability issues associated with syntality measures are manifoldly more severe.

Single-Variable Indicators of Power

Recognizing the complexity of the concept of national power, observers of international relations have sought to approximate it by means of a shortcut: a single aggregate variable. Those interested in capabilities immediately available for the conduct of war generally rely on military personnel or military expenditures. Thus, Norman Z. Alcock and Alan G. Newcombe (1970, p. 339) list as one of their four indexes of national power Emile Benoit's (1968) data on "military expenditures . . . in millions of purchasing-power-equivalent dollars."[2]

Others, concerned more with long-term capabilities (e.g., Knorr, 1956), point to economic indicators as the best candidate. National income is the most frequent of these. The demographer Kingsley Davis (1954, p. 208) terms national income "perhaps the best" index of national power, since it "expresses the grand result of all the productive forces of a nation's command." A. F. K. Organski (1958, p. 436) also, after listing three determinants of power (size of the nation-state's population, skill and efficiency of its government, and level of economic development) turns to national income as "the best index of power available." Bruce M. Russett (1968a), by contrast, after exploring a number of variables concludes that total consumption of fuel and electric energy could best indicate this elusive concept.

Single-variable indicators have the advantage of simplicity and widespread availability. Those who favor them usually argue that multivariate data sets are unnecessary and complex mathematical manipulations are not needed. This advantage nevertheless extracts a price. Critics have had a field day attacking single-variable indicators for their lack of "realism." A high national income (or national income per capita) can imply a country's long-term ability to influence others, but not if it means that the population is less willing and even less able than others to engage in activities such as wars that might jeopardize its high standard of living. A healthy, skilled population may be a capability; an equally large but disease-ridden and illiterate population can diminish a government's capacities. Generals never tire of telling us that even the best-equipped army is ineffective without good leadership and high morale. Is energy used to drive television sets and compact-disk players equivalent to energy used for industrial production? Without strong evidence that a single-variable indicator predicts (or postdicts) relevant outcomes, it is difficult to answer the complaints of "realists" who point to a more complex world than any single indicator suggests.

Multivariate Indexes of Power

Knorr: War potential of nations. The first significant multivariate approach to national power in quantitative terms came with Klaus Knorr's (1956) investigation of national war potential. By the term "war potential" Knorr means a nation-state's "potential military power" (p. 41), that is, "the capacity of nations to provide quantities of military manpower and supplies in the event of war" (p. 41). This rests on economic capacity, administrative competence, and motivation for war. Knorr provides a checklist of factors—both summational and syntality variables—which brought to the literature of strategic studies a significant new orientation. While stressing caution on the issue of measurement—"precise measurement and comparison are impossible at our present state of knowledge"—he nevertheless urges researchers and policymakers to work toward improving instruments for generating relevant data, to narrow "the area of uncertainty and the margin of error" in estimating qualitative determinants of military potential, and to develop "fairly accurate indices" of its quantitative determinants (pp. 48–49). "It should be possible," Knorr concludes (p. 50), "to improve such measuring techniques and thereby discipline the element of guesswork on which any over-all estimate must in part, and often in large part, rest."

Although Knorr indicates that multiple factors must be considered in assessing a nation-state's power, he does not tell us how those factors should be combined. Like Knorr, subsequent researchers have identified sets of factors but have gone on to suggest ways in which these attributes interact to produce power. While the sets of indicators identified by these analysts overlap, though they are by no means identical, the functional rules used to combine the variables are different.

Alcock and Newcombe: Perceptions of national power. A straightforward *linear* index is provided by Alcock and Newcombe (1970). Primarily interested in popular perceptions of national power, they also developed two multivariate indicators to ascertain the validity of perceptions.[3] They begin with regression analyses using the variable loading highest on each of the three largest orthogonal factors found in Russett's (1968c) factor analysis of the Yale Data Program's findings: (1) gross national product per capita, (2) population, and (3) population density. The data comprising these summational variables are then apparently converted into rank orders (to make them more comparable) and the rankings used to obtain logarithms and standard scores which are then fed into regression equations.

Using different sets of independent variables, Alcock and Newcombe provide three regression equations, the latter two of which they consider promising for assessments of *relative power*:

$$\text{Relative power} = -16.1 + 0.69 \text{ population} + 0.49 \text{ GNP/cap}$$
$$+ 0.08 \text{ area/cap}; \tag{1}$$
$$\text{Relative power} = -8.85 + 0.67 \text{ population} + 0.47 \text{ GNP/cap}; \tag{2}$$
$$\text{Relative power} = 9.4 - 0.09 \text{ population} + 0.93 \text{ GNP}. \tag{3}$$

Equation (1) can be eliminated as inefficient: it contains a variable (area/cap) that adds little to the predictive capacity of the regression equation. "Equation (2) involves reanalyzing the data after the least important item, the one with the smallest coefficient, has been dropped" (p. 338). For the sake of convenience we refer to Equation (2) as emphasizing *size*, with "population" as its highest coefficient, and Equation (3) as *income*, with gross national product as its highest component.

Singer: Correlates of war. A simple linear index composed of summational variables was formulated within the context of J. David Singer's Correlates of War Project. Of particular concern to the COW Project is the impact of national power capabilities on both involvement in war and the outcome of wars. Are states with greater capabilities more likely than others to become involved in war? To what extent do varying national power capabilities predict which countries win and which lose the wars that occur? In the most complete published statement on the first question to emerge from the project, Singer and his colleagues (Singer et al., 1972; cf. Bremer, 1980;

Wayman et al.,1983) examine for every quinquennial period from 1820 to 1965 the impact of national capabilities on nation-states' involvement in war.[4] Their conceptualization of national power, although not specifically spelled out in the article, centers on the demographic, industrial, and military capabilities of nation-states. Each dimension of capability is operationalized in terms of two indicators:

Demographic capabilities:
Total population
Urban population (cities of 20,000 or larger)
Industrial capabilities:
Energy consumption (after 1885), measured in coal-ton equivalents
Iron production (1820–1895) and steel production (1896–1965)
Military capabilities:
Total military expenditures
Size of the armed forces, excluding reserves

A nation-state's power is assessed in terms of these six summational variables by adding up the world's total on each dimension and then expressing a particular nation-state's value as a percentage of the world total. If the world in 1965 had an estimated population of 3276 million inhabitants, and Indonesia had 105 million (or 3.2%), its score on the variable "total population" would be 0.032. Similarly, China's score would be 0.229, the Soviet Union's 0.070, and that of the United States 0.059 (Taylor and Hudson, 1972, p. 295). Finally, Singer and his colleagues average each nation-state's scores on the six dimensions to obtain its composite score.

More Complex Indexes of Power

Fucks: Formulas of power. Although Singer and his collaborators use percentages, their power index is essentially a linear combination of the six attributes. A more elaborate, *nonlinear* index was proposed by Wilhelm Fucks (1965). He argues that national power derives from three summational variables: population size, energy production, and steel production. Experimenting with different ways to weigh and combine population size (p) first with energy production and then with steel production (each labeled z in the separate formulas), he generates nine formulas for national power (M), such as:

$$M = p^2z,$$
$$\text{or } p^{3/2}z,$$
$$\text{or } p^{1/2}z,$$
$$\text{or } pz^{1/3}.$$

Each formula is applied to data on 29 industrialized countries. Eyeballing the results he concludes that the last formula listed above "fits" best ($M = pz^{1/3}$). Using estimates of future growth rates in population, energy, and steel production, the formula enables him to project the relative power of each country to the year 2040. On a scale that accords the most powerful nation-state (the United States) the score of 100 in 1960, Fucks predicts that growth in U.S. power will taper off and reach 200 by the year 2040. Meanwhile, China's power will outstrip that of the United States in about 1975 and reach a score of approximately 3000 in the year 2040.

Cline: World power trends. A second nonlinear index based on a larger number of *both* summational and syntality variables was proposed by Ray S. Cline (1980, cf. 1975). His basic formula makes perceived power (P_p) the product of capabilities and commitment. Although most of the variables that make up "capabilities" are summational—the exception being two of the factors that enter the formula for military capability—the two factors that compose "commitment" are syntality variables:

$$P_p = \text{capabilities x commitment.}$$

The two overarching variables comprising "perceived power" are

$$\text{capabilities} = (C + E + M)$$

and

$$\text{commitment} = (S + W).$$

"Capabilities" in turn include

$$C = \text{critical mass} = \text{population + territory;}$$
$$E = \text{economic capacity} = \text{income + the production of five resources}$$
$$(= \text{energy + critical nonfuel minerals}$$
$$+ \text{ manufacturing + foods + trade);}$$
$$M = \text{military capability} = \text{strategic balance + combat capabilities}$$
$$+ \text{ bonus for effort.}$$

"Commitment" includes

$$S = \text{national strategy coefficient}$$

and

$$N = \text{national will coefficient} = \text{equal part levels of (1) national integration}$$
$$+ (2) \text{ strength of national leadership}$$
$$+ (3) \text{ relevance of strategy to national interest.}$$

Thus, the formula for perceived power becomes

$$P_p = (C + E + M)(S + W).$$

Cline defines an upper bound for each of the variables and then *judgmentally* determines where a particular nation falls on a given variable. The upper bounds for the scales of each of the variables are

Capability scores

Population	50
Territory	50
Income	100
Resources	100 (20 each)
Strategic balance	100
Combat capabilities	100
Effort bonus	10
	510

Commitment scores

National strategy coefficient	1.0%
National will coefficient	1.0%
	2.0%

Since the overall "capability" score cannot exceed 510 points and the overall "commitment" score cannot exceed 2.0%, a nation-state's maximum "perceived power" score is 1020 (i.e., 510 x 2.0% = 1020). Cline's final ranking of 77 countries lists as the most powerful the Soviet Union (458 points), United States (304), Brazil (137), West Germany (116), and Japan (108).

Although judgmental procedures are justifiable for measuring some of the variables, it is noteworthy that Cline adopts such procedures to assess most of the variables.[5] This raises questions about the overall reliability of the resulting indices. The most serious reliability questions, however, emerge from the two syntality variables: "national strategy" and "national will." Small changes in either of them can mean substantial differences in a nation-state's final score and hence its power ranking. Cline defines *strategy at the national level* as "the part of the political decision-making process that conceptualizes and establishes goals and objectives designed to protect and enhance national interests in the international environment" (1980, p. 143). This is operationalized by determining the extent to which a nation-state has "clear-cut strategic plans for international exercise of power and aggrandizement of influence" (p. 145). Nation-states that in Cline's judgment have "an integrated, truly global strategic concept" attain scores on this coefficient as high as 0.9 (Israel) or 0.8 (Taiwan, Vietnam, North Korea, East

Germany, and Switzerland). The Soviet Union scores 0.7, China 0.4, and the United States 0.3.

National will, Cline states, "is the degree of resolve that can be mobilized among the citizens of a nation in support of governmental decisions about defense and foreign policy" (p. 143). As noted above, it sums three equally weighted elements (p. 167):

1. Level or degree of cultural integration of the people in a feeling of belonging to a nation, which includes assessments of both cultural uniformity (ethnicity, language, religion) and popular identification with a territory (with cultural integration weighted three times as heavily as territorial integration).
2. Effective strength of national leadership, comprising equal parts of governmental policy capability and level of social discipline.
3. Relevance of strategy to national interest.

Nation-states with a high degree of national will, "the foundation upon which national strategy is formulated and carried through to success" (p. 143), have scores of 0.9 (Taiwan) or 0.8 (Brazil, West Germany, Japan, Israel, and Switzerland). The Soviet Union scores 0.5, the United States 0.4, and China 0.2 points.

Judgments by different analysts on these syntality variables could vary widely. One wonders whether the judgments made by Cline and his assistants could be replicated by independent, equally well-trained observers, or whether area specialists would produce the same scores as would generalists.

German: World power. A more complex index comes from F. Clifford German (1960). Nonlinear, like Fucks' and Cline's indexes, it contains, like Cline's, both summational and syntality variables and involves some judgmental factors. German argues that a country's power rests on four dimensions—land, population, industrial base, and military size—which in turn are strongly affected by the country's possession of nuclear weapons:

$$G = \text{national power} = N(L + P + I + M),$$

where N = nuclear capability
L = land
P = population
I = industrial base
M = military size.

Each of these five variables is further broken down into a series of factors. *Nuclear capability* (N), a syntality variable, is scored 2 if the state has nuclear weapons and 1 if not. Its multiplicative nature creates a large gap between the three nuclear powers of the late 1950s, when the study was conducted, and indicates the importance of this variable for German.

The summational variable *Land* (*L*) consists of not only sheer area but how the land is used. "Room for dispersal and maneuver," German notes (p. 139), "are considerable assets, and their value is enhanced if they are facilitated by the possession of adequate communications; empty space and inaccessible areas are virtually liabilities." Accordingly,

$$L = T/D,$$

where T = territory (in 1000s of km^2)
      D = density = $d_p d_r$.
The latter, "density," in turn comprises modification based on two characteristics:

$$d_p = \text{population density}$$

scored as   5 if population density > 200/km^2
           10 if 30/km^2 ≤ population density ≤ 200/km^2
           20 if population density < 30 km^2;

$$d_p = \text{railway density,}$$

scored as   1.00 if each km of rail net serves ≤30 km^2
            1.25 if each km of rail net serves 31–75 km^2
            2.00 if each km of rail net serves 76–150 km^2
            3.00 if each km of rail net serves ≥151 km^2.

The variable "land" (*L*) illustrates an important aspect of German's formula. Factors can enter the power calculation as either a capability or a load. From the above we see that two countries of equal size (say, 100,000 km^2), where one is densely occupied (20.1 million people and 3500 km of track) and the other sparsely occupied (3 million people and 650 km of track), would obtain scores on the variable "land" of 20 for the first country and 1.7 for the second.

The third variable, *population* (*P*), also constitutes a set of further factors (p. 139), one, the active working population (*W*), added, and the other, "the number of the total population surplus in home-produced food supply" (*E*) deducted:

$$P = WE + A,$$

where *W* = workforce (in millions)
      E = technical efficiency,

scored as   1 if $C < 0.5$
2 if $0.5 \leq C < 1.5$
3 if $1.5 \leq C < 3.0$
4 if $3.0 \leq C < 5.0$
5 if $C \geq 5.0$,

where C = national consumption of energy measured in terms of tons of coal equivalent per head per year;

and

$$A = \text{adjustment on workforce} = a_m + a_s + a_f$$

where a_m = adjustment for workforce in manufacturing
a_s = adjustment for morale
a_f = adjustment for food surpluses or deficits.
While the variables W and E can be considered summational, the workforce adjustment is clearly an overall assessment of a national characteristic, that is, a syntality variable.

The fourth variable, *industrial base* (I), is likewise composed of a further complex breakdown of factors:

$$I = RS + B,$$

in which

$$R = \text{resources} = r_t + r_c + r_l + r_o + r_e,$$

where r_t = steel production in metric tons per year (millions)
r_c = coal production in metric tons per year (millions)
r_l = lignite production (5,000,000 metric tons per year)
r_o = crude oil production (million metric tons per year)
r_e = hydroelectricity in millions of ton coal equivalent;

and

$$S = \text{presence or absence of directed economy},$$

scored as 2 if directed
1 if nondirected;

and

$$B = \text{adjustment on resources} = b_s + b_o + b_m + b_e,$$

where b_s = index of surplus or deficit in steel
b_o = index of surplus or deficit in oil
b_m = index of surplus or deficit in minerals

b_e = index of surplus or deficit in engineering;

and each is scored using the following criteria:

0.10 (RS) if large surplus
0.05 (RS) if surplus
0.00 (RS) if neither surplus nor deficit
−0.05 if deficit
−0.10 if large deficit.

Finally, the fifth variable, *military* (*M*), is obtained by a simple count of military personnel in terms of 100,000s.

Of the power indexes considered, the German index is the most complex. It consists of a multitude of variables, both summational and syntality, a series of scoring schemes, and several instances in which judgments must be made. Given the multiplicative factor of nuclear power, it is not surprising to find that the top three among the 19 industrialized countries scored are the United States (6459 points), the Soviet Union (6321), and the United Kingdom (1257). China (999) follows fairly closely behind Britain, mainly because of its large size and population. The remaining 15 countries range far behind, from West Germany (663.5) and Canada (498) to Sweden (116) and Belgium (112).

Which Variables Are Measured?

Undoubtedly there are other power indexes. We have not attempted here a thorough comparison of the underlying principles and procedures of all such power indexes. We focus on only two aspects: (1) the extent to which some of the more complex indexes touch on similar or different variables and (2) the difference in the findings they generate.

The most complex indexes are those proposed by Singer, Fucks, Cline, and German as well as the two regression equations of Alcock and Newcombe. They span an intriguing variety of dimensions. We move from the relatively simple two-variable index of Fucks to the twenty-variable index of German, and from the relatively straightforward, linear composition of Singer's six-variable index to the various nonlinear versions introduced by Fucks in terms of power and Cline or German in terms of multiplicative factors.[6] The diversity of variables considered and functional forms used to compose the indexes is striking. It would appear that the concept of power has many faces.

The degree of overlap in the variables these indices include, however, is equally impressive. From index to index certain variables seem to appear and reappear, albeit sometimes in slightly different forms. This sense of overlapping continuity is even more dramatic if we consider variables more generically, that is, if we do not distinguish between population and urban population, among the forms of energy (such as coal and steel and oil), between national leadership or integration and morale, or between strategic balance and nuclear capablity. Table 2.1 indicates the degree of generic similarity.

Do the Indicators Have Different Outcomes?

The combination of variation and similarity leads us to ask: Is there a significant difference in outcomes among these various indexes? If we move from the relatively simple, two-variable index of Fucks—or the still more straightforward variables of Alcock and Newcombe—to the more complex, twenty-variable index of German, has the additional work inherent in obtaining more data and subjecting them to more calculations produced a more useful, or even different, result? What, in short, is gained by more variables and more complex functional forms?

A partial answer is obtained by comparing results across the various indexes. To make this comparison we focus on both the four indexes discussed in the previous section and four additional indexes offered by Alcock and Newcombe (1970). They are:

1. Alcock and Newcombe: Canadians' perceptions of national power.[7]
2. Alcock and Newcombe: size (population + GNP per capita).[8]
3. Alcock and Newcombe: income (population + GNP).[9]
4. Alcock and Newcombe: military expenditures in purchasing-power-equivalent dollars.
5. Singer and Bremer: demographic, industrial, and military expenditures.[10]
6. Fucks: population and energy production, $M = pz^{1/3}$.
7. Cline: fifteen combined variables of capabilities and commitment, $P_p = (C + E + M)(S + W)$.
8. German: combined variables of nuclear capabilities, land, population, industrial base, and military, $G = N(L + P + I + M)$.

Two caveats are in order. First, the individual studies cite the power ranking for anywhere from 19 (German) to 103 (Alcock and Newcombe) countries. To compute the correlations we compared all countries ranked by the pair of studies being correlated. Second, the studies refer to different time periods. Since the world changed from1950 (cited in the Singer–Bremer analysis) to 1978 (cited by Cline), the time spans covered by the studies, we may be comparing the power value of a country in two different time frames.

Table 2.1 Main Variables of Five Indicators

Variable	Cline	German	Alcock–Newcombe[a]	Singer	Fucks
Population (quantitative and qualitative, e.g., workforce character	X	X	X	X	X
Energy (industrial base)	X	X	—	X	X
Military	X	X	X	X	—
Territory	X	X	—	—	—
Strategic balance (nuclear factors)	X	X	X	—	—
National leadership (morale)	X	X	—	—	—
Income	X	—	X	—	—

[a]Alcock and Newcombe (1970) use four separate indexes, three of which include one or two of the variables listed in this table: population and GNP per capita ("size"); population and GNP ("income"); and military expenditure in millions of purchasing-power-equivalent dollars. The fourth index measures Canadian public perceptions.

Nevertheless, as a first approximation, these temporal differences do not appear problematic.

In each study the researchers provide *rank orders* of power among a set of countries. To what extent do the rank orders differ from study to study? Table 2.2 presents the rank-order correlation coefficients between all possible pairs of indexes. The most striking result in this table is the similarity among the power rankings of the studies. With the possible exception of the correlations between Alcock–Newcombe and Singer–Bremer on the one hand and Cline on the other, the indexes produce very similar results. The overall average score is $r_S = .821$.[11]

In some studies the researchers report *absolute amounts* of power. That is, the score values for each country are entered instead of their world ranking. In this case comparing the data with Pearson's product-moment correlation coefficient, as seen in Table 2.2, reveals results that are even more dramatic. The average correlation between the absolute scores, $r = .926$, shows even greater congruence than do the rank-order scores.

A closer examination of the studies reveals a persistent variance. We divided each rank-order or absolute score into split halves and recalculated their coefficients. For example, Singer–Bremer and Cline reported data on the same 72 countries. Taking into account the data only for these 72 countries, we tabulated rank-order coefficients separately for the 36 top-ranked (i.e., more powerful) countries and the 36 bottom-ranked (i.e., less powerful) countries.[12] The results on the rank-order data on the split halves are shown in Table 2.3.

This procedure reveals that the average scores of lower-ranked countries are substantially different from those of upper-ranked countries. Scores for

Table 2.2   Rank-Order Correlations (Spearman's r_s)[a]

	1 Canada	2 Size	3 Income	4 Military	5 Singer–Bremer[b]	6 Fucks	7 Cline	8 German
		Alcock–Newcombe			Singer–			
1. A-N, Canada	—							
2. A-N, Size	.851	—						
3. A-N, Income	.854	.995	—					
4. A-N, Military	**.918**	**.880**	**.890**	—				
5. Singer–Bremer	.657	.802	.830	**.814**	—			
6. Fucks	.875	.908	.927	**.867** (.960)	.935	—		
7. Cline	.573	.601	.612	**.635** (.865)	.657	.786 (.883)	—	
8. German	.853	.893	.911	**.868** (.981)	.907	.921 (.944)	.758 (.921)	—
Average[c]	.797	.847	.860	**.839** (.935)	.800	.888 (.929)	.660 (.890)	.873 (.949)

[a]Linear correlations (Pearsonian r) in parentheses.
[b]Singer's Correlates of War data are found in Bremer (1980).
[c]For rank-order correlations, average scores are a study's total scores divided by seven. Thus, for the Alcock–Newcombe (1970) military expenditures (boldface), scores across row 4 are .918 + .880 + .890 = 2.688, and down column 4 are .814 + .867 + .635 + .868 = 3.184; the average is (2.688 + 3.184)/7 = 5.872/7 = .839. For linear correlations (in parentheses), average scores are a study's total scores divided by three.

Table 2.3   Rank-Order Correlations of Upper Versus Lower Rankings[a]

	1 Canada	2 Size	3 Income	4 Military	5 Singer–Bremer[b]	6 Fucks	7 Cline	8 German	Average
		Alcock–Newcombe			Singer–				
1. A-N, Canada	—	.731	.758	.743	.773	.853	.614	.817	.755
2. A-N, Size	.491	—	.994	.802	.830	.833	.698	.833	.817
3. A-N, Income	.506	.969	—	.823	.850	.875	.702	.900	.843
4. A-N, Military	.708	.561	.583	—	.865	.862	.614	.859	.795
5. Singer–Bremer	.279	.093	.154	.377	—	.951	.635	.833	.827
6. Fucks	.308	.578	.688	.365	.527	—	.943	.811	.875
7. Cline	.392	.384	.426	.295	.495	.305	—	.458	.666
8. German	.292	.409	.417	.384	.617	.858	.484	—	.794
Average[b]	.425	.498	.535	.467	.358	.518	.392	.494	

[a]The upper, right-sided quadrant represents average scores of the top half of each pair of "power" rankings (with an overall average score of .796). The lower, left-sided quadrant represents average scores for the lower half (with an overall average of .459).
[b]Average scores are a study's total scores divided by seven; see Table 2.2.

more powerful countries ($r_S = .796$; $r = .920$) are almost twice as consistent between studies than scores for less powerful countries ($r_S = .459$; $r = .538$). Why is this the case? The most reasonable explanation is that the analysts are more knowledgeable about, interested in, and hence better able to assess the degree of power among the world's more powerful states. Comparative data on the ranking of weaker states are most likely to be inaccurate.

Given the overlapping variables in the various studies, the findings of congruence among the data are not altogether surprising. Yet it will be recalled that, from index to index, the researchers used somewhat different operational measures for the same variable concept. Table 2.1 merely creates an artificial similarity by collapsing such categories as national integration, leadership, and morale. Even so, the degree of congruence suggests a further conclusion. As we move from two-variable to twenty-variable studies, or from simple linear formulas to more complex functional forms, we find no appreciable change in outcome. This is true even when the methodological procedures are problematic—as in the Alcock–Newcombe regression equations involving logarithmic transformations of rank-ordered variables, and the arbitrary choice of functional forms by Fucks. The variation that occurs seems to stem more from the researcher's level of information about the less powerful countries than from different conceptualizations or analytic procedures. Generally, it appears that needless additional data and arithmetic computation have been introduced without an increase in payoff.

How Can We Measure Power?

Thus, we return to full circle: What do we wish to say (and hence measure) about the power of a nation-state?

A general answer to this question underpins much of the research cited in this chapter. It envisions a *universal scale,* a more or less complex but nevertheless standardized index that measures each nation-state's power relative to that of all other nation-states. Power in this view is akin to a currency of politics (cf. Deutsch, 1963, p. 120). Just as economists evaluate economic transactions in terms of a standardized unit of currency, the dollar, so political analysts might see an absolute scale along which the "value" of one nation-state can be assessed with respect to another.

However challenging intellectually, our search for a universal scale of power poses some severe analytic difficulties. First, judging from available research results, no general agreement tells us which variables best indicate power relationships. Occasionally, it is as though the researcher grasps the best-available straws which are then given an ad hoc justification. Second, still less agreement addresses the methodological procedures for linking the variables. In some cases these procedures are at best questionable. This pair of issues has resulted in neither conceptual clarity nor substantive wisdom. Third, implicit in the search for a currency is the assumption that power, like money, is fungible. An individual can use $1000 for a variety of purposes, ranging from groceries to capital investments and vacations to the Caribbean. If power is truly a currency,[13] then it follows that a government could use it for equally manifold purposes: to war with a neighboring nation-state, influence votes in the United Nations, prevent another country from dumping its products, and pursue still more goals. Seen from this perspective, the requirements of analysts seeking to predict the outcome of a pending dispute between two nation-states are minimal: They need only to assess whether or not A is more powerful than B. If it is, then the consequence is straightforward: A will prevail.

The reality, however, is different. As we know from the recent experience of the United States in Vietnam and the Soviet Union in Afghanistan, even superpowers can find it difficult to translate their putative power base into effective action. Nor is such experience a new thing. Weak actors have long been able to tweak the tails of more powerful tigers—albeit often at some cost to themselves. No doubt it was this kind of consideration that led Cline to place such weight on national strategy and national will. Even so,[14] no data-based research to date has been able to deal adequately with the fact that power is fungible only in some circumstances.

A more useful but more difficult answer to our question about the meaning and measurement of power is *theory based*. The nature of our theory of international politics determines how we conceptualize power. Examples of such a nexus are to be found in the balance of power, Organski's and Jacek Kugler's (1980) power challenger, and Bruce Bueno de Mesquita's (1981) rational expectation model. In each the attributes of the power concept are linked directly to arguments made within the theory. The emphasis thus focuses on data applicable to individual theories rather than the search for a universal, all-purpose scale of power relationships.

Notes

1. This issue underlies the analysis by Paul R. Pudaite and Gretchen Hower in Chapter 4 of this book.

2. Alcock's and Newcombe's two additional, multivariate indexes, size and income, are discussed below. This chapter does not consider in detail their fourth index: In accordance with the idea that power is in the mind of the beholder, they report how a sample of 38 Canadians ranked 122 nation-states "in order of their power as they think of them" (p. 336).

3. Alcock and Newcombe find that their perceptual index, the Canadian sample's view of power relationships, closely correlates with three other indexes: size, income, and military expenditures. These findings of congruence are very similar to those reported in Table 2.2.

4. Since the most convenient listing of Singer's Correlates of War data on national characteristics appears in an article by Stuart A. Bremer (1980), here and later our references to Singer's findings are to be found in Bremer's article.

5. Thus, in the "critical mass" variable, scores on both the "population" and "territory" subvariables are based on arbitrary rank orders that do not preserve the interval attribute characteristic of the variable: "population" scores are modified in some cases by the size of per capita gross national product; and a "territory" score receives a "bonus weight" if the country occupies an area of strategic importance. Of the other subvariables, only "income" preserves the interval.

6. A further difference of importance separates Singer's index from the others: by expressing each nation-state's score on a given variable in terms of world percentages, that score automatically reflects its world ranking. In each of the other four cases, resulting scores must be further ranked to determine a particular nation-state's standing in relationship to the rest of the world.

7. "The rank ordering of 117 nations of the world as perceived by our 38 Canadian subjects" (Alcock and Newcombe, 1970, p. 338).

8. "Relative power = -8.85 + 0.67 Population + 0.47 GNP/cap" (Alcock and Newcombe, 1970, p. 338).

9. "Relative power = 9.4 - 0.09 Population + 0.93 GNP" (Alcock and Newcombe, 1970, p. 338).

10. Correlates of War data derived from Bremer (1980).

11. All scores are statistically significant at the $p = .001$ level. Not surprisingly, adding variables that essentially preserve the ranking of the nation-states does not change the power index value of a given country even under rather different mathematical transformations. Indeed, it can be shown that the inclusion of new variables that preserve the rank order will not affect the rank orders that a mathematical operation produces, provided that that operation is monotonically increasing in each variable.

12. For a somewhat different but consistent approach, see Chapter 3 by Charles S. Taber in this volume.

13. For an alternative view, see Baldwin (1985).

14. Using data for 1978, Cline (1980, p. 173) finds the United States with 7.8 times as much perceived power as unified Vietnam; Afghanistan is not among his 77 nation-states.

3

Power Capability Indexes in the Third World

Charles S. Taber

For centuries, scholars, philosophers, and practitioners of politics have sought valid and reliable power rankings of the states in their worlds. The more recent efforts in this tradition have benefited from published national data and modern measurement techniques, but questions of validity and reliability persist. Indeed, though one finds considerable agreement across these lists for the higher rank positions, an impressionistic survey across these same lists for the lower rank positions shows much less agreement. In this chapter, I argue that the commonly used power capability indexes do not adequately tap the underlying concept because they work well only among more developed countries (MDCs) but fail among the less developed countries (LDCs).

The problem of power capability measurement is of considerable theoretical interest. In a survey of political scientists, John Vasquez (1983, p. 36) found that power was ranked first in importance among disciplinary concepts. Indeed, Charles McClelland asserted that if the idea of power was prohibited "the field would be struck dumb" (1971, p. 60). For Bertrand Russell (1938), "the fundamental concept in social sciences is power, in the same sense in which energy is the fundamental concept in physics." Despite its centrality in political science, a generally accepted theory of power has not emerged. Several leading scholars consider the concept theoretically bankrupt (March, 1966; McClelland, 1971).

Though my empirical investigation concerns just one aspect of power—capability indexing—my general concern is with the contribution of power measurement to power theory. Studies of measurement tools often provide theoretical and conceptual benefits (Blalock, 1982). An understanding of the reasons for the success or failure of power capability indexes may reveal much about the power capability concept.

The accurate ranking of LDCs by power capability would also facilitate research into international power processes. Consider the curious impotence experienced by the superpowers in some of their relations with LDCs. For example, Cuba has apparently gained disproportionate power in the Third World in recent years. Accurate indexes that reflect the sources of this success might help researchers predict and model the relations of superpowers in the Third World. If Cuba's power is a function of its salience as a communist nation in the Western Hemisphere or of its role as a conduit for Soviet power, and these factors were considered in the power measurement, then the outcomes of conflicts involving Cuba might be better predicted.

For similar reasons, accurate power capability measurement would be useful for the policymaker. Because of the uncertain conversion of potential power into actual power, however, even perfect power capability rankings would not generate perfect conflict outcome predictions. But if policymakers understood power balances in the Third World and what factors contribute to greater power capability, they would be able to make better use of foreign aid. Perhaps most important, they would be able to temper their informal heuristics (general world view, mind set, organizational bias, etc.), which often lead to perceptual error, with more solid information about power capabilities in the world. Presumably, better informed policymakers would be less prone to error.

Conceptualizing Power

Unfortunately, as Charles McClelland asserts, many proponents of power explanations in international relations "have only a misty notion of what they are talking about" (1971, p. 60). Much of the problem stems from a failure to explicate different aspects of power. Indeed, different conceptual meanings are often given the same label. Power is used as both an attribute and a relation, for example.

The problem runs much deeper than semantics. Some scholars are predisposed to view power as an attribute of nations while others see it as a set of relationships in an international system. Furthermore, proponents of one approach often deny the validity of alternative approaches. To my mind, the disagreements between these groups on the meaning of power simply reveal the underlying differences in their ways of doing business. We should recognize that, though they often use the same word "power," systems theorists and national attribute theorists are not talking about the same concept.

I distinguish four concepts of power, ranging from the attributional concept to the relational concept. This partitioning of the conceptual space into a descriptive model has the advantage of relating, rather than opposing, different power concepts and is a prerequisite to theoretical development.

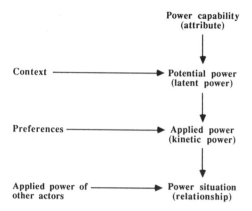

Figure 3.1 A descriptive analysis of power

   Most international relations scholars would agree that a concept exists
with the following meaning: *a causal relationship between an actor and a
desirable outcome* (see Figure 3.1). Thus, actor *A* is said to cause outcome *O*
(actively or through anticipated activity). Following Thomas Hobbes (1839,
1971), Herbert A. Simon (1953), James G. March (1955, 1957), Robert A.
Dahl (1957, 1965, 1968), and Jack H. Nagel (1975), among others, I will
label this concept *power.*
   As with all causal relationships, power is a *necessary* relationship (when
all conditions have been specified), stemming from some "inherent and
essential aspects" of actors.[1] Two essential aspects of actors for understanding
power causation are power capability and actor preferences..

   Power Capability. Capability is attributional, a characteristic of actors
that enables them to act. It may be defined as the possession of "power
sufficient for an act; as, that man is *capable* of lifting over 300 pounds"
(*Webster's New Twentieth Century Dictionary*, 1983, p. 267). I define power
capability as an inherent and essential property of an actor that tends to give
that actor control over outcomes, though the actor's preferences and the
situation are not specified.
   Potential Power. There are two important strands to the meaning of
potential employed in the term potential power. One is attributional, the
other contextual. Consider an analogy from physics. Potential energy refers
to "energy stored in the situation or condition of matter, as in raised weight"
(Riban, 1982, p. 640). There are two components to the energy stored in a
raised weight: the mass of the object (attribute) and the position of the object
(context). Similarly, there are two components to potential power in
international relations: the power capability of the nations (attribute) and the
particular situation (context). Potential power is power capability in context.

Applied Power. Potential power has not yet been "put into motion" (indeed, it need not be). Before it is applied, potential power must be directed by the actor's preferences. Strictly speaking, this direction may be conscious or not, for it need only be anticipated by other actors to be effective.

Nagel (1975, p. 29) defines power as a "causal relation between the preferences of an actor regarding an outcome and the outcome itself." This definition is insufficient because it fails to distinguish theoretically between situations where preferences do lead to the desired outcome and situations where they do not. I define applied power as potential power that has been directed by actor preferences.

Power Situation. The potential power, the direction of the preferences, and the intensity of the preferences of all relevant actors (i.e., their applied powers) cause the outcome, and this set of causal relationships is the power in the situation.

J. David Singer (1963, p. 422) distinguishes between influence attempts and influence outcomes in a similar way. An influence attempt depends on the predictions, preferences, and capabilities of one actor and corresponds to my applied power. The influence outcome, on the other hand, depends also on the predictions, preferences, and capabilities of other relevant actors. It results from a complete power situation.

Operationalizing Power Capability

My concern is with the measurement of power capability, which I have defined as an undirected property, with no context specified, that tends to give an actor control over outcomes. Many researchers, at least implicitly, define power capability similarly and propose attributes that, in their estimations, capable nations have (e.g., German, 1960; Fucks, 1965; Knorr, 1970; Cline 1975, 1980; Hart, 1976). Some of them emphasize military attributes (Knorr, 1970; Maoz, 1983), while others find economic and demographic indicators more appropriate (Fucks, 1965; Organski and Kugler, 1978, 1980). Several develop quite complicated formulas for national capability (German, 1960; Cline, 1980), while others use a single indicator (Organski, 1965, 1968; Rosen, 1972).

A feature common to all of these attribute schemes is that they use indicators of capability to measure surrogate attributes of nations. These surrogates may be factors contributing to an actor's power capability, consequences of it, or both. For example, a large developed economy may contribute to a nation's power position relative to future outcomes, or it may be the result of a favorable power position in the past.

Concept measurement is always an indirect process relying on auxiliary measurement theories. Unfortunately, this process is rarely explicit, making the comparison and validation of different measurement approaches very difficult. One must infer the index builder's measurement theory from the index itself. Many measurement theories would be consistent with the scale's observed behavior.

Indirect measurement makes the measurement task inseparable from conceptualization and theory development. Since these tasks have been separated in the power literature, I make two assumptions to pull them together. I assume that different index builders intend to measure power capability as I have defined it, and I assume that their indexes represent theoretical statements.

The approaches taken by index builders differ along two dimensions. They disagree about what attributes capable actors tend to have, and about how many of these attributes must be included in a valid index of power capability. The first difference comes from the difficulty in identifying surrogates for capability, while the latter difference is due to different solutions to the trade-off between validity and simplicity.

I have selected five indexes from the literature as test operationalizations of power capability. Each of these indexes has received significant attention in the international relations literature. In addition, they represent a broad spectrum of approaches (see Appendix A for specific operationalizations).

F. Clifford German. German (1960) constructed an index that combines many of the attributes theorists have considered important to power capability. He selected four basic dimensions that he believed represent the relevant factors that produce "gross national strength": industrial base, land, population, and military capability (including nuclear capability).

Wilhelm Fucks. Fucks (1965) developed an index using population, energy production, and steel production. Believing that these attributes were most likely interactive, Fucks multiplied rather than added them. He tried various exponential weights on the combination of population and energy production and the combination of population and steel production. He then selected the weighting scheme that matched his intuitive idea of the rankings of five powers.

J. David Singer, et al. Singer and the Correlates of War Project devised one of the most popular indexes, the Composite Index of National Capability, based on a nation's share of six capability resources (Singer et al., 1972; Bremer, 1980): population, urban population, steel production, fuel consumption, military personnel, and military expenditures. A nation's percentage share of the total amount of each resource available in the international system is computed and then its six shares are averaged. Unlike German, Singer et al. saw no theoretical reason to differentially weight the components of their index. In addition, they differ from Fucks in their implicit view that the six components are not interactive, that they should be added rather than multiplied.

Ray S. Cline. Like German, Cline (1975, 1980) includes many national attributes in his index. Some of the attributes are treated as interactive, while others are not. Many of the components in Cline's index, however, are completely subjective and nonreplicable. Rather than attempt to reproduce his estimates of such intangibles as "strategy," "effort," and "will," I use Cline's 1980 rankings.

GNP. Several power theorists have argued that power and property are virtually synonymous (e.g., Berle, 1967). Indeed, Alcock and Newcombe (1970, p. 342) found that "perceived national power is some function of GNP" for nonwarring nations. Organski and Kugler (1978, p. 144; 1980) argued for the use of GNP as an index of power capability, despite its weaknesses, because of the "parsimoniousness of the measure as well as quality and availability of data." Many studies of power or influence in international relations have used GNP alone as an indicator of capability.

Validity Tests

To review briefly, the research question concerns the validity of extant indexes of power capability, of which these five are representative. I have suggested that they do not work as well for LDCs as they do for MDCs. Clearly, a good general index of power capability should not systematically err along any dimension of nations. It should be valid for all types of nations.

Generating the Rankings

The first step is to rank the nations of the world in order of power capability for each of the five indexes. Using 1980 data, I computed these power capability scores for each nation. Since the raw scores generated by the indexes are not directly comparable, I standardized each index with the U.S. score as base. For example, Cline's index gives the United States a raw score of 304, the Soviet Union a score of 458, and South Africa a score of 40. These scores translate into standardized scores of 1000, 1509, and 130. The standardized scores and the rank orders are reported in Table 3.1. Where data were unavailable, preventing the calculation of one of the indexes for a nation, that nation was eliminated from the analysis. This procedure yielded a sample of 73 nations.

Dichotomizing the Nations

Using a measure that is not included in any of the indexes, I must divide the nations of the world by level of development. I would run the risk of tautology if I used a development indicator (such as GNP) that is included in one of the indexes, for the validity tests are performed on these indexes.

The number of telephones per capita is often used as a measure of development. It is easily accessible and is not included in any of the power capability indexes. Using the median of the telephone/capita ranking (median=5.6/100) as the cutoff point, the countries of the sample (N=73) were split into two parts. The countries above the median point were defined as developed, those below as underdeveloped. This procedure yielded ten rankings: one for LDCs and one for MDCs for each index.

Face Validity

Three tests of measurement validity are common in the literature. One is the intuitive, or "face validity," test. The researcher simply eyeballs the ranking, judging its validity on the basis of prior knowledge. The researcher might select a panel of "experts" and tap their knowledge to establish face validity.

Alcock and Newcombe (1970, p. 336), for example, asked 38 Canadian subjects to rank 122 nations "in order of their power as they think of them." They wished to compare perceptions of national power with the political and social indicators of power derived by Bruce M. Russett (1967) through factor analysis. Alcock and Newcombe found that the subjects' perceptions correlate strongly with GNP.

These perceptual data afford an initial opportunity to test my general hypothesis, which suggests that the Canadian subjects' perceptions of national power should agree more closely with attributional measures among MDCs than they do among LDCs. This is the case for 1970 GNP data (MDCs: r_s = .785; LDCs: r_s = .603; p < .075 that this difference occurred by chance).

Similarly, I drew on the expertise of the graduate students in political science and area studies at the University of Illinois. Forty countries were selected as a test sample, ten each from developing Asian, African, and Latin American countries, and ten from developed countries.

I distributed thirty-five response forms to graduate students who have done research in African, Latin American, or Asian studies or in general international relations. Each of the sixteen respondents ordered the ten developed nations and one of the Third World lists according to his or her perception of power capability. I divided the developing countries regionally

Table 3.1 Power Capability Ranks (1980 Data)

Nation	GNP Rank	GNP Norm	Cline Rank	Cline Norm	Singer Rank	Singer Norm	German Rank	German Norm	Fucks Rank	Fucks Norm
I. Developed (above 5.6 telephones/100 people)										
United States	1	1000	2	1000	2	1000	2	1000	1	1000
Soviet Union	2	469	1	1509	1	1127	1	1253	2	577
Japan	3	406	5	355	3	356	3	220	4	197
West Germany	4	319	4	380	4	238	6	128	5	101
France	5	253	7	243	5	187	5	207	8	65
United Kingdom	6	200	8	224	6	166	4	217	7	76
Italy	7	152	14	111	7	142	8	120	9	50
Brazil	8	95	3	452	8	127	7	120	10	48
Canada	9	95	9	200	9	93	12	44	6	76
Spain	10	81	13	128	11	83	11	59	3	26
Mexico	11	70	17	74	12	78	9	71	12	19
The Netherlands	12	62	16	75	19	44	19	23	19	11
Australia	13	56	6	288	17	47	20	21	15	16
Poland	14	54	19	65	10	93	10	65	11	28
Argentina	15	48	15	105	20	42	15	29	22	8
East Germany	16	47	21	54	15	59	14	30	14	18
Belgium	17	46	28	29	16	54	22	15	23	8
Sweden	18	45	23	51	22	33	25	12	16	14
Switzerland	19	40	26	37	30	15	29	9	24	6
Czechoslovakia	20	35	26	37	14	61	17	27	17	13
Austria	21	31	31	17	28	20	28	10	25	6
South Africa	22	27	11	130	17	47	16	28	13	18
Denmark	23	25	21	54	32	12	30	6	31	3
Yugoslavia	24	23	24	42	21	38	18	27	18	11
South Korea	25	21	10	152	13	74	13	39	21	9
Norway	26	21	18	69	30	14	32	5	20	9
Finland	27	19	29	21	29	15	31	5	27	5
Hungary	28	17	34	11	25	24	23	15	29	4
Greece	29	16	29	21	26	23	26	11	30	3
Bulgaria	30	14	33	15	23	25	24	12	26	5
Kuwait	31	13	32	16	37	5	36	1	35	1
Colombia	32	13	25	39	27	21	21	17	28	5
United Arab Emirates	33	11	36	7	34	6	37	1	37	0
New Zealand	34	9	20	58	35	6	33	4	33	2
Portugal	35	9	37	3	33	11	27	10	32	2
Israel	36	8	12	129	24	25	35	3	34	1
Singapore	37	4	35	7	36	6	34	3	36	1
II. Developing										
China	1	116	1	275	1	782	1	2858	1	212
India	2	62	6	117	2	366	2	694	2	73
Saudi Arabia	3	46	4	128	9	47	28	5	13	3
Rumania	4	33	18	49	8	56	5	33	3	13
Iran	5	32	17	53	10	45	10	29	8	5
Nigeria	6	31	9	74	12	34	11	25	14	2
Indonesia	7	27	2	181	3	78	3	89	7	5
Turkey	8	24	15	59	5	61	8	31	6	6
Venezuela	9	24	27	29	18	23	16	11	5	6
Algeria	10	15	13	66	23	18	22	9	20	1
Iraq	11	14	20	45	16	27	18	10	15	2

Table 3.1 Continued

Nation	GNP Rank	GNP Norm	Cline Rank	Cline Norm	Singer Rank	Singer Norm	German Rank	German Norm	Fucks Rank	Fucks Norm
Phillippines	12	14	8	79	14	32	7	32	10	5
Thailand	13	13	13	66	15	32	12	24	12	4
Libya	14	12	15	59	31	6	32	2	28	0
Chile	15	11	7	81	25	16	26	7	18	2
Egypt	16	10	3	150	11	44	6	33	11	4
Pakistan	17	10	9	74	6	61	4	52	9	5
Malaysia	18	9	31	16	26	13	19	10	17	2
North Korea	19	8	11	69	29	57	27	18	25	6
Peru	20	7	21	43	22	19	21	9	16	2
Morocco	21	7	24	33	24	16	17	11	23	1
Cuba	22	7	34	8	21	20	20	10	19	1
Syria	23	5	18	49	19	22	24	7	27	1
Bangladesh	24	4	23	37	13	33	9	30	24	1
Vietnam	25	3	4	128	4	69	14	19	22	1
Sudan	26	3	22	41	27	12	23	8	31	0
Kenya	27	3	25	9	30	7	29	5	30	0
Burma	28	2	33	13	17	24	13	20	29	0
Zaire	29	2	11	69	29	8	27	5	25	1
Zimbabwe	30	2	28	24	32	5	31	3	26	1
Tanzania	31	2	25	30	28	9	30	4	34	0
Ethiopia	32	2	29	23	19	5	25	3	32	1
Zambia	33	1	31	16	33	5	33	2	21	1
Guinea	34	1	30	18	36	1	36	0	36	0
Mongolia	35	1	34	8	34	3	34	1	33	0
Liberia	36	0	36	5	35	1	35	1	35	0

because I thought it unlikely that any single respondent would know enough about nations from all of these regions to rank them. By assigning each nation a score equal to its rank number and adding the scores, I consolidated the lists of perceived power capability into one "mean" list. The nation with the lowest score in each of the four categories was ranked first, second lowest was ranked second, and so on. Thus, if the United States received thirteen first ranks, and three second ranks it would be assigned a cumulative score of $(13 \times 1) + (3 \times 2) = 19$. If this cumulative score was the lowest in the developed category, the United States would be ranked first on the consolidated expert list of perceived power capability for that category.

To do this, I must assume that the rank differences are comparable, that the difference between ranks 1 and 2 is about the same as the difference between ranks 9 and 10. I must also have some confidence in the agreement of the respondents—if their rankings are too different the consolidated list will reflect nobody's wisdom. I know of no way to test the validity of the first assumption, but Kendall's τ_b can check the second. I find that agreement across experts is significant in all four categories, though weak in Africa (Table 3.2), and the number for all correlations are small.

Table 3.2   Concordance (τ_b) of Experts' Predictions

	N	τ_b	χ^2	p
Developed	12	.833	89.911	.000
Africa	7	.308	19.397	.022
Latin America	3	.800	21.612	.010
Asia	8	.700	50.430	.000

Within each of the four categories, a ranking was generated by each of the five test capability indexes. This allowed each index to be compared separately to the expert rankings. If the hypothesis is correct, I should find less agreement between the indexes and expert perceptions of power capability rankings in the Third World categories than in the developed category. The results in Table 3.3 suggest that the experts and the indexes do agree significantly more for rankings of MDCs than for LDCs.

There is at least one problem with the face validity test, however. What reason do I have for accepting intuitive judgments as more valid than those generated by the indexes? How do I know that the respondents are capturing power capability any more than attributional data do? In fact, there is some cause to believe that experts base their judgments on what they know about national attributes (Alcock and Newcombe, 1970). In other words, the indexes may be more valid than the perceptions used to test them.

Cross-Correlation of Indexes

Another test of validity found in the literature is the cross-correlation of indexes that purport to measure the same thing. I can simply (1) correlate the five indexes for developed nations with each other, (2) correlate the five indexes for developing nations with each other, and (3) compare the results. The hypothesis predicts that the correlations will be quite high for MDCs but less high for LDCs.

Using Spearman's rank correlation coefficient (r_s), pairwise correlation matrices were generated for the five indexes in each development condition. The results in Table 3.4 show consistently (and significantly) lower correlations in the underdeveloped condition than in the developed one, though the difference is not large. Since r_s must be squared for interpretation, however, the difference in strength is greater than it appears. Indeed, when values of r_s fall to .7, less than 50% of the variance in one rank list could be predicted from variance in the other. In this light, it seems apparent that these indexes do not strongly agree about power capability in the underdeveloped category. Though German and Singer and GNP and Fucks have reasonably strong correlations with each other, all other pairings are tenuous.

Table 3.3 Face Validity

a. Spearman's correlations (experts by indexes)					
	GNP	Cline	Singer	German	Fucks
Developed	.939	.903	.927	.819	.879
Africa	.770	.649	.212[a]	.273[a]	.830
Latin America	.873	.058[a]	.408[a]	.408[a]	.524[a]
Asia	.699	.906	.906	.578[a]	.855

b. Significance of correlation differences (LDC region by MDCs)					
Region by LDCs	GNP	Cline	Singer	German	Fucks
Africa	1.327	1.337	2.659	1.634	0.343
	.092	.090	.004	.052	.367
Latin America	.718	2.676	2.251	1.331	1.477
	.236	.004	.012	.092	.074
Asia	1.481	0.032	0.225	0.841	0.167
	.069	.488	.409	.201	.433

[a]$p > .05$.
[b]The first entry in each cell of Section b of this table is Z; the second entry is the probability p that the correlations are from the same population.

Certainly there is support for the research hypothesis in these findings. Nevertheless, it is somewhat puzzling that the differences between development conditions are not larger. One possible explanation is that the power capability indexes work better at the extremes of development than for the nations clustered in the middle. Perhaps the most *and least* developed nations are more easily indexed. I tested this possibility by dividing the nations into four groups (1 to 4 from most to least telephones/capita) rather than two and repeating the tests. The results in Table 3.5 indicate that there was indeed a subgroup of the underdeveloped dimension where the five indexes were less strongly correlated (Group 3).

In sum, there is a significant difference between the strength of correlations among LDCs and MDCs. Though some of the paired indexes agree more than others, none of the pairs were correlated as highly among underdeveloped nations as they were among developed nations. A test of the significance of these differences found some marginal levels, but the overall results justify rejecting the null hypothesis that there is no difference.[2]

The Confrontation Test

The outcome of confrontations is often used to test the validity of power capability indexes (Organski and Kugler, 1978; Wayman et al., 1983; Ray

Table 3.4 Cross-Correlation of the Indexes

	GNP	Cline	Singer	German
		a. Spearman's r		
		Developed Nations (N = 37)		
Cline	.775	1.000		
Singer	.893	.802	1.000	
German	.882	.759	.958	1.000
Fucks	.929	.797	.926	.917
		Underdeveloped Nations (N = 36)		
Cline	.685	1.000		
Singer	.735	.707	1.000	
German	.697	.586	.891	1.000
Fucks	.856	.628	.805	.797
		b. Significance of the Difference		
Cline	0.794			
	.215			
Singer	2.023	0.911		
	.022	.181		
German	2.136	1.256	2.032	
	.016	.104	.021	
Fucks	1.527	1.440	2.131	1.960
	.063	.075	.017	.025

Average rank order correlations $Z = 1.485$, $p = .068$

Note: The first entry in each cell in Section b of this table is Z; the second entry is the probability p that the correlations are from the same population.

and Vural, 1986). Those who use the confrontation test look at conflicts of various kinds among nations, ascertain the balance of capabilities, and check predictions made on the basis of this balance against the historical outcomes. The assumption is that "God is always on the side of the larger battalions" and that we can infer the relative size of the battalions by observing which side God was on.

This validity test ignores the distinction between undirected and noncontextual power capability and applied power. To use it properly, one must build a theoretical model of the power process that specifies the conversion of capability into potential and then into applied power.[3] Without such a model, the confrontation test is inappropriate; it will not be employed here.

Table 3.5 Four Development Categories

	GNP	Cline	Singer	German
		a. Spearman's r		
		Group 1		
Cline	.817	1.000		
Singer	.944	.739	1.000	
German	.960	.753	.973	1.000
Fucks	.900	.814	.902	.898
		Group 2		
Cline	.705	1.000		
Singer	.893	.827	1.000	
German	.915	.752	.938	1.000
Fucks	.926	.752	.946	.959
		Group 3		
Cline	.605	1.000		
Singer	.812	.603	1.000	
German	.573	.342[a]	.725	1.000
Fucks	.847	.434	.837	.810
		Group 4		
Cline	.826	1.000		
Singer	.810	.832	1.000	
German	.843	.738	.934	1.000
Fucks	.827	.788	.827	.792
	b. Significance of the Difference Between Groups 1 and 3			
Cline	1.241			
	.108			
Singer	1.789	0.694		
	.037	.254		
German	3.587	1.735	3.423	
	.000	.041	.000	
Fucks	0.628	1.879	0.760	0.934
	.264	.030	.224	.176

Average rank order correlations (GR1, GR3): $Z = 1.508$, $p = .066$

[a]$p > .05$.
[b]The first entry in each cell in Section b of this table is Z; the second entry is p.

Discussion

The evidence presented in this chapter supports the hypothesis that the indexes of power capability commonly used by analysts of international relations do not adequately measure power capability. Though these indexes may be reasonable measures of power capability for some nations, they fail when applied to Third World nations. Several explanations are possible for this failure.

Oversimplification

Individual national attributes that serve as surrogates for power capability might correlate more highly among developed nations than among underdeveloped ones. Thus, simpler indexes would adequately represent the power capabilities of developed nations but not underdeveloped ones because, though all the attributes that contribute to (or are consequent on) power capability are not included, they are so redundant among MDCs that any one would do.

For example, suppose that national attributes A, B, and C are crucial to a nation's power capability. Capable nations must have all three. Index X is a combination of all three attributes, but index Y includes only A. If A, B, and C have a .99 correlation with each other for developed nations but correlate .25 among LDCs, then they are highly redundant among the developed nations—any one of them would be an accurate indicator for all three. In contrast, an accurate index for LDCs must contain all three. Index X would do well for both MDCs and LDCs, but index Y would systematically err when level of development changes.

Of course, this only explains the failure of simple indexes. If this explanation is true, the German, Singer , and Cline indexes would do "better" in the tests than Fucks or GNP, because they are more inclusive. Looking across the significance levels in Table 3.5, there is no clear trend. The problem is that not only do they include more attributes in their indexes, they include different attributes, and they combine them in different ways. In terms of my simple example, index X is a product of A, B, and C, while index Y is the average of B, D, and E.

Noncomparability

The relationships among crucial indicators of power capability may be different for different ranges of their values, making indexes noncomparable in these different conditions. Blalock (1982, pp. 66–67) points out several ways that measures may be noncomparable. First, it is possible that the relationship between indicator and concept is opposite under different conditions. Second, the empirical relationship may be nonlinear though the measurement theory is linear. Third, parameters in a linear relationship may vary across conditions though they are treated as constants by the index. Finally, the stochastic elements in the measurement theory may differ under different conditions.

Each of these sources of noncomparability could be responsible for the findings. For example, GNP could be an important predictor of capability when it is large but may be less important as it grows smaller. Other indicators might be more important when they are small than when they are large. If this is the case, the measurement theory should treat the weighting parameters on GNP and other indicators as variable.

Real Fluctuation

Perhaps the rate of change of the crucial attributes is much greater for LDCs than for MDCs. Developing countries are undergoing cultural, political, and economic transformations. This constantly changing milieu, so the argument goes, cannot be captured accurately by indexes that measure at one time point. Predictions made on the basis of the situation at time t may not be relevant at time $t + 4$.

It seems clear, however, that many researchers have been successful in the use and interpretation of data from this "ever changing milieu." Consider an analogy. A zoologist may not be certain what color a chameleon will be at any given time, but knowledge about its adaptive nature will allow predictions about what color it will be in a particular environment. Similarly, students of the third world can extrapolate current "readings" into the future and enhance the predictive power of capability indexes in the developing world.

Unreliability

The reliability of the indexes could be questioned rather than the validity. Perhaps scale insensitivity, which is hidden by the magnitude of differences among the higher ranks, becomes more important when capability differences are smaller and more clustered on the scale.

Every scale of measurement has an error tolerance—the range of uncertainty that surrounds each measurement point. After weighing a tomato on a grocer's scale, for example, I might conclude that it weighed one-quarter pound, plus or minus 5 ounces. The same tomato, weighed on an electronic laboratory scale, might weigh 113.3975 grams, plus or minus 0.00005 gram. The grocer's scale has an error tolerance of 5 ounces, and the laboratory scale has an error tolerance of 0.00005 gram.

The failure of the power capability indexes for LDCs might be explained by their inability to distinguish between nations whose values on the measured attributes are very close together. The error tolerance of the scales might be too large to make this distinction; they might work well only for nations whose values (measured attributes) are far apart.

In fact, I found earlier that the indexes worked better for the top scale positions (Groups 1 and 2) and the bottom scale positions (Group 4) than they did for the middle (Group 3). Significantly, the raw scores for Group 3 are far closer together than either of the extremes.

Compounding this problem, national attribute data collected in the Third World are often less reliable than comparable data for developed nations. Not only may the measurement scales used for all nations be insensitive, but the Third World data are noisy.

Conclusion

For many reasons, political scientists have long been interested in the measurement of nations' power capabilities and their relative rankings along this dimension. The evidence presented here suggests that the indexes developed to perform this task systematically err. They work well for developed nations, but they fail when applied in the Third World.

I have suggested several explanations for this failure. The underlying problem is the lack of a theoretical basis for the indexes (see Chapter 5 in this book). Indeed, tests of the internal validity of an indicator, such as those in this chapter, must be very crude without a theoretical model that specifies the linkages among the crucial variables (Carley, 1981, p. 68; Blalock, 1982, p. 40). More conclusive tests of the validity of the power capability indexes must wait upon a causal model that relates the four power concepts and specifies operational links to the empirical world. Measurement of power capability cannot be separated from conceptualization and theory building.

In conclusion, I suggest that this subject has barely been explored, despite its centrality to political science. Many political scientists have succumbed to the extreme temptations of fatalistically accepting capability indexes and applying them indiscriminately or rejecting them out of hand. We need to develop and use power capability indexes, but with a healthy skepticism. Systematic work on basic issues of conceptualization and operationalization are essential if power is to be a useful explanatory concept.

The following data sources were used for this chapter:

Central Intelligence Agency, *The World Factbook* (1985); SIPRI, *Stockholm International Peace Research Institute* (1984); Ruth Sivard, *World Military and Social Expenditures* (1983); United Nations, *Energy Statistics Yearbook* (1983); United Nations, *Industrial Statistics Yearbook* (1982); United Nations, *Yearbook of International Trade Statistics* (1983); United Nations, *National Account Statistics* (1983); United Nations, *Statistical Yearbook* (1984); World Bank, *World Development Report* (1984a).

Appendix: Index Operationalization

German

$$X_G = N(L + P + I + M), \tag{1}$$

in which

$L = f_1(\text{territory, use of territory})$
$\quad = T/d_p d_r,$

where T = territory in 1000s of km^2
$\quad d_p$ = 5 if population density > 200/km^2
$\quad\quad$ = 10 if 30/km^2 < population density < 200/km^2
$\quad\quad$ = 20 if population density < 30/km^2
$\quad d_r$ = 1.0 if rail density < 30 km/km^2
$\quad\quad$ = 1.5 if 30 km/km^2 < rail density < 75 km/km^2
$\quad\quad$ = 2.0 if 75 km/km^2 < rail density < 150 km/km^2
$\quad\quad$ = 3.0 if rail density > 150 km/km^2;

$P = f_2 (\text{workforce, use of workforce})$
$\quad = WE + a_m + a_s + a_f,$

where W = workforce (age 15–60)
$\quad E$ = efficiency
$\quad\quad$ = 1 if energy consumption < 0.5 ton coal/capita
$\quad\quad$ = 2 if 0.5 ton < energy consumption < 1.5 tons
$\quad\quad$ = 3 if 1.5 tons < energy consumption < 3.0 tons
$\quad\quad$ = 4 if 3.0 tons < energy consumption < 5.0 tons
$\quad\quad$ = 5 if energy consumption > 5.0 tons
$\quad a_m$ = 5(workers in manufacturing industry)
$\quad a_s$ = W/3 if "morale" higher than average
$\quad\quad$ = W/2 if "morale" very high"
$\quad a_f$ = F(total population) – (total population)
$\quad F$ = percentage of food consumption grown at home;

$I = f_3(\text{resources, use of resources})$
$\quad = RS + B,$

in which

$R = r_s + r_c + r_l + r_o + r_e,$

where r_s = steel production in 10^6 metric tons/year
$\quad r_c$ = coal production in 10^6 metric tons/year

r_l = lignite production in 5×10^6 metric tons/year
r_o = crude oil production in 10^6 metric tons/year
r_e = hydroelectricity in coal equivalent
S = 2 if economy is "directed"
   = 1 if free market economy;

and in which
$$B = b_s + b_o + b_m + b_e,$$

where b_s = steel surplus or deficit
b_o = oil surplus or deficit
b_m = mineral surplus or deficit
b_e = engineering surplus or deficit.

All coded as

+ 0.10(RS) if large surplus
+ .05(RS) if surplus
0 if no surplus or deficit
–0.05(RS) if deficit
–0.10(RS) if large deficit;

M = 10(military personnel) in millions;
N = 2 if nuclear armed; 1 if not.

Fucks

$$X_F = \frac{(EP^{1/3}) + (SP^{1/3})}{2}. \tag{2}$$

where E = energy production
P = population
S = steel production

Singer

$$X_S = \frac{(R_1 + R_2 + R_3 + R_4 + R_5 + R_6)}{6}, \tag{3}$$

where R_1 = (national population/world population) x 100
R_2 = (national urban population/world urban population) x 100
R_3 = (national steel production/world steel production) x 100
R_4 = (national fuel consumption/world fuel consumption) x 100
R_5 = (national military personnel/world military personnel) x 100
R_6 = (national military expenditures/world military expenditures) x 100.

Cline

$$X_C = (C + E + M)(S + W), \tag{4}$$

where C = critical mass = population + territory
  E = economic capability
  M = military capability
  S = strategic purpose
  W = will to pursue national strategy;

  $C = P + T,$

where P = 5 for countries with population over 100 million
  = 4 for countries between 50 and 100 million
  = 3 for countries between 20 and 50 million
  = 2 for countries between 15 and 20 million
  = 1 for countries between 12 and 15 million
  = 0 for countries below 12 million
  T = 5 for countries with area over 3.5 million miles^2
  = 4 for countries between 1 and 3 million miles^2
  = 3 for countries between 0.5 and 1 million miles^2
  = 2 for countries between 250 and 500 thousand miles^2
  = 1 for countries between 94 and 250 thousand miles^2
  = 0 for countries with area below 94 thousand miles^2;

  $E = e_1 + e_2 + e_3 + e_4 + e_5 + e_6,$

where e_1 = income
  e_2 = energy
  e_3 = minerals
  e_4 = industry
  e_5 - food
  e_6 = trade;

  $M = m_1 + m_2 + m_3,$

where m_1 = strategic balance
  m_2 = conventional balance
  m_3 = effort.

Notes

I am grateful to Richard Merritt, Dina Zinnes, Claudio Cioffi-Revilla, Steven Seitz, Gretchen Hower, Paul Pudaite, Michael D. Ward, and Richard Stoll for their helpful comments on the manuscript.

1. This tautological nature should not distress. Indeed, the physical sciences demonstrate the utility of tautologies in explanation and prediction. Causal laws are necessarily true and are implied by the properties of things. But, as all conditions and relevant causes can never be fully specified, empirical causation cannot be completely traced. In general, tautological *arguments* should present no theoretical problem; they are simply logical identities. Tautological *tests*, however, are a serious problem, for circularity nullifies the purpose of testing.

2. Several other statistical tests were run. I repeated the analysis using the raw scores generated by the indexes (interval measurement) rather than the ranks, finding a more pronounced difference between Group 3 and the other groups. I also did the analysis using a different criterion for development—physicians per thousand. Dividing the nations into two groups with the median number of physicians/1000 as the cutoff point, I again found a significant difference between the strengths of rank correlations for LDCs and MDCs (MDCs: average $r_s = .826$; LDCs: average $r_s = .602$; significance of the difference: $Z = 1.97$, $p = .024$).

3. In addition, one would have to establish that a particular nation A caused a given outcome O. One must be sure that outcome O would not have happened in the absence of A. this is a very difficult thing to demonstrate in history and in most cases must be highly speculative. In a power relationship, of course, many causal links exist other than the ones under consideration. These other links must be explored to evaluate the causal link of interest. As a minimum requirement for a causal analysis—a requirement I could not currently meet using the confrontation test—all the "significant causes in a given context" must be specified (Bohm, 1957, pp. 7–10).

4

Choosing Among Measures of Power: A Review of the Empirical Record

Jacek Kugler and Marina Arbetman

Power provides the foundation for relations among nations in the global system. Power is a persistent, elusive concept widely used in the analysis of international politics, whose deep theoretical roots interconnect major efforts to understand conflict and cooperation. Power is an integral element in the classic analysis of Kautilya (circa 310 B.C./1967), Thucydides (circa 450 B.C./1951), Niccolo Machiavelli (1513/1950), or Thomas Hobbes (1651/ 1957) and provides the thread that joins the very different approaches of Edward Hallett Carr (1951), Hans Morgenthau (1962), A. F. K. Organski (1968), Inis L. Claude Jr. (1962), Henry Kissinger (1957), Kenneth Waltz (1979), Robert Gilpin (1981), Robert Keohane (1984) or Bruce Bueno de Mesquita (1981) to mention just some of the most prominent and diverse exponents.

Power is not simply of interest to academics. National leaders have an undeniable desire to estimate their power in relation to that of potential opponents hoping that such sounding will reflect on their ability to impose on, or withstand pressures by competitors. It is somewhat surprising therefore that despite this long theoretical and practical interest in power there is still so little consensus regarding the definition of this basic concept and particularly its measurement. In this chapter we attempt to define the concept of power for use in world politics, evaluate the reliability of alternate measures, and tentatively explore the validity of such indicators.

Definition of Power

Within the field of international politics several definitions are used concurrently. Morgenthau (1962, p. 28) proposed that "when we speak of power, we mean man's control over the minds and actions of other men."

This abstract conception still prevails in many sectors despite the obvious difficulty of defining and the impossibility of measuring the influence of one person over the "mind" of another. An alternate definition is provided by Organski (1968, p. 104), who argues that "power...is the ability to influence the behavior of others in accordance with one's ends." This conception requires knowledge of an actor's capabilities to achieve a goal and the actor's preferences regarding the desirability of alternate outcome. Karl W. Deutsch (1968, p. 22) attempts to reduce the concept further and argues that "power, put most crudely and simply, is the ability to prevail in conflict and overcome obstacles." This definition restricts power to evaluations of conflicts and overlooks its role in cooperation. We feel that a middle ground is the appropriate starting point for this discussion of power.

In world politics, power refers to the capability a society to produce resources and to the ability of national elites to apply such capabilities in conflictual or cooperative environments. Capabilities are the objective aspects of power. Economic, political, military, technological and demographic components are used to evaluate the potential capability of a nation to influence another. The ability of elites to mobilize resources in the pursuit of national goals is a more elusive target that reflects political capacity. Much of the controversy over the measurement of power centers on the interaction between these two components and requires clarification before any attempts to assess reliability and validity can proceed.

Gregory King (1696/1973, p. 36), in one of the first attempts to measure national power by aggregating economic and demographic indicators, provides us with a vivid and surprisingly modern evaluation of national capabilities:

> If to be well appraised of the true state and condition of a nation—especially in the two main articles, of its people and wealth—be a piece of political knowledge, of all others at all times, the most useful and necessary; then surely, at a time when a long and very expensive war against a potent Monarch . . . seems to be at its crisis; such a knowledge of our own nation must be of the highest concern. But, since the attaining thereof . . . is next to impossible, we must content ourselves with such near approaches to it as the grounds we have to [rely] upon will enable us to make.

King was aware that national capabilities—even when fully estimated and adequately integrated—would fail to indicate what proportion of such capabilities could be applied in a particular situation. Klaus Knorr (1956) expands on this point when he distinguishes between actual and potential power. Actual power is the resources mobilized at a given point in time. Potential power is the resources that elites have the capacity to mobilize.

Actual power and potential power are equal only during the stress of a total war. A serious confusion stems from the lack of agreement over which of these two concepts represents power.

We believe that potential power is the appropriate concept for empirical measurement because it captures the structural constraints of decisionmaking. Potential power remains relatively constant in the short run. It is not possible to infer from potential power how much of this resource will be applied in a given situation. Thus, variations in the outcomes of confrontations are due in part to potential power and in part to measurable variations in perceptions or commitments that cannot be anticipated without direct reference and knowledge of a particular confrontation. For this reason some choose to use the term capabilities rather than power (J. David Singer et al., 1972).

This view of power is not universally accepted and some argue that perceptions and involvement must also be added (Morgenthau, 1962; Raymond Aron, 1966; Michael D. Ward and Lewis L. House, 1988). Ray S. Cline (1980), for example, argues that power combines capabilities and commitment to a given goal, expressed by the will of elites and the resolve among mobilized supporters of the government to pursue the strategy established by such elites. Along a slightly different line, King (1696/1973, p. 31), foreshadowing current arguments about perceptions, points out that "the vanity of people in over evaluating their own strength is so natural to all nations, as well as ours, that it has influenced all former calculation of this kind, both at home and abroad." Likewise, Robert Jervis (1976) argues that "misperception" is critical since actors do not behave according to reality but on their perceptions of reality. The implications of distortions of power created by perceptions are summarized by Ole Holsti (1962, p. 245):

> Decision makers act upon their definition of the situation and their images of states—others as well as their own. These images are in turn dependent upon the decision makers's belief system, and these may not be accurate representations of "reality." Thus, it has been suggested that conflict frequently is not between states, but rather between distorted images of states.

Such distortions cannot be denied. However, resources mobilized in response to threats and perceptual distortions can be approximated independently, allowing the reconciliation of potential power and actual power. Here we agree with Bruce Bueno de Mesquita (1981) that the concept of power should be restricted to the structural constraints that measure the probability of success. The importance or salience of specific issues that reflect the willingness of elites to use capabilities at their disposal, and the propensity of such elites to accept risk, which captures the willingness of actors to accept uncertain gains, should be evaluated separately. For example, recall that risk takers distort objective probabilities by "gambling" that their chances of success in a confrontation are unreasonably high. In anticipation of a confrontation, pure risk takers perceive that they are stronger than objective estimates indicate, wager that third parties will help, and concurrently perceive their opponents as weaker than in actuality and discount the probability that a third party will come to their aid (Bueno de Mesquita et al., 1985; James Morrow, 1987). Pure risk-averse actors, on the other hand, underestimate their own chances while overvaluing that of their opponents. Combinations of such distorted views of reality lead actors to take steps that cannot be anticipated objectively by calculations of potential power. Indeed, quite distinct decisions can be made by elites of two equally powerful nations because they perceive potential outcomes very differently (Kugler and Frank Zagare, 1987).

Moreover, the disparity between objective and perceived power is impossible to assess outside the boundaries of actual events. When a confrontation escalates to war, distortions generated by perceptions of power are superceded by objective measures, which in turn determine the outcome. Thus, misperception affects decisions only as long as power remains untested.

To use power as a variable over time one cannot aggregate structural constraints with temporal pursuits of specific objectives. We know that power is seldom used to its fullest. Indeed, even belligerents are rarely willing to commit all their capabilities *unless* each party anticipates that the vanquished will have to endure political occupation and territorial dismemberment (Kugler and William Domke, 1986). Limited conflicts do not justify the full use of available power. Contrast, for example, the performance of the United States in conflicts against Japan and North Vietnam. In the war with Japan the United States committed its forces fully, endured heavy losses, and demanded unconditional surrender to end the war. During the conflict with North Vietnam, by contrast, the American commitment was limited, heavy losses were avoided, and defeat was accepted even when unilateral escalation by the United States was still viable. In raw capability terms, the United States was weaker in relation to Japan during the 1940s, than in relation to North Vietnam during the 1960s and 1970s. Yet, the United States defeated Japan and withdrew from Vietnam under pressure. The outcome in each of these conflicts was not decided by power constraints but by the ability of elites in the United States to mobilize resources in pursuit of their goals. Using the actual power exercised, one can argue that the United States was not powerful enough to defeat North Vietnam but was strong enough to vanquish Japan. The problem with such a conception is that power is not a variable but a relative measure that gauges the chosen level of reaction in particular situations.

In summary, the limitation of potential power is that other elements must be included to analyze the outcomes of limited confrontations or to understand cooperative behavior. Only in the rare instance of total war are the outcomes well understood because salience and risk attain extreme values. Potential power can therefore only outline the necessary but not sufficient conditions for conflict or cooperation and requires additional indicators to account for the resolution of most other events. Thus, potential power provides a base for analysis without regard for the specific context of an event and is relatively consistent measure across peaceful and conflictual situations.

Alternative Measures of Power

Even when the concept of power is narrowly defined, the alternatives for measurement are vast. Richard L. Meritt and Dina A. Zinnes (see Chapter 2 in this book) provide a very recent overview of alternatives. They divide the field between those that advocate single indictor measures and those that view the problem as far more complex. One tradition attempts to provide parsimonious single indicators of power. Claude (1962), Deutsch (1968), and many others propose that military capacity is a good approximation to power. In historical evaluations, the size of naval forces have been used, but more complex measures of military strength, including expenditure, army size, and nuclear capability are now available (ACDA, 1986; Modelski and Thompson, 1987). Energy consumption sometimes augmented by fuel consumption is another parsimonious and cross-nationally comparable way to measure power (Bruce Russett, 1968; Oskar Morgenstern et al., 1973). Following the lead of King (1696/1973), Kingsley Davis (1954), Organski (1958), and Charles Hitch and Roland McKean (1960) advocate total output as an indicator of power because, unlike energy consumption, GNP can be used to aggregate or disaggregate additional elements useful for power.

Critics of single-indicator measures recognize their simplicity and parsimony but argue that they lack realism and suggest that more intricate measures can express more fully the complexity of power. Organski and Jacek Kugler (1980) argue that total output should be augmented by the addition of foreign aid and that each of these elements should be weighed by the political capacity of national elites to mobilize the pool of resources available in a society. Wilhelm Fucks (1965) proposes a weighted, interactive measure of power that combines population, energy consumption, and steel production. Cline (1980) incorporates in his capability element (1) critical mass measured by territory and population, (2) economic capacity indexed by income and production of energy, critical nonfuel minerals, manufacturing, foods, and trade, and (3) military capacity composed of combat capabilities, the strategic balance, and an effort indicator. All these elements are equally weighted and added to attain a total score for a given nation. After this point the total is then adjusted for the commitment of a nation by taking into account judgments on national strategy and national will. Another complex index is proposed by F. Clifford German (1960), who argues that power is reflected by a rather intricate interaction between land, population, industry, military capabilities, and the availability of nuclear weapons. These components are aggregated through additive and interactive structures to attain a measure of power.

Despite their variety, few of the proposed power measures are used beyond a single cross-sectional evaluation. Indeed, an informal review of research using power shows that GNP, the index proposed by the Correlates of War (COW) Project, and variations of these two are the most widely used measures of power in current research. Therefore, to evaluate the cross-temporal reliability and then to address the more difficult question of validity of power indexes, these two measures and their variations are used.

Our first goal is to determine whether these indicators are reliable in the sense of measuring the same phenomena. If reliability is established, the results of studies using alternate indicators are comparable—if not, the measures themselves may account for important differences. We consider whether military effort and nuclear weapons are critical as explicit elements in the assessment of potential power and whether distance plays a critical role. Our second goal is to take a step in the direction of verifying the accuracy of these indicators in evaluations of total conflict. Meritt and Zinnes (see Chapter 2 in this book) call for precisely this kind of investigation, because regardless or reliability of alternate measures it is important to show that such indicators capture the power of nations.

Indicator Reliability

To test the reliability of power indicators, we compare the national capabilities of the major powers from 1850 through 1980. The constant sample of countries selected for this comparison—United States, Russia/Soviet Union, Germany/West Germany, France, United Kingdom, and Japan—includes all the critical major power for over a century. We keep the sample of countries constant over time because otherwise only cross sectional comparisons are accurate. The reason is that when a major power is excluded (i.e., Austria–Hungary for lack of a successor state or China for lack of data) the proportional capabilities of the remaining nations in the sample are overestimated in relation to their real capabilities after the year such nations are excluded.

National capabilities change at a relatively slow pace. Many estimates are used to compile the data (see Tables 4.1–4.5 in the appendix at the end of this chapter for details) and to avoid undue precision, we compare alternate estimates of capabilities at 10-year intervals starting in 1850. However, since we are equally interested in the cooperative and conflictual behavior of major powers, the performance of these countries in war periods is critical. Unfortunately, COW data for critical war years are still incomplete. To capture in part the differences caused by the anticipation of conflict and crisis we include 1913 and 1938, because they mark the initiation of World Wars I and II, and use 1925 rather than the end of that decade for the interwar period, because this year reflects partly the devastation from World War I and the distortions caused by the Great Depression.

Comparison of Base Capabilities

The basic comparison to be made is between the COW Index and GNP to ascertain whether complexity is a critical element in the construction of reliable indicators of capabilities.

Gross National Product represents the total value of output in a society. By this device one measures the performance of the total economy including the private and governmental sectors. The items included in Gross National Product are a set of sector accounts: households, firms, government, and the rest of the world. The latter is excluded in Gross Domestic Product. In each sector account, "expenditures by final buyers on currently produced goods and services, and income earned in the process of current production" are recorded. By aggregating the expenditure side of these sector accounts, "a measure of market value of currently produced goods and services" is obtained with the purpose of measuring the total output. A further adjustment is made to translate the measure of output in money terms into a measure of output in real terms. This is done by deflating for price level changes, which leaves a measure of real output change over time (R. Musgrave, 1959, pp. 184–185; see also Table 4.1 in the chapter appendix). Recall that Gross Output was originally developed by King (1696/1973) to compare the strength of nations rather than to monitor economic performance because total output expresses concurrently the results of all productive factors and encompasses the contribution of demographic factors.

A more complex basic measure of capabilities is proposed by the Correlates of War Project (COW) headed by J. David Singer. The COW Index is a linear combination of (1) demographic capabilities measured by total population and urban population in cities larger than 20,000;

(2) industrial capabilities reflected by energy consumption and iron production (1820–1895) or steel production (1896–1980), and (3) military capabilities indexed by military expenditures and size of active armed forces. These indicators are weighted equally, converted into proportions, and aggregated into a single measure by adding, separately, the proportions of each element held by a nation and dividing that total by the number of indicators. The composite score weighs all factors equally (Singer et al., 1972).

To allow direct comparisons with the COW Index, GNP is standardized by calculating what proportion of the total each major power held at each time point (see Tables 4.1 and 4.2 in the chapter appendix). Since the sample of countries remains constant these proportions measure the relative standings and changes in such standings over time for each nation.

The congruence between indicators is assessed by ordinary least squares. This approach is very useful because the two series measure national capabilities in exactly the same way—when the constant is zero, the regression coefficient is one and the correlation coefficient approaches unity. Deviations from this pattern indicate specific disparities among the two measures. Consider the first set of results.

Relationship between the COW Index and GNP: 1850–1980

$$\text{COW Index} = 1.72 + .90 \text{ GNP} \tag{1}$$
$$(1.34) \quad (.07)$$

$R^2 = .69,$ cases $= 78,$ significance $= .0001.$

The relationship between these two basic measures of capabilities is strong. The GNP accounts for almost 70% of the variance in the COW Index. The intercept is located slightly above the 1% mark but it is not significant, indicating that GNP and the COW Index score the average nation equally. This slight understatement by GNP translates into a 2% distortion since the largest nations in this sample hold approximately 40% of total capabilities. Finally, change is not reflected very accurately. The two measures vary at the same rate when a one-to-one relation is established. The regression coefficient suggests that changes in capabilities measured by GNP are 10% less pronounced than similar changes measured by the COW Index.

Still, the high standard error attached to the constant and the relatively high error associated with the rate of change in GNP suggests that there is wide internal dispersion between these two indexes of power. To identify whether these results are produced by differences in rank or dispersion within the variable, we concentrate on the rate of change alone:

Relationship between the COW Index and GNP without a constant: 1850–1980

$$\text{COW Index} = \underset{(.035)}{.97 \text{GNP}} \tag{2}$$

$R^2 = .91,$ cases $= 78,$ significance $= .0001.$

These two measures of capabilities now co-vary consistently. The variance explained exceeds 90%, and the critical rate of change is not significantly different from the anticipated slope of one (the difference between 1.00 and the estimated b of .97 is not significant at .04). We therefore conclude that cross-sectional ranking based on the COW Index and GNP is the source of the differences. Once a rank is established, changes in the relative capabilities among major powers are identified in the same way by either measure.

The practical implication of results in Equation (2) is that the COW Index and GNP are compatible in time series analysis. Parsimony does not affect temporal reliability as some have suggested; rather, the two measures are equally serviceable in cross-temporal analysis (see Merritt and Zinnes, 1988 p. 143). However, the dispersion in ranking among these two indexes is relevant for cross national research because here discordance among the two indexes will lead to different results. A simple plot (Figure 4.1) of the two measures of capabilities identifies the main differences.

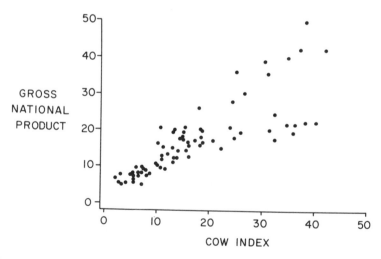

Figure 4.1   Relationship Between the COW Index and GNP: 1850–1980

GNP tends to underestimate the capabilities of the largest among the major powers. Indeed, among nations that hold more than 20% of all major power resources, there is a noticeable divergence that produces two clear clusters. Scores among the bulk of the smaller major powers are very consistent. However, the two indexes measure the strength of hegemons and their immediate challengers very differently. To explore these differences further, we considered military factors.

Impact of Military Factors on Basic Capabilities

The reason for concentrating first on military factors is that the COW Index and GNP are composed of similar elements with the exception of military factors. Recall that both include economic and demographic dimensions. They differ, however, in basic design because the COW Index incorporates explicit measures of military components, while GNP includes such factors implicitly.

Theoretical reasons are given for this disparity. Singer and his colleagues (1972) argue that the COW Index includes military elements to reflect the difference in cross-national allocations to defense. Countries that do not exert their military muscle are considered less capable of influencing others. Hitch and McKean (1960), among others, contend that GNP does not need to account explicitly for military allocation because money is fungible and nations will allocate resources to the military according to their perception of threats. Adding military expenditures to economic indicators or productivity amounts to double counting.

The difference between these two approaches is illustrated with the case of Japan. In the past, Japan made a serious commitment to the military but since 1945 this country has only spent a token 1% of their GNP on the military. Using total output as an indicator of capabilities, Japan emerges as one of the most powerful nations and will soon rival the Soviet Union; while using the COW Index, Japan's capabilities are substantially discounted since on army size and military expenditures—two out of six components in the index—Japan ranks last in the sample. Presumably, then, the main reason for the difference in ranks among these two indicators may be found in the military element.

Military effort in a given year is estimated by the difference between the percentage distribution of military expenditures in the group of nations considered minus the percentage distribution of GNP in the same group (see Table 4.5 in the chapter appendix for data and sources). When military effort is positive, countries "overspend" by committing a larger proportion to the military than their proportion of GNP warrants. When the military effort is negative, major powers "underspend" on the military in relation to their

GNP. The overall impact of military allocations on measures of national capabilities is detailed below:

Relationship between the COW Index, GNP, and relative military effort: 1850–1980

COW Index = .94 + .94 GNP + .31 Military Expenditures   (3)
　　　　　(1.13) (.06)　　　(.06)
R^2= .78,　　　cases = 78,　　　significance = .0001.

Military buildups have an important effect on the two indexes. The relationship between the COW Index and GNP remains close to anticipated patterns. The intercept is not significant, the rate of change suggests a one-to-one relationship. Moreover, military expenditures account for a substantial portion of the remaining variance and improve the fit among these two indicators by 10%. The COW Index is therefore capturing aspects of power mobilization that are not included in GNP.

Recall that GNP and the COW Index diverge for the largest among the major powers. Perhaps these nations also spend more on the military than their weaker counterparts. To investigate this possibility we consider—separately—the relationship between these two indicators for countries that underspend and overspend on the military:

Relationship between the COW Index and GNP by levels of relative military expenditures: 1850–1980

COW Index = 0.0 DU + .98 GNPU + .39 MEU
　　　　　　(**)　　　(.09)　　　(.16)
　　　　　 + 1.28 DO + .93 GNPO + .42 MEO   (4)
　　　　　　(**)　　　(.11)　　　(.11)
R^2 = .79,　　　cases = 78,　　　significance = .0001.
where
DO　 = Dummy for nations with military overexpenditures (value = 0)
DU　 = Dummy for nations with military underexpenditure (value = 1)
GNPO = GNP for nations with military overexpenditures
GNPU = GNP for nations with military underexpenditures
MEO　 = military expenditures for nations overspending on the military
MEU　 = military expenditures for nations underspending on the military
** Coefficient is not significant

National capabilities are measured most consistently and reliably when military expenditures are underemphasized. Among major powers that underspend on the military, the relationship between the COW Index and GNP is completely congruent with theoretical expectations. The intercept is not significant and the rate of change is not meaningfully different from the expected one-to-one relation. However, the impact of military underexpenditures is barely significant. Thus, for nations that underspend, either measure of power is equally effective.

Quite a different picture emerges among countries that overspend on the military. The rank difference among the two indicators still centers on zero, but the rate of change now indicates that GNP attenuates changes by 10% in relation to the COW Index. Moreover, large military efforts account for much of the variance among these two indicators, creating systematic distinctions among nations. Thus, COW Index credits the nations for military mobilization, while GNP is not directly affected by such allocations. The underlying characteristics of this relationship can be further explored with the aid of Figure 4.2.

Circles indicate a proportional underallocation to military expenditure given overall resources, while squares indicate proportional overallocations. The size of each circle or square indicates the level of under- or overallocation to military expenditures.

Figure 4.2 can be conveniently divided into two sectors. Levels of military effort are not a useful discriminator among major powers that hold less than 20% of national capabilities. However, among major powers that hold more than 20% of total capabilities and compete for hegemony in the international arena, a diverging pattern emerges.

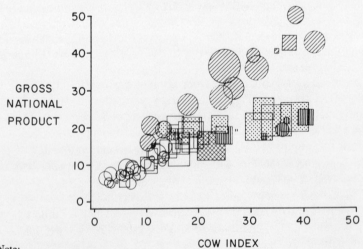

Note:
Circles indicate undercommitment to military expenditures.
Squares indicate overcommitment to military expenditures.

USA ▨   Russia/USSR ▦   Great Britain ▥   Germany ▧

Figure 4.2   Relationship Between GNP, COW Index and Military Expenditures: 1850–1980

We explore whether these differences can systematically be related to military expenditures. Consider first the Soviet Union. This nation would hardly qualify for superpower status after 1938 based on its GNP. The COW Index, on the other hand, assigns the Soviet Union a very high ranking reflective of its military effort. The evaluation of U.S. performance provides a sharp contrast. Both the COW Index and GNP show the same pattern even though the United States consistently underemphasizes the military sector. Thus, the Soviet Union, like Germany prior to each world war, compensates for its economic weakness by building its military arm in the post-World War II period. On the other hand, the United States whose economy is much more productive, like Britain in the 19th century, allocates resources elsewhere without loss in its capability rank.

This pattern is not completely consistent. Military effort does not account for the performance of Britain. The military effort of Britain prior to World War II fluctuates between mild overexpenditure and underexpenditure, yet the COW Index ranks British capabilities consistently higher than GNP. Indeed, the largest distortions occur between 1850 and 1880 when Britain was undergoing industrialization rather than militarization (see Tables 4.1 and 4.5 in the appendix to this chapter). It is difficult to conclude, given the performance of Britain, that all divergences between the COW Index and GNP are due to military effort. Yet, the COW Index reacts quickly to military allocations while GNP provides a consistent indicator whether the country is at peace or war. The results for the United States and Britain seem to contradict Paul Kennedy's (1987: 514-535) recent highly acclaimed thesis that military overexpenditure leads to the decline of dominant powers (for further details see Kugler and Organski, 1988).

The more important question is whether the explicit inclusion of military effort simply reflects mobilization for war or more realistically indicates potential power. A review of the periods of military mobilizations provide a partial answer. Britain—never an overwhelming economic power—also does not emphasize the military sector until its dominance of the international order is threatened by Germany in the early 1900s. By contrast, the Soviet Union compensates with military effort for a weak economy during the Cold War. Finally, the United States does not overspend until the Vietnam conflict. Therefore, among the leading major nations, military effort seems to coincide with the perception of international threat. However, it is difficult to translate such evaluations into power since preparation for war may indicate weakness as well as strength. The data at hand show that these power indicators differ in their evaluation of large major nations, but it is still an open question whether a militarily mobilized country is stronger than one not yet mobilized. We return to this point, tentatively, when we explore the validity of these indicators.

Let us review results thus far. When the military is not stressed, the two measures of capability are very closely associated; when they are stressed, capabilities tend to diverge. Military effort therefore differentiates among these two ways of measuring capabilities. Some of the most serious distortions that systematically affect the largest of major powers are accounted for by military effort, yet this effort is insufficient to account for other equally systematic and sizable disparities. Military factors are responsible for average differences between these two indicators in the range of 10%. However, such differences are much stronger for large countries in competition for dominance. And among such countries the use of alternate indicators can produce different results (Singer et al., 1972; Nazli Choucri and Robert North, 1974; Organski and Kugler, 1980; Hank Houweling and Jan Siccama, 1988). When the emphasis shifts to an analysis of cooperation, distortions are minimal, causing little difference in results due to measurement problems.

Impact of Nuclear Weapons on Basic Capabilities

The need to adjust capabilities for the presence or absence of nuclear weapons was suggested from the outset of the nuclear age. Bernard Brodie (1946) argued that nuclear weapons increased destructive capacity by such a wide margin that war could no longer be the continuation of policy by other means, rather, in the atomic era, nuclear weapons could only be used to avert conflict and maintain stability. Thus, Brodie anticipated a dramatic reduction of conflict and its replacement by cooperation because of the impact of nuclear weapons on power.

How should nuclear capacity affect power? Karl W. Deutsch (1968) once suggested that capabilities in the current age are nuclear capabilities. Constructing an index on this basis would suggest that the United States was omnipotent in the late 1940s and early 1950s, that the United States only had to share this dominance with the Soviet Union in the late 1950s, 1960s, and early 1970s, and since that time these two actors have to consider China and perhaps France and England in their evaluations (see Table 4.6 in the chapter appendix). This view does not seem to square well with the application of power in the international arena.

The record of success for nuclear powers since 1945 is mixed. Nuclear weapons have proliferated, and their destructive capability has steadily been enlarged and diversified. It is true that following the destruction of Hiroshima and Nagasaki no conflict has been waged with nuclear weapons. However, there is increasing evidence that the possession of such capabilities does not reduce the likelihood of conflict nor does it secure success in conventional confrontations (Kugler, 1973; Kugler and Zagare, 1987; Paul Huth and Bruce Russett, 1988). Nuclear weapons may not be the absolute weapon originally anticipated, still it should be an element in the complex equation of power.

Charles Doran and William Parsons (1980) argue that if capabilities are a composite of many resources, clearly nuclear weapons with their unusually high destructive capability should be incorporated as a distinct element of the COW Index (see also German, 1960). Their inclusion would stress the difference between true superpowers and other nations. No such adjustments are required for total output, since nuclear weapons, like other military expenditures, can be disregarded because funds will be allocated in response to threats and according to the effectiveness of alternate weapon systems.

It is possible to test the impact of nuclear weapons rather easily since the number of nuclear powers is still very small. Only five overt players—the United States, the Soviet Union, China, France, and England—have admitted to the deployment of nuclear weapons. In addition, three or four less overt ones—India, Israel, South Africa, and Pakistan—have deployed or can in a very short time deploy such weapons. A score of others have the potential to do so in the foreseeable future (Stephen Meyer, 1984).

To show how nuclear weapons affect the structure of capabilities among the major powers, we add nuclear weapons as one more element in the COW Index. The sample we are surveying is very appropriate for this task since four of the five nations with overt nuclear capabilities are included. Since nuclear weapons were introduced in 1945, we restrict comparisons to the last 40 years. To calculate the nuclear capabilities of major powers we use the percentage of nuclear warheads deployed on delivery vehicles with an appropriate range (Tables 4.2 and 4.6 in the chapter appendix) and add them to the COW Index following the same procedure used for other variables.

To show the impact of nuclear weapons on capabilities we contrast first the COW Index against the same measure that now includes nuclear capabilities:

Relationship between the COW Index excluding and including nuclear weapons: 1945–1980

$$\text{COW Index} = \quad 2.32 + \quad .86 \, \text{Nuclear COW Index} \qquad (5)$$
$$\phantom{\text{COW Index} =} (.76) \quad (.03)$$
$$R^2 = .97, \qquad \text{cases} = 24, \qquad \text{significance} = .0001.$$

Adding nuclear weapons to the COW Index produces the most measurable differences recorded thus far, even though the two measures are very strongly related. Nations that do not have nuclear weapons are—as expected—undervalued once nuclear weapons are included. Moreover, there is a constant rank adjustment of slightly over two percentage points for the average nation. Given the potential impact of nuclear weapons in waging wars, these results seem rather attenuated.

The reason for the attenuated impact of nuclear weapons, however, is found in the construction of the COW Index. As the number of indicators increases, the overall impact of each additional indicator declines. Therefore, when nuclear weapons are added as the seventh independent indicator, even the nuclear hegemony by the United States between 1945 and 1960, or, after 1960, the preponderance shared by the United States and the Soviet Union, affects overall estimates of capabilities at the margin. Is this an effective reflection of the impact of nuclear weapons on world politics? No direct answer to this question is possible. However, an indirect way to assess the strength attributed to nuclear weapons can be gained by reviewing the relation between the nuclear adjusted COW Index and GNP:

Relationship between the COW Index including nuclear weapons and GNP: 1950–1980

$$\text{Nuclear COW Index} = \quad -1.00 + \quad 1.06 \text{ GNP} \tag{6}$$
$$\qquad\qquad\qquad\qquad (1.70) \qquad (.08)$$
$$R^2 = .89, \qquad \text{cases} = 24, \qquad \text{significance} = .0001.$$

The relationship between the nuclear adjusted COW Index and GNP is *stronger and more precise* than without such adjustments. Despite a vastly reduced number of cases, the variance explained now approaches 90% contrasted with the 70% previously reported, and the fits of rank and change both improve [see Equation (1)]. Indeed, much of the disparity attributed to military effort since 1945 may simply be due to the development of nuclear weapons. A more detailed look at the direct impact of nuclear warheads is therefore due:

Relationship among the COW Index including nuclear weapons, GNP, and nuclear warheads: 1950–1980

$$\text{Nuclear COW Index} = \quad -.66 + \quad 1.02 \text{ GNP} + \quad .10 \text{ Nuclear warheads} \tag{7}$$
$$\qquad\qquad\qquad\qquad (2.64) \quad (.23) \qquad\qquad (.17)$$
$$R^2 = .89, \qquad \text{cases} = 24, \qquad \text{significance} = .0001.$$

These results confirm that GNP already reflects nuclear capabilities. Note that there is no improvement in the strength of the relationship due to the inclusion of nuclear warheads and—most important—the relationship between the adjusted COW Index and nuclear warheads, controlling for GNP, is not significant. There is ample room to believe therefore that GNP already implicitly includes the impact of dramatic technological developments. An evaluation (Figure 4.3) of the three-dimensional relationship among these variables confirms this judgment and adds further detail.

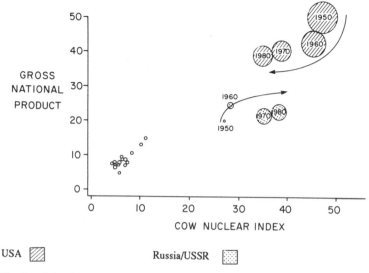

USA [⫽⫽]   Russia/USSR [▦]

The size of the circles indicates the relative number of nuclear warheads.

Figure 4.3   Relationship Between the Nuclear COW Index and GNP, Controlling for Nuclear Warheads: 1950–1980

As in Figure 4.2, the size of the circle reflects the proportion of nuclear warheads held by each country. The main impact of nuclear weapons is, as expected, that they separate the two superpowers from the pack. Also, the size of the circles suggests that the high score accorded to the United States by GNP does not undervalue its relative capability. However, no major changes in rank take place. GNP effectively reflects each nation's relative ability to produce nuclear weapons, and unlike in the case of military effort, neither country gives ground in this area. Thus, Hitch and McKean's (1960, Chap. 1) argument that monetary resources are fungible and are allocated to any activity that is deemed profitable seems to hold very well for nuclear weapons. Figure 4.3 also shows that the deployment of nuclear weapons is recorded accurately by both GNP and the COW Index. In both, the United States shows a small decline in capabilities after nuclear weapons are deployed by the Soviet Union, and this action brings a commensurate rise in the capabilities of the Soviet Union.

The analysis suggests that GNP implicitly and effectively incorporates the effects of nuclear weapons deployment, and that such effects can also be well reflected by the explicit inclusion of nuclear weapons into the COW Index. These results reinforce the perception that for the subset of major powers, either the COW indicator adjusted for nuclear weapons or GNP is an equivalent gauge of power in the nuclear era. However, GNP may be preferred since it is somewhat more responsive to technological changes and does not require adjustments to account for nuclear weapons.

Impact of Distance on Power

Kenneth Boulding (1962) proposed that the power a nation can exercise against an opponent is linked in large part to the distance between the two antagonists. He argued that nations face a "power gradient," which produces a decline in national capabilities due to distance. Various reasons are given for such results, among them the difficulty of maintaining extended supply lines, the lack of familiarity with distant territory, the reduced speed of reinforcement, and the complexity of commanding troops at a distance. Perhaps, the most vivid representation of distance effects can be found in a classic graph, reproduced by Edward Tufte (1983), which shows how during the invasion of Russia, the capabilities of Napoleon's army were depleted as the distance from their home base increased, while concurrently, the capabilities of the Russian army increased as its supply lines grew shorter. The same graph shows, in turn, how this decline in capabilities was directly translated into casualties inflicted on French troops and led to their eventual defeat.

Bueno de Mesquita (1981) suggests that to adjust for this decay in national capabilities one should account for the distance between the capitals of all actors and take into consideration the time required to travel this distance. He argued simply that the farther the target in real terms, the weaker is a country's capacity to exercise influence. To implement this adjustment Bueno de Mesquita (1981, p. 105) proposes the following model:

$$\text{Adjusted capability} = \text{capability}^{\log[(\text{miles/miles per day}+(10\text{-}e)]}$$

This formulation controls for two effects of distance. First, the sheer separation among contenders is taken into account by the distance in miles among the capital of two nations. Second, since the efficiency of transportation varies over time, the effects of sheer distance are reduced when more effective means of transportation are introduced. The faster one can travel on the average, the less will capabilities decline with distance. Thus, this model proposes that if the target is far away, and the average distance that can be covered in one day is short, this adjustment should affect substantially overall capabilities. The inverse is true when distance is short or travel very fast.

There is little doubt that distance has an effect on capabilities. Bueno de Mesquita justifies the exponential expressions used because they have convenient mathematical properties but independent tests have not demonstrated the accuracy of this particular weighting. However, the structure reflects accurately the principle that the farther the home base the more severe is the decline in capabilities, and the slower the means of transportation the larger is the decline in capabilities. Overall trends can therefore be assessed effectively.

What is the effect of such comparisons? We present results only for the COW Index because distance adjustments affect both indicators in the same way. Evaluations of adjusted and nonadjusted COW Index centered on Germany are used to demonstrate their extent (for details on this index see Table 4.3 in the chapter appendix).

Relationship between COW Index adjusted and not adjusted for distance: 1850–1980

$$\text{COW Index} = \quad 2.39 + \quad .86 \text{ COW Index Adjusted for distance} \qquad (8)$$
$$(.64) \quad (.03)$$
$$R^2 = .91, \qquad \text{cases} = 78, \qquad \text{significance} = .0001.$$

For the major powers, most of whom are in Europe, the effects of distance are minimal. The two indexes are strongly related. Ranks are altered only by slightly more than 2%. The two measures co-vary, but the index adjusted for distance changes at a slower rate. This accurately reflects the fact that very powerful members of the international arena—including the United States, the Soviet Union, and Japan—could not exercise their power fully on Germany—located in the center of Europe.

These effects can best be seen over time among distant nations. Indeed, the changes in relative capabilities of the United States in relation to Germany over the last century show marked disparities (Figure 4.4).

The distance adjustment in 1860 is severe. The United States could exert only 30% of available capabilities on Germany. However, the effects of distance drop dramatically with improvement in means of transportation and by 1970 the United States could exert almost 90% of its capabilities on Germany. Thus, distance affected power much more in the past and in traditional societies today than it does among developed nations. Capabilities in the modern period are increasingly impervious to distance since the power of modern states—particularly those that rely heavily on nuclear weapons—are simply not affected by distance. For practical purposes, then, distance adjustments are important for historical research and are worth exploring in long-term cross-temporal analysis. They may be disregarded with little loss in accuracy in current cross-national evaluations, except in very extreme circumstances such as those found in the recent Falkland–Malvinas war.

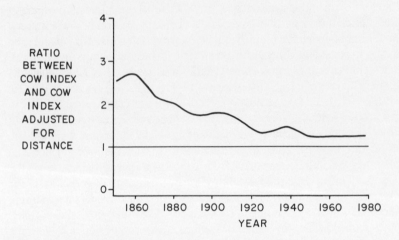

Figure 4.4   Capability Convergence Between the United States and Germany Due to Changes in Transportation Technology

Indicator Validity

The validity of power indicators is always in question. We have shown that alternate, widely used and available indicators are reliable for major powers. However, this may not be so for developing societies. Previous work by Kugler and Domke (1986) and Organski and Kugler (1980) strongly suggested that adequate evaluations of power should include, along with objective components of capabilities, political factors that account for the ability of governments to extract and allocate available resources. In simplified form, this work suggests that power should be conceived as follows:

Power = domestic capabilities + external capabilities,
where
Domestic capabilites = GNP x relative political capacity
and
External capabilities = foreign aid x political capacity of the recipient.

Political capacity transforms capabilites into potential power. A first approximation of national power can be obtained by combining the total pool of human and material assets of a society with the support provided by allies and by weighing these factors by the political capacity of government to use resources. In the empirical work, total population serves as proxy for the size of the working and fighting force, GNP per capita is used to reflect the economic productivity of individuals in a society, foreign aid is a proxy for external contributions, and political capacity is obtained by calculating the ratio of available revenues (in the broadest possible sense of that term) that governments obtain from their societies over expected revenues given the economic constraints faced by that society (Organski and Kugler, 1980, pp. 68–100).

The first three indicators have already been detailed. The measure of political capacity, which is essential to this work, is far less well known. For this reason we provide a brief sketch of the way the index of political capacity is obtained. Government revenues rise and fall because of the interaction between the productivity of the economy and the capacity of the government to extract and allocate available resources. To obtain a measure of political capacity, one must separate the economic from the political aspects embedded in government revenues. A simple device is to take the ratio of what a government actually extracts and what such a government should be able to extract given the wealth of the society:

$$\text{Relative political capacity} = \frac{\text{actual revenue extraction}}{\text{expected revenue extraction}}.$$

Actual extraction measures performance by the revenue extracted. The estimate includes revenues collected through direct and indirect taxes, profits from governmental enterprises or monopolies, and government borrowing. Expected extraction is an econometric estimate of potential revenues based on economic factors that ease or render more difficult the task of a government to obtain revenues. This adjustment places countries on an even economic field. In developing nations where one can assume that governments extract all they can, controls are introduced for reliance on exports, productivity of populations, share of agricultural production, and reliance on mining. In advanced societies one adds controls for commitment to public welfare and education.

RPC captures the difference between what is politically and economically achieved, and what is theoretically feasible on economic grounds alone. Thus, RPC provides a shadow measure of governmental performance that identifies the *relative* ability of a government to perform political tasks given the record of other governments in countries that have achieved the same socioeconomic level of development (see Organski and Kugler, 1980, pp. 227–233; Organski et al., 1984, pp. 140–141; and Kugler and Domke, 1986, for details on measurement and specification). By construction, when the RPC ratio is unity, a nation's political performance is average or normal; when it falls under one, its performance is poor; and when it rises above one, its performance is above expectations. Used as a multiplier, RPC increases the capabilities of politically advanced nations, does not affect that of average performers, and reduces those of poor political performers.

The effectiveness of this political adjustment of the capability base has been tested rather extensively. Organski and Kugler (1980) demonstrate that the outcome of conflicts between developed and developing nations and among developing nations can be effectively accounted for, while in similar circumstances the COW Index and GNP fail. Kugler and Domke (1986) extend this work and show that for the succession of major wars in the 20th century the outcomes can be accounted for much more effectively by the use of capabilities weighted by political capacity than by GNP (recall that the COW Index is not available for these periods). Additional tests done in real time on current conflicts such as the Falkland–Malvinas War, the Iran–Iraq War, and the Russian invasion of Afghanistan, strongly suggest the generality and predictive value of this approach. For example, the outcome of the war in Afghanistan was estimated several days after the Russian invasion took place. At that time it was forecasted as a serious war that would last, like Vietnam, until the withdrawal of foreign troops. The government of Afghanistan could not succeed because it lacked the political capacity to mobilize and utilize domestic or foreign resources. This forecast, rejected at the time, is now coming true.

Few power measures have been exposed to such explicit tests designed to assess the validity of the indicator itself; rather, their assessment is indirect and depends on the validity of a power theory that is under review (Ray and Vural, 1986). We hoped to make a direct cross-temporal comparison with the COW Index for the major powers, but this is not possible at this time because data for the war periods are still being collected. However, the Iran–Iraq conflict provides an opportunity for a partial but detailed evaluation of the validity of these indicators.

The Iran–Iraq conflict is an excellent test of the validity of potential power measures because actual and potential power should approach each other: the Iran–Iraq confrontation is a total, severe, bilateral conflict among two developing nations where external aid does not determine the outcome. We portray this conflict as a total war because both sides are committed fully and wish to avoid defeat for fear of the consequences. Thus, like World War I or II, the outcome of this conflict will be decided by available capabilities and not, like Vietnam or Afghanistan, by the unwillingness of one party to fully commit available resources. Moreover, we argue that this conflict is bilateral and allows one to overlook external capabilities because, unlike in Korea, Vietnam, or Afghanistan, the help of third parties is not the critical element that affects the progress of this war. The analysis uses simple graphic comparisons (Figure 4.5) between these two competitors because they present the best picture of the progress in this conflict.

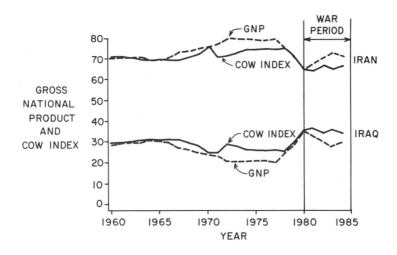

Figure 4.5   Comparison of Capabilities of Iran and Iraq Using the COW Index and GNP

Note that the COW Index and GNP trace the performance of both countries almost identically. For Iran, GNP slightly overestimates capabilities in relation to the COW Index, while for Iraq the opposite is true. Figure 4.5 confirms our previous results that both indicators co-vary closely even for developing nations and are reliable. However, are they valid?

Both comparisons suggest that Iran should have easily defeated Iraq—the initiator—because of an overwhelming advantage. Indeed, prior to the war, Iran has a two-to-one advantage or better. At the point of initiation, Iran is stronger by more than 30%. Slight discrepancies occur after this point. The COW Index suggests that the gap between these two countries drops slightly after the initiation of conflict, while GNP suggests that Iran increases its lead to over 40%. One wonders how Iraq, in spite of such a large disparity in the capability base against it, chose to initiate the war, was successful in the first phase, and continues to maintain a draw. Clearly, such measures cannot be valid.

Contrast these results with those obtained using GNP adjusted for political factors. In Figure 4.6—initially reported immediately after Iraq invaded Iran—both the reasons for that conflict and its long duration emerge. Iraq gains power in relation to Iran because the political collapse of the Shah's regime reduces Iran's political capacity . Indeed, Iraq finds itself in a temporary power transition with Iran—which provides the necessary but not

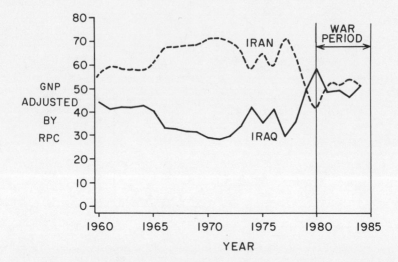

Figure 4.6   Comparison of Capabilities of Iran and Iraq Using GNP Adjusted for Political Capacity

sufficient conditions for initiating a serious confrontation (Organski and Kugler, 1980; Houweling and Siccama, 1988). The success of Iraq in the early stages of the conflict is accounted for by the substantial, if short-lived, power advantage Iraq holds over Iran in the early stage of the war. The subsequent recovery of Iran is not due to increased productivity (see Figure 4.5) but to Iran's political recovery.

Despite lasting economic losses and the initial destruction of the political environment caused by Iran's revolution, Figure 4.6 shows that the Ayatollah Khomeini's regime is able to mobilize more from the remaining product of the population than its predecessors, and it is this political recovery that accounts for the changing fortunes of war. Note finally that in the last year available for scrutiny, Iraq again draws even with Iran overcoming the deficiencies in power that were present during the previous 3 years. Again, this variation is due to politics and accounts for the change in war fortunes.

A criticism of political capacity is that it reflects the mobilization of societies during conflict and is therefore a surrogate for excluded military factors. We can explore this possibility by contrasting the performance of Iran and Iraq given their military effort (Figure 4.7). The symbols used follow the pattern of earlier evaluation of military expenditures (see Figure 4.2), where the size of the squares indicates the overcommitment to military expenditures and the size of the circles indicates the relative undercommitment, given the proportion of GNP held by each country. In

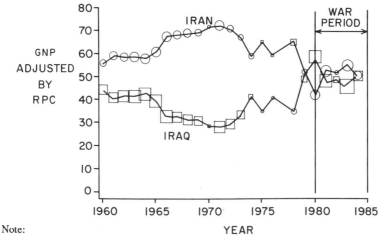

Note:

The size of the squares indicates the relative overcommitment to military expenditures and the circles indicate the relative undercommitment given the proportion of GNP held by each country in this pair.

Figure 4.7   Comparison of Capabilities of Iran and Iraq Using Power Controlling for Military Expenditures

peace time, Iraq allocates substantially more to the military than Iran, but these differences diminish prior to the initiation of conflict. Once the war starts, however, Iraq—the smaller country in basic capability terms—again *overspends*, while the larger Iran *underspends* on the military in relative terms. Such performance is congruent with the requirement of bringing these two nations to an even keel. However, note that despite a relatively low military effort Iran *gains* ground on Iraq. Thus, political capacity has a strong overall impact that overwhelms the effects of military effort on power and identifies a different aspect of mobilization. Indeed, political capacity rather than military effort is the more accurate indicator of success and failure in conflict.

Conclusion

A step in the direction of King's dream of evaluating the strength of nations has clearly been made in this generation. Indicators are more parsimonious and improved measures are effectively converging. We show that, for major powers, a number of indicators used in international politics to index power are highly related. Whether one chooses to use GNP, the COW Index, or adjust these for military expenditures is not critically relevant for the analysis of relations among major powers over time. This choice affects cross-sectional analysis since rank varies at one point in time but even here the average disparity is on the order of 10%.

The inclusion of military effort creates some disparity between GNP and the COW Index. When military considerations are included, prewar mobilization is directly reflected. However, we find no such effects when nuclear weapons are added. GNP, the more parsimonious indicator, reflects accurately the contents of the COW Index with the addition of nuclear weapons.

We therefore show that explicit adjustments are not necessarily superior to implicit ones. Our evaluations suggest that complex composites of numerous variables do not produce outcomes that are superior to simpler constructs, but rather, they produce series that are relatively immune to temporal variation. Using Imre Lakatos' (1978) criteria of parsimony, since little is added by complexity, why complicate it?

More serious are the effects of distance, which can affect the capabilities of noncontiguous nations. Yet, our evaluation also shows that distance adjustments are most important in historical analysis where variations in the speed of transportation distorted substantially estimates of power. In current analysis such adjustments are justified only in exceptional circumstances (i.e., Falkland–Malvinas War) and can usually be disregarded.

Efforts to verify the validity of alternate measures of power support the need to account for political factors. The analysis of the Iran–Iraq conflict shows many phases that can be understood only when political elements are included in the evaluation of power. Indeed, the effects of political elements are both different and more important than military effort. When political elements are excluded the power of contenders is seriously distorted.

Such distortions could have serious implications for decisionmakers. Is it possible that American elites were lured into Vietnam because analysis of capabilities produced unreasonably high expectations of success? Is it possible that the same fate befell elites in the Soviet Union who anticipated a short and successful confrontation in Afghanistan? Is it possible that Iraq's elites decided to initiate conflict on similar grounds before running into a long and devastating war? One cannot say for sure. However, our research shows that critically diverse evaluations of potential outcomes are obtained in each situation with alternate measures of power, while only those adjusted for political factors are eventually confirmed by the outcomes of conflict.

What are the implications for future research on power? Indexes of the capability base are adequate but, without political adjustments, such indexes can seriously distort assessments of outcomes. Future research should perhaps stress the testing rather than the specification of new and more complex measures of the capability base and should emphasize the specification and evaluation of alternate political components in the assessments of power.

Appendix: Data and Sources

Table 4.1   Percentage Distribution of Gross National Product Among the Major Powers, 1850–1980

Year	United States	Japan	Germany	Britain	Russia/Soviet Union[a]	France
1850[b]	15.9	9.5	12.3	21.9	19.9[a]	20.5
1860	20.5	7.7	11.1	22.6	18.0	20.1
1870	19.6	6.7	16.8	19.3	19.8	17.8
1880	26.1	5.4	16.3	17.5	19.1	15.6
1890	28.2	5.0	15.7	19.3	17.7	14.1
1900	30.6	5.3	16.4	17.8	17.1	12.8
1913[c]	36.0	5.5	17.0	14.3	16.9	10.3
1925[c]	42.5	8.0	12.2	12.6	15.1	9.6
1938[c]	36.3	9.2	15.0	11.7	20.8	7.0
1950	50.0	5.0	7.1	10.6	20.1	7.2
1960	42.5	7.8	9.2	8.6	24.8	7.1
1970	40.4	13.1	9.6	7.8	21.7	7.4
1980	39.2	15.0	8.9	6.5	22.6	7.8

Sources: Data for 1870–1960 are based on the work of Angus Maddison. Data for 1970–1980 are from the World Bank *World Tables* and National Foreign Assessment Center (1979), *Handbook of Economic Statistics.* Maddison's conversion is used to calculate a constant base year and control for territorial changes (See Angus Maddison, 1969, 1982, for additions; see Kugler, 1973, for adjustments; see Maddison, 1982, pp. 160–161).

[a]Data for Russia/Soviet Union are estimated.
[b]In 1850, data are for Prussia. For 1950–1980, data are for West Germany.
[c]The years prior to the initiation of World Wars I and II are used to determine the relative capabilities of opponents as close as possible to the outbreak of conflict. We chose 1925 to evaluate the interwar period despite the lingering effects of World War I to avoid the larger distortions introduced by the Great Depression.

Table 4.2   Percentage Distribution of the COW Index Among the Major Powers, 1850–1980

Year	United States	Japan[a]	Germany[b]	Britain	Russia/Soviet Union	France
1850	10.2	6.1	13.7	36.6	18.6	15.3
1860	10.7	3.1	13.0	40.2	14.7	18.3
1870	13.1	2.1	17.2	35.9	13.3	18.4
1880	17.9	2.7	15.9	32.4	15.0	16.1
1890	24.3	3.2	18.2	25.9	14.4	14.0
1900	26.6	4.1	18.7	24.7	15.0	10.9
1913	31.0	5.6	20.7	15.5	17.2	10.0
1925	41.7	7.1	13.2	16.1	11.2	10.7
1938	24.9	11.5	22.3	10.9	23.9	6.5
1950[c]	38.0	7.0	8.1	9.8	31.4	5.7
1960	37.0	8.7	7.5	7.9	32.3	6.6
1970	34.7	12.0	7.2	6.4	34.7	5.0
1980	30.3	13.0	7.7	5.5	38.1	5.4

Sources: Estimates of the COW Index from 1850 to 1938 are based on the data compiled before 1980 (from Singer et al., 1972). For 1950 to 1980 we use preliminary updates, kindly provided by J. David Singer.

[a]The data for 1850 is estimated based on GNP. The data for 1950 corresponds to 1952.
[b]In 1850 and 1860, Germany includes Baden, Bavaria, Prussia, Hanover, Hesse Electoral, Hesse Grand Ducal, Meckelnburg Schwerin, Saxony, and Wuerttemburg.
[c]The data for 1950 are an extrapolation from 1955.

Table 4.3 Percentage Distribution of the COW Index Adjusted by Distance Among the Major Powers Using Germany as the Target, 1850–1980

Year	United States	Japan	Germany	Britain	Russia/Soviet Union	France
1850	4.3	2.6	15.0	41.7	19.3	17.1
1860	4.6	1.2	13.6	45.4	14.8	20.4
1870	6.7	1.1	18.9	40.0	13.3	20.0.
1880	10.3	1.2	18.4	36.8	14.9	18.4
1890	16.3	1.2	20.9	30.2	15.1	16.3
1900	17.8	1.2	22.6	29.8	15.5	13.1
1913	23.0	1.2	25.2	19.3	19.3	12.0
1925	37.2	3.5	15.1	18.6	12.8	12.8
1938	19.8	5.8	25.6	12.8	27.9	8.1
1950	34.8	3.4	9.0	11.2	34.8	6.7
1960	34.1	4.5	7.9	9.2	36.4	7.9
1970	31.9	7.9	7.9	6.8	39.8	5.7
1980	27.7	8.0	9.2	5.7	43.7	5.7

Sources: Sources for the COW Index are the same as those reported for Table 4.2. Adjustments for distance were performed using Mike Horn's TOLSTOY program that incorporates data and equations used in Bueno de Mesquita's (1981, 1985) work.

Table 4.4 Percentage Distribution of GNP Adjusted by RPC Among Major Countries, 1900–1980

Year	United States	Japan	Germany	Britain	Russia/Soviet Union	France
1900	24.8	3.8	29.0	25.4	10.0	7.0
1913	25.6	11.0	17.7	14.2	20.4	11.0
1925	28.8	11.6	16.0	20.0	10.6	13.0
1938	21.2	18.0	23.1	12.5	19.6	5.5
1950	43.1	5.0	8.4	13.3	25.2	5.0
1960	46.4	6.7	9.8	9.7	20.6[a]	6.8
1970	42.8	10.8	9.1	8.6	22.4[a]	6.3
1980	42.9	11.2	9.0	6.8	24.1[a]	6.0

Sources: Data for 1900–1950 from Kugler and Domke (1986); data for 1960–1980 from Organski et al. (1984).

[a]An average political performance (1.0) for the Soviet Union is assumed since estimates of RPC are unavailable.

Table 4.5 Percentage Distribution of Military Expenditures Among the Major Powers, 1850–1980

Year	United States	Japan	Germany	Britain	Russia/Soviet Union	France
1850	7.5	1.0	9.6	20.2	32.4	29.3
1860	8.4	0.9	8.4	29.6	22.2	30.5
1870	8.4	0.3	28.2	12.7	12.7	37.7
1880	10.2	2.3	17.3	19.1	21.8	29.3
1890	9.8	2.7	24.5	19.3	19.7	24.0
1900	17.2	5.5	16.4	26.3	17.8	16.8
1913	15.4	9.2	21.6	16.6	20.9	16.3
1925	27.8	8.1	7.0	27.4	14.4	15.3
1938	6.1	9.4	40.1	10.1	29.3	5.0
1950	40.4	1.0	4.9	6.6	43.0	4.1
1960	48.2	0.5	3.1	4.9	39.2	4.1
1970	41.2	0.8	3.2	3.1	48.6	3.1
1980	33.2	2.2	6.1	6.2	46.2	6.1

Source: Correlates of War Project data provided by J. David Singer.

Table 4.6 Distribution of Warheads Among the Major Powers in the Nuclear Era,
1950–1986

Year	United States	Japan	Germany	Britain	Soviet Union	France
1950	17	0	0	0	0	0
1960	8,603	0	0	180	415	0
1970	4,000	0	0	148	2,419	20
1980	10,100	0	0	164	6,000	148
1986	12,000	0	0	180 (est.)	10,000	200 (est.)

Sources: Robert Berman and John C. Baker (1982, pp. 42–43); Ruth Leger Sivard (1987,
p. 17); Christy Campbell (1984, Chap. 7). See also Kugler (1983) for definitions and procedures.

Table 4.7 Alternate Estimates of GNP for Iran and Iraq in Constant
1982 Dollars, 1980–1984

Year	Series 1: Estimates Using Constant U.S. Dollars		Series 2: Estimates Using Constant Domestic Currency	
	Iran	Iraq	Iran	Iraq
1980	89,201	48,879	89,201	48,879
1981	87,186	42,067	78,871	42,067
1982	94,597	40,563	101,529	54,786
1983	102,464	38,899	129,719	55,691
1984	99,798	41,068	141,758	56,750
1985			194,993	57,620

Sources: For 1950–1974, World Bank and Internatinal Monetary Fund data detailed in
Organski et al. (1985). For 1974–1980, United Nations *Statistical Yearbook*, Table 25.
For Iran 1959–1974 and Iraq 1965–1974, *International Financial Statistics, 1981* (in
constant domestic currencies). For 1974–1984, ACDA (1986). All estimates are in constant
1983 dollars. Estimates of total output for Iran and Iraq are of poor quality. Series 1,
used in our analysis, is estimated from increases reported in ACDA (1986) starting in 1982.
The last year available in our longer series is 1980. The change from 1980 to 1981 is not
used because the reported drop in total GNP of 56% seemed excessive. This variation is more
likely to be due to the use of different series rather than to real differences in total output
from year to year. To confirm our evaluation we constructed Series 2, which is estimated with
changes in constant domestic currency from the United Nations *Statistical Yearbook*.
Differences in inflation across the two countries are disregarded but estimates in Series 2
indicate that Series 1 reflects changes in GNP within each country rather accurately for the rest
of the period except 1980–1981. We use the change in Series 2 in Series 1 to evaluate the link
between 1980 and 1981.

5

National Capability and Conflict Outcome: An Application of Indicator Building in the Social Sciences

Paul R. Pudaite and Gretchen Hower

In this chapter we develop an explicit model[1] relating national capability to conflict outcome and then use this model to build an indicator for national capability from (1) raw indexes (such as military expenditures or population) and (2) the results of international wars. This indicator is developed under the assumptions of, and is intended specifically for, the expected utility theory of war described by Bruce Bueno de Mesquita (1981). This indicator, however, may be suitable for the testing of other theories, but if found inappropriate for a particular theory, then the method used in this chapter can be adapted to develop an indicator of national capability appropriate to the theory.

We believe that research in the social sciences will benefit from a more thorough application of the available methodology of operationalization. To address this situation, we begin by reviewing the essential components in the process of indicator building as they appear in the social science literature. These sources argue that the primary requirement for successful operationalization is that the indicators must be located within an explicit theoretical framework. This in turn requires "the explicit specification of the nature of the causal linkages within a model" (Carley, 1981, p. 68).

We then discuss one particular difficulty that confronts the researcher attempting to build indicators for a theory. This difficulty occurs whenever the theory permits more than one realization for a particular conceptual relationship. In order to build the explicit model that this approach requires, the researcher is compelled to make a specific choice without any further help from the theory. In this case it is possible that a poor choice of a given relationship may bias the model away from relationships that would represent the empirical situation more accurately. To address this problem, we draw upon a method developed in information theory that helps us choose an explicit relationship which accurately reflects the uncertainty due to theoretical ambiguity, and which does not ignore any of the possible relationships allowed by the theory. We also propose some refinements that address certain shortcomings of this method.

Finally, we apply the entire operationalization process, building an indicator of national capability for the expected utility theory of international conflict developed by Bueno de Mesquita in *The War Trap* (1981). We present some preliminary empirical results which suggest that military expenditures alone are a better indicator of the concept of national capability within Bueno de Mesquita's theory than any positive linear combination of military expenditures, population, and fuel consumption.

Because this approach to indicator building maximizes the ability of a theory to use its formal knowledge to obtain unbiased empirical information, we recommend employing this approach in any theory that intends to be empirically relevant.

The Operationalization of Theoretical Concepts

Theoretical Ambiguity

In this section, we draw primarily on Abraham Kaplan (1963), Michael Carley (1981), and Steven T. Seitz (1983) to review the operationalization process. These methodologists motivate the use of explicit models to facilitate the operationalization of concepts within scientific theories and to enable more precise testing of these theories. An explicit model for a theory is one that fully specifies the functional form of every relationship among the theory's concepts. However, the relationships among concepts in social science theories are often ambiguous, permitting a variety of mathematical representations for each relationship. This makes it impossible to develop an explicit model for the theory without making ad hoc choices of specific relationships. Thus, when an explicit model is developed for an ambiguous theory, the specific mathematical representations of these relationships will have been chosen without further guidance from the theory. The resulting model may end up being a poor approximation of the theory it is intended to represent. Because explicit models are essential for effective indicator building, much of this section will focus on the process of developing explicit models for ambiguous theories.

To illustrate the main ideas in this section, we use as our primary example a theory that addresses the relationship between two concepts: a nation's capability C, and the probability P that it will win a war with another nation. The theory proposes that P increases as C increases. This theory displays ambiguity because there are many explicit models for the theory which are consistent with the relationship between the two concepts proposed by the theory. For example, we could propose a linear or an exponential model. Both are consistent with the theory. Clearly, many more models could be proposed that are consistent with the theory's proposition that "the probability of winning for a nation increases as its capability increases."

Ambiguities like the one displayed above are common in the social sciences. When researchers attempt to test theories containing such ambiguities, they do develop explicit models that are consistent with the relationships proposed in the theory. For example, linear models are often used to represent increasing relationships. After assigning indicators for the variables, the model can then be tested by using linear regression. But how do we interpret the results if the linear model fails to support the theory's hypothesis? Is it because the theory is false, or because the linear model is a poor representation of the actual relationship? This chapter suggests methods for developing explicit models that more accurately represent the theory, so that statistical tests can be interpreted less equivocally.

Although theoretical ambiguities are undesirable for indicator building and empirical testing, they still serve two important purposes. First, theories gain generality through ambiguity (e.g., a theory may want to subsume both the linear and exponential cases above within a single hypothesis). Second, ambiguities may accurately reflect the uncertainties in our theoretical knowledge. In both cases, the techniques we propose enable the researcher to take advantage of such ambiguities in theoretical elaboration, while eliminating these ambiguities when building indicators or conducting empirical tests.

Operationalization in the Social Sciences

The fundamental requirement in developing useful indicators is that they must represent the concepts of a theory. Carley (1981, pp. 67–68) presents the following argument in the context of "social" indicators, but his remarks clearly apply to indicators in any scientific research.

> Social indicators, virtually by definition, specify causal linkages or connections between observable aspects of social phenomena, which indicate, and other unobservable aspects or concepts, which are indicated. This can only be accomplished by postulating, *implicitly* or *explicitly*, some causal model or theory of social behaviour which serves to relate formally the variables under consideration. All social indicator research represents, therefore, some social theory or model, however simplistic.

Because an indicator represents a concept in a theory, "the operational indicator should approximate as closely as possible the function performed by the concept in the theory" (Seitz, 1983, p. 6-2). Successful operationalization will produce an indicator that reflects "a reasonable understanding of what work the theory requires from the concept" (Seitz, 1983, p. 6-3).

Seitz (1983, p. 6-3) cautions that

> operational indicators for apparently similar abstract concepts may in fact be dramatically different, depending upon the theory being tested. Thus, an operational indicator . . . cannot be judged against other operational indicators of the same or similar terms, because the appropriate referent is not the concept, *per se*, but its function in the theory being tested.

Because indicators are theory specific, researchers should recognize that adopting an indicator developed for another theory actually represents an additional hypothesis that must be tested. Here is an example from the physical sciences:

> Newton introduced the concept of mass in two contexts. . . . The inertial mass is a kinematic quantity having to do with motion. The gravitational mass, on the other hand, is a "charge": an object feels a gravitational force in proportion to its gravitational mass, just as it would feel an electromagnetic force in proportion to its electric charge.

> Although they are completely different concepts, Newton maintained that the two types of mass, inertial and gravitational, are equivalent. To test the idea he did experiments with pendulums. . . . Newton verified the equivalence principle to a precision of one part in 1,000. (Goldman, et al., 1988, p. 49)

In order to build an indicator for a concept so that the indicator accurately reflects the concept's function in the theory, Carley (1981, p. 68) argues that we must develop an explicit model of the theory:

> the failure to make explicit an underlying theory or model impedes the development of social indicators. . . . Only the explicit specification of the nature of the causal linkages within a model allows hypothesis-testing and thus the opportunity to establish the likelihood that some indicator indeed indicates that which it claims to indicate.

Explicit models provide three advantages in theory testing. First, an explicit model allows the researcher to utilize more powerful techniques in empirical testing. Recall our example of a theory that asserts that the probability of a nation winning a war increases with its capability. No generic test for such a relationship is currently available. The development of an explicit model, for example, the specification of a linear relationship between the probability of winning a war and national capability, would allow us to use linear regression together with appropriate statistical tests to determine if the slope is significantly positive. The explicit model allows us to test relationships that may be directly untestable in a less explicit form.

A second advantage of explicit models is that their logical structure enables the researcher to develop indicators for a theory efficiently and without logical inconsistency. We first illustrate this process by elaborating on our ongoing example and then describe the process in more general terms.

Consider the probability P of an attacking nation with capability A defeating a defending nation with capability D. Assume that P is completely determined by A and D, that is, $P = f(A, D)$ for some bivariate function f. If we have an explicit model for the relationship between A, D, and P, that is, if we know the functional form of f, then after we develop $\hat{A}$ and $\hat{D}$ (indicators for A and D, respectively), we can derive $\hat{P}$ (an indicator for P) by applying f to $\hat{A}$ and $\hat{D}$.[2] What we have done is to exploit the relationship (provided by the explicit model) between the *primitive* concepts of A and D and the *derived* concept of P.

Conversely, consider the following example from kinematic theory. The basic concepts of time t, distance d, and velocity v obey the relationship $v = d/t$. If, after developing $\hat{t}$ and $\hat{d}$, indicators for time and distance (i.e., by building clocks and rulers), we were to develop a separate indicator $\hat{v}$ for velocity (i.e., build a speedometer), we would run the risk that $\hat{v} \neq \hat{d}/\hat{t}$. Similarly, if we do not have an explicit model for the relationship between A, D, and P, then we will not be able to derive $\hat{P}$ from $\hat{A}$ and $\hat{D}$. Instead, we will have to develop an indicator for P separately from our indicators of A and D. This produces the potential for logical inconsistency between our indicators: $\hat{P}$ need not display any functional relationship to A and D, let alone the correct functional relationship.

Assigning an indicator to a primitive concept is an *indication hypothesis*: an assertion about the relationship between a model and the real world. Explicit models reduce the number of indication hypotheses that are implicitly incorporated in the testing of a theory. Qualitatively speaking, the less ambiguous a model for a given theory is, the fewer the number of primitive concepts. Thus, an explicit model provides the most efficient way to operationalize a theory and minimizes the potential for logical conflict between indicators for a theory's concepts.

A third advantage of explicit models is that we can use the relationships to develop and calibrate a composite indicator for a single concept. This composite indicator is built by aggregating a number of indicators for a single concept into a single indicator that replicates the theoretical role of that concept more accurately. The relationships between the concepts must be explicit in order to assess the precision with which their indicators capture the role of the concepts in the theory. Later in this chapter, we illustrate this process when we operationalize the concept of national capability from a number of raw indexes (viz., military expenditures, population, and fuel consumption).

To clarify the relationship between the theory and the explicit model for the theory developed to build indicators, we find it useful to use Kaplan's distinction between two kinds of model. One kind of model is the *formal model*, "a model *of* a theory which presents the latter purely as a structure of uninterpreted symbols" (Kaplan, 1963, p. 268). The formal model of a theory is a representation of the theory's logical or deductive information. As a formal object, the information in a formal model is contained in the set of assumptions that determine the relationships between its symbols. In order to be an accurate model of the theory, a formal model must not include assumptions that are not provided by the theory.[3]

Typically, a formal model may have several interpretations which are consistent with its assumptions. These interpretations have also been called models. Kaplan (1963, p. 268) calls this kind of model an *interpretive model*, "providing an interpretation *for* a formal theory." In our previous example, both the linear model and the exponential model represent interpretive models for the formal model which specifies only that the probability of winning a war increases with a nation's capability.

Another example is a theory that might postulate that the variable X is a random variable. One interpretive model may assume that X follows a normal distribution, while another may assume that X follows an exponential distribution. Both of these interpretive models would be consistent with the relationship postulated by the theory; even though they might produce different conclusions, they would both be valid interpretations for the formal model of the theory.

To make use of the advantages provided by a completely explicit model, we will want to develop an interpretive model for the theory that makes explicit every relationship within the formal model of the theory. There are three ways in which the researcher can approach this issue.

One way to deal with this problem is to find propositions that are true for all interpretive models for the formal model. In the previous example, this would entail proving theorems that held for any possible distribution of the random variable X. This approach would unify the study of the various interpretive models for the formal model. Certainly, formal unification is an important scientific goal.

However, unification does not produce an explicit model. Consequently, as noted above, any attempt to operationalize and test the ambiguous formal model (1) will be restricted to weaker statistical tests which can be employed, (2) may result in logical conflicts among the indicators (mutually contradictory indication hypotheses), and (3) will not be able to guide composition of indicators. Carley (1981, p. 86) concludes the following:

Although direct work on unified theory may have some value, progress will mainly be made by concentrating much attention on explanatory models which are at a low level of generalisation and thus close enough to reality to allow empirical testing to take place.

A second way to deal with lack of specificity in the formal model is to make an ad hoc selection of a particular conceptual relationship from the various relationships allowed by the theory. In our example of the random variable, we noted that the researcher could choose a particular distribution for X in the model, such as a normal distribution. This choice would be consistent with the theory because of the theory's silence on the matter. But it would ignore other possibilities permitted by the theory. This has two implications. First, since this choice was not required by the theory (other distributions could have been chosen), any axiomatic basis for this choice would have to include assumptions that did not originate within the theory. Thus, the resulting interpretive model would contain information that had no theoretical basis (our next section gives a concrete example of this effect). This is one reason why ad hoc specification of the model is undesirable. Second, by ignoring other possibilities, these ad hoc choices might bias the model and, subsequently, the indicators, away from those relationships which more accurately reflect the empirical world where the theory is to be applied. This potential for bias gives rise to the equivocal interpretation of hypothesis testing that we noted in introducing this section (is the theory wrong, or is the model a poor representation of the theory's intent?).

But in order to obtain an explicit model for the theory, we cannot avoid this problem of choosing specific conceptual relationships. The only thing we can do is make sure our choices reflect the uncertainty underlying the theory. The third way to deal with a lack of theoretical specificity that we would like to discuss recognizes both the need to choose a specific relationship and the distortion of the theory that such a choice necessarily introduces. It is this method, based on the principle of maximum entropy, that we suggest be incorporated into the standard process of operationalization.

Ambiguity and the Principle of Maximum Entropy

Silviu Guiasu and Abe Shenitzer (1985) present arguments that motivate using the principle of maximum entropy to select specific relationships in theories with probabilistic components. Applying this principle to a random variable produces a distribution that is "the most uncertain one" and that "ignores no possibility subject to the constraint given by" the theory. Thus, this approach provides a balance between the need to choose a specific relationship, and the need to avoid the introduction of information bias which would result in ad hoc specificity.

One important motivation for using the principle of maximum entropy is that negative entropy can be used as a measure of information (Shannon, 1948). Thus, in our example of the random variable X, we can assess the amount of nontheoretical information introduced by the selection of any specific distribution for X. From this perspective, the principle of maximum entropy enables us to choose the relationship that minimizes the introduction of nontheoretical information, while still producing an explicit model. Also, because the principle of maximum entropy does not ignore any theoretically consistent possibility, it reduces tendencies toward bias.

Unfortunately, it is possible for a theory to be so ambiguous that the principle of maximum entropy cannot select a relationship. In our example of the random variable, suppose that the theory only specifies that the domain of X is $[0,+\infty)$. The method of Lagrange multipliers shows that maximum entropy is not achieved by any probability density function (p.d.f.; see Appendix at end of this chapter for details). Thus, if all we know about X is that it can take on any positive value, we will not be able to find a distribution for X that achieves maximum entropy.

To overcome this additional difficulty, we suggest a method that has been used to solve many types of variational problem: the introduction of additional variables with undetermined value. In our example, we could introduce the expected value of X as an additional variable. If we let $\mu = E[X]$, then the principle of maximum entropy will select the exponential probability density function (p.d.f.) for X's distribution (Guiasu and Shenitzer, 1985, p. 47), that is,

$$f(x) = \frac{1}{\mu} e^{-\frac{x}{\mu}}. \tag{1}$$

Although μ is not specified, it can be determined empirically.

Although we do not have a formal justification for this method, it does appear to be consistent with the goal of minimizing the introduction of nontheoretical information when developing an explicit model for a theory. In the above example, adding the variable μ essentially asserts that the expected value of X exists. Thus, the arbitrary choice we made to produce an explicit model was one of only two possibilities: existence versus nonexistence of the expected value of X. This binary choice, which can be represented by 1 bit of information, seems far less restrictive than, say, the choice of a linear model out of the uncountably infinite number of models that are capable of representing an increasing relationship.

Summary of this Section

Further development of the theory based on empirical findings would complement the approach we have outlined in this section. Because the explicit interpretive model for a theory developed using maximum entropy would not ignore any possibility allowed by the theory, successive incorporation of empirical and formal research using these techniques should be able to detect and correct any biases that are introduced. Ultimately, it should be possible to attribute empirical failures to theoretical shortcomings rather than to errors in operationalization.

To summarize, there are three contributions to the process of operationalization discussed in this section. First, we wish to apply the principle of maximum entropy to determine an explicit model for an ambiguous theory. This method produces a model that accurately reflects the uncertainty underlying the theory. Second, when the theory is so uncertain that even the principle of maximum entropy cannot be successfully applied, we suggest using mediating variables with undetermined value. Finally, we suggest a method for combining several empirical indexes for a single concept into a composite indicator for that concept.

An Explicit Model for National Capability and Conflict Outcome

For simplicity, we have chosen to examine and rework a subset of Bueno de Mesquita's operationalization of the expected utility theory, which he developed in *The War Trap*. This subset, found in a section entitled "Measuring Probability" (Bueno de Mesquita, 1981, pp. 101–109), deals with the relationships among and measurement of the following concepts: national capability, probability of "gaining or losing" in a conflict, and distances between nations. We restrict our analysis to the relationship between national capability and conflict outcome, and the operationalization of national capability. To control for the effect of distance, our empirical work is restricted to conflicts in which Bueno de Mesquita (1981, pp. 106–107) concludes that "the debilitating impact of distance" is negligible.

In Bueno de Mesquita's theory of international conflict the proposed relationship between capability and conflict outcome is that the greater the nation's capability, the higher its probability of winning against a particular opponent. While Bueno de Mesquita defines, but does not derive, an explicit model relating national capability to war outcome (Bueno de Mesquita, 1981, p. 108), our approach is to draw out the assumptions underlying Bueno de Mesquita's theory and develop an explicit model for these assumptions from an axiomatic basis. Bueno de Mesquita's model appears to make the following simplifying assumptions about the relationship between national capability and conflict outcome:

1. After controlling for distance, the probability of one nation or alliance of nations defeating another nation or alliance of nations in a conflict is completely determined by the two nations' capabilities.[4]

2. National capabilities are measured on a comparable scale across nations (e.g., two nations with the same level of capability have the same probability of winning a conflict against a third nation) and for both initiators and defenders (e.g., two nations with the same level of capability will have equal probability of winning a conflict against each other, regardless of which nation initiated the conflict).[5]

3. National capabilities are nonnegative.[6]

4. National capabilities are additive (e.g., the combined capability of two allies equals the sum of their individual capabilities). This is an important factor in evaluating whether or not to use proposed indicators for capability.[7]

These simplifying assumptions tell us what we can ignore by restricting the domain of inquiry. Our model will adhere to these assumptions, as well as the following constructive assumptions, which guide the development of an explicit model.

The probability of nation i defeating nation j in a conflict must take the form

$$P_{ij} = f(\text{cap}_i, \text{cap}_j)$$

where $f(x, y)$ has domain $\{ (x, y) : 0 < x, y < +\infty \}$ and satisfies the following properties: (1) $0 < f(x, y) < 1$ (i.e., $f(x, y)$ is a probability); (2) $f_x(x, y) > 0$ (probability of victory for nation i increases with i's capability); (3) $f_y(x, y) < 0$ (probability of victory for i decreases with j's capability).

These assumptions appear to exhaust the amount of information about the precise relationship of the concepts contained in Bueno de Mesquita's original treatment. The relationship between the two concepts is clearly ambiguous, since there are many formulas that can satisfy these assumptions.

Bueno de Mesquita "defines" the probability of nation i winning a bilateral conflict, P_{ij}, in terms of the national capabilities of nations i and j, cap_i and cap_j, respectively, by setting

$$f(\text{cap}_i, \text{cap}_j) = \frac{\text{cap}_i}{\text{cap}_i + \text{cap}_j}$$

In addition to satisfying the three properties listed above, this formula also satisfies another property: (4) scale invariance (probability of victory can be determined using only the ratio of the two nations' capabilities, without referring to their absolute levels). It is quite possible that this formula may satisfy other interesting properties. Note that nowhere above was scale invariance required of the formula. This illustrates how selecting an interpretive model for a formal model introduces additional information not contained in the formal model.

The theory posits a relationship between conflict outcome, a dichotomous random variable, and national capability, which is a continuous, deterministic variable. In order to find an explicit relationship between national capability and conflict outcome, two transformations are required: one from deterministic to random, the other from continuous to dichotomous.

We build the formula by applying these transformations one after the other and then composing the two transformations. This involves introducing an additional variable (which we call "applied capability"): the first transformation will map national capability to applied capability; the second transformation will map applied capability to conflict outcome. The order in which the transformations are applied determines the characteristics of applied capability: if the transformation from deterministic to random is applied first, then applied capability will be a continuous, random variable; if the transformation from continuous to dichotomous is applied first, then applied capability will be a dichotomous, deterministic variable. We have chosen to use the first alternative because the second alternative collapses into a deterministic transformation in which the nation with greater capability always wins. The sequence of transformations is depicted as follows:

National capability		*Applied capability*		*Conflict outcome*
Deterministic	$\rightarrow$	Random		Random
Continuous		Continuous	$\rightarrow$	Dichotomous

The first transformation carries the concept of national capability (deterministic, continuous) to applied capability (random, continuous). The second transformation carries applied capability to conflict outcome (random, dichotomous).

Applied capability shares with national capability the properties of being continuous, positive, and directly related to the probability of winning a conflict, but unlike national capability it is a random variable. By arbitrary choice of the unit of measurement of applied capability, we can assume that for any nation i with national capability cap_i, and applied capability A_i, the expected value of i's applied capability $E[A_i] = cap_i$, that is, in terms of probability theory it is an unbiased estimator. The principle of maximum entropy motivated us to assume that A_i has an exponential p.d.f. with the required mean value [recall Equation (1)]. Thus, the first transformation carries cap_j to A_j, a random variable with exponential p.d.f. whose mean value is equal to cap_j.

We have transformed national capability into the intermediate concept of applied capability and established a distribution function for A_j. It remains to develop a formal relationship between applied capability and conflict outcome and to compose these two relationships to form an indicator for national capability.

The relationship between applied capability and conflict outcome must satisfy the assumption that there is a direct relationship between applied capability and the probability of winning. There is no need to introduce further uncertainty by making this relationship probabilistic, so we assume that it is deterministic. Only one deterministic relationship can satisfy these two assumptions: if nation i defeats nation j whenever A_i is greater than A_j. This is the result of the second transformation which carries (A_i, A_j) to P_{ij}.

The last step is to compose the formal relationships between national capability and applied capability and between applied capability and conflict outcome to form an explicit model that relates the concept of national capability to the concept of conflict outcome (see Appendix A for details). Surprisingly, composing these relationships replicates formula (2):[8]

$$\text{Prob}[A_i > A_j] = \frac{cap_i}{cap_i + cap_j}$$

Thus, Bueno de Mesquita has defined the particular relationship between national capability and conflict outcome that is consistent with the assumptions listed above, while minimizing the addition of nontheoretical information.

Of course, given the wide range of possible relationships available, it is doubtful whether ad hoc choices can always be this successful. Furthermore, if we can make the theoretical relationship between national capability and conflict outcome more complete, this will generate a different formula which reflects the additional, theoretically justified information. For example, Charles S. Taber (see Chapter 3 in this book) suggests that indicators of national capability are not as precise for Third World nations as they are for developed nations. If we incorporate this information into the model of the theory, the relationship between national capability and conflict outcome in this model will not be scale invariant. Since this violates property (4) above, we will *not* obtain formula (2) when we derive the relationship in the revised model. As another example, consider the influence of distance on capability and conflict outcome as discussed by Bueno de Mesquita (1981, pp. 83–84). We may discover that the impact of distance may vary among the indexes that are combined to assess national capability. This would be reflected in the formula for adjusted capability which Bueno de Mesquita develops.

Measurement and Testing of National Capability

We now use the explicit model we developed relating national capability to war outcome to help build an indicator for national capability. Many prior indicators have been developed without specifying the theoretical role of the concept they are intended to indicate. The method we have described shows how a researcher can build an indicator using his theory rather than having to choose arbitrarily among already existing indicators. In particular, whereas Bueno de Mesquita uses the composite capabilities index from the Correlates of War Project as his indicator for national capability, our method produces an indicator for national capability that is developed under the particular assumptions of Bueno de Mesquita's theory of international conflict. The indicator we develop can also be used without alteration by another theory provided that the assumptions relevant to that theory's concept of national capability are consistent with (i.e., do not contradict or supplement) the assumptions used to derive this indicator. More generally, the method we display in this section can be adapted to develop an indicator of national capability for a given theory.

We treat conflict outcome as a primitive concept in our model of the theory, which may thus be associated with an empirical referent as an indication hypothesis. We follow Bueno de Mesquita by using the categorization of winners and losers devised by J. David Singer and Melvin Small (1972). However, it should be noted that in the expected utility theory as a whole, the concept and evaluation of conflict outcome are not primitive but are actually based on the primitive concept of utility. Within this enlarged context, conflict outcome should be measured on a ratio scale in order to be consistent with the ratio scale utility measurement, rather than as a dichotomous variable. Because Bueno de Mesquita operationalizes utility as the congruence of interests observed in military alliances, our approach to operationalization suggests that the indicator for conflict outcome should be measured by observing the change in this congruence produced by the conflict. [This may have already been done. See, for example, James D. Morrow (1985), who models conflict outcome as a continuous variable. In his article, Morrow considers the implications for empirical tests but does not actually operationalize war outcome.]

We consider national capabilities to be a primitive concept also, but one that can potentially be "tapped" through several real-world indexes. We use the relationship between national capabilities and conflict outcome to determine the most accurate combination of these various indexes.

As a consequence of simplifying assumptions (3) and (4) from the previous section, an indicator for national capability must be a linear combination of positive quantities. Thus, the capability of nation i will take the form

$$cap_i = \sum_{k=1}^{n} \beta_k \; x_{ik} \; ,$$

where the x_{ik} are (real-valued, positive) attributes of nation i, and the β_k are positive constants.

The sample over which we measure and test the concept of national capability consists of all wars recorded by Singer and Small involving contiguous nations from 1948 to the present, and for which there was a clear-cut victor.[9] This left us with a small sample of $N = 9$ wars. We also gathered data for military expenditure (x_{i1}), total population (x_{i2}), and fuel consumption (x_{i3}) of each war participant i (see Table 5.1 for the raw data and the sources from which they were collected).

Table 5.1 Raw Data for Capability Indexes[a]

Year	Participants[b]	Military Expenditure[c]	Total Population[d]	Fuel Consumption[e]
1979	China	52.7	933	579
	Vietnam	1.64	51.6	6.33
1974	Turkey	0.808	39.1	24.5
	Cyprus	0.007	0.639	0.860
1973	Israel	2.42	3.28	9.48
	Egypt,...[f]	4.268	62.5	32.4
1971	India	1.85	548	102
	Pakistan	0.746	65.0	11.6
1969	El Salvador	0.0295	3.39	0.570
	Honduras	0.0149	2.49	0.470
1967	Israel	0.562	2.92	6.08
	Egypt,...[g]	0.935	60.8	11.0
1965	Pakistan	0.538	102	9.19
	India	1.57	487	87.3
1962	China	5.60	710	407.8
	India	1.00	453	73.1
1948	Israel	0.0284	0.717	0.671
	Egypt,...[h]	0.129	28.1	5.64

[a]Quantities are given to three significant digits (if available).
[b]Winner is listed first.
[c]Military expenditures in billions of U.S. dollars. *SIPRI Yearbook.*
[d]Total population in millions of people. U.N. *Statistical Yearbook.*
[e]Fuel consumption in millions of metric tons of coal equivalent. U. N. *Statistical Yearbook.*
[f]Egypt, Iraq, Jordan, Saudi Arabia, and Syria.
[g]Egypt, Jordan, and Syria.
[h]Egypt, Iraq, Jordan, Lebanon, and Syria.

Using these data together with formula (2), we maximized the probability of observing the war outcomes (victory/defeat) in our sample through regression over composite capabilities of the form:

$$\text{cap}_i = \sum_{k=1}^{3} \beta_k x_{ik}$$

with $\beta_k \geq 0$.

We found that the likelihood of observing the sample is maximized when $\beta_2 = 0$ and $\beta_3 = 0$. β_1 can be set to 1 after scaling.

Thus, for this sample, military expenditure is a better measure of a nation's capability to win a war than any positive linear combination of all three indexes. Therefore, we hypothesize that military expenditure is the appropriate measure for national capability in the Bueno de Mesquita model.

Next, we tested to see whether we could distinguish this hypothesis (H_1) from the null hypothesis (H_0) that war outcome is unrelated to military expenditure. We used the following test statistic:

$$S = \sum_{i=1}^{N} (p_i - W_i)^2$$

where p_i is the probability that the superior side (the side with greater capability) wins, and W_i equals 1 or 0, respectively, if the superior side wins or loses. The expected value of S given H_0 is $E[S \,|\, H_0] = 3.102$, with variance $\text{Var}[S \,|\, H_0] = 0.852$. Under the alternative hypothesis, we expect a lower value of S. The observed value is $S_{\text{obs}} = 2.235$.

Given the null hypothesis, the probability that S is less than what we observed, is $\text{Prob}[S \leq S_{\text{obs}}) \,|\, H_0] = 0.17$. Thus, we cannot reject the null hypothesis with 95% confidence; but this is not surprising because of the small sample size. If the same effect (reduction of S from that expected under H_0) persists when we are able to obtain more data, then we would require a sample of about 30 wars to reject the null hypothesis at 95% confidence, or a sample of about 60 wars to reject at 99% confidence. Note that Singer and Small document over 100 international wars since 1816.

Because the data we used were insufficient to reject the null hypothesis, we did not proceed to measure the precision of military expenditure as an indicator for national capability. To assess the precision of an indicator, we need to determine confidence regions for the regression parameters (the β_k). The confidence regions are in turn determined by the sensitivity of the sample's likelihood with respect to the parameters. Because we cannot reject the null hypothesis at a 95% level of confidence, the 95% confidence region for the parameters obtained from our meager sample includes the point at which they vanish. If, using a larger sample, we are able to reject the null hypothesis, we would consequently obtain nontrivial confidence regions for the parameters.

Conclusion

The indicator of national capabilities and the indicator-building approach developed in this chapter can both contribute to the study of power in political science. The most direct application is to estimate an indicator of national capabilities based on all international wars on record, rather than the small sample of nine used in this chapter. This indicator can subsequently be used to test Bueno de Mesquita's expected utility theory of war. Whether or not this indicator is appropriate for application within other theories can be partially assessed empirically, but, as usual, negative results are equivocal because either the theory and/or the indication hypothesis may be incorrect.

A more productive approach would be to follow the indicator-building approach we have described: the researcher must identify the logical relationships within the theory and incorporate these relationships into the development of indicators. For example, A. F. K. Organski and J. Kugler (1980) look at the role of national capabilities not only in victory and defeat in wars, but more importantly in the conditions for war initiation, which include the relative rates of growth of nations and the influence of national capabilities on national growth. Because the information we have used to develop our indicator of national capabilities in this chapter does not incorporate the relationship between national capabilities and national growth, it is quite possible that empirical tests employing our indicator may fail to substantiate the theory proposed by Organski and Kugler. These shortcomings can be rectified by incorporating the additional theoretical information provided by Organski and Kugler to develop an indicator of national capabilities which explicitly reflects its effect on national growth.

In general, the operationalization and measurement of power or capabilities in political science theories can be facilitated by methods that aid in producing explicit models of ambiguous theories without introducing arbitrary assumptions. Since many important theories in political science either display some degree of ambiguity (e.g., verbal theories) or arbitrary specification (e.g., assumptions of linearity in place of monotonicity), there is a great need for methods such as those presented in this chapter which increase our efficiency in obtaining empirical information and consequently promote progressive elaboration, specification, and application of political science theories.

Appendix A: Probability $[X > Y]$ for Exponential Random Variables

Assume X and Y are exponential random variables with mean value a and b, respectively. That is, X and Y have p.d.f.'s $f_a(x)$ and $f_b(y)$, respectively, where

$$f_k(z) = \frac{1}{k} e^{-\frac{z}{k}} .$$

Then

$$\text{Prob}[X>Y] = \int_0^{+\infty} f_a(x) \int_0^x f_b(y) \; dy \; dx$$

$$= \frac{1}{a} \int_0^{+\infty} e^{-\frac{x}{a}} \left(1 - e^{-\frac{x}{b}} \right) dx$$

$$= 1 - \frac{1}{a} \int_0^{+\infty} e^{-x \left(\frac{1}{a} + \frac{1}{b} \right)} dx$$

$$= 1 - \frac{1}{a} \left(\frac{1}{\frac{1}{a} + \frac{1}{b}} \right)$$

$$= 1 - \frac{a\,b}{a(a + b)}$$

$$= \frac{a}{a + b} .$$

Notes

1. This research was assisted by an award to Paul R. Pudaite from the Social Science Research Council of an SSRC–MacArthur Foundation Fellowship in International Peace and Security.

2. We may not necessarily want to use $\hat{P} \equiv f(\hat{A}, \hat{D})$. For example, suppose our indicators are intended to be maximum likelihood estimates (MLEs). If $f(A, D)$ is nonlinear, then it is unlikely that $f(\hat{A}, \hat{D})$ will be the MLE of $\hat{P} \equiv f(\hat{A}, \hat{D})$. But we will still have to derive an MLE of P using f and the distributions for which $\hat{A}$ and $\hat{D}$ are MLEs. Nonetheless, $f(\hat{A}, \hat{D})$ may be an adequate

approximation of $f(A, D)$ for the purposes of empirical testing.

3. We note in passing that a complete model of the theory may be too complicated to study effectively, and that the researcher may need to simplify the model by excluding some of the assumptions. We do not address this problem here.

4. See Bueno de Mesquita (1981, pp. 83–86, 101–109).

5. This is inferred from the assumption that the capabilities for all nations can be measured by the same indicator (see Bueno de Mesquita, 1981, pp.102–103).

6. Because Bueno de Mesquita's formula for the probability of winning a war (see Bueno de Mesquita, 1981, p. 108) does not make sense with negative capabilities, we have inferred the assumption that capabilities are nonnegative.

7. This assumption is implicit in Bueno de Mesquita's formulation for probabilities for nations with allies (see Bueno de Mesquita, 1981, pp. 108–109).

8. This model is known in the statistical literature as the Bradley–Terry model, although it was apparently first proposed by E. Zermelo (see Stob, 1984). What we have done is to provide motivation for this model using the principle of maximum entropy.

9. Data on the war participants as well as winners and losers were obtained from the J. David Singer and Melvin Small *Wages of War* (1816–1980) data base.

PART 2

Reconceptualizing Power in World Politics

6

Power in the International Political Economy

James A. Caporaso and Stephan Haggard

As the other chapters in this book attest, the nature of power remains a central puzzle for international relations theory. On the one hand, the concept is ubiquitous in writing on world politics, central not only to realism (Morgenthau, 1948; Waltz, 1979) but to work on economic interdependence as well (Keohane and Nye, 1977). On the other hand, "power" is not a concept around which knowledge has grown and converged. The role of power in the international economy raises numerous questions. Is a separate theory of economic power required? Should economic power be understood as one component of a broader domain of power, or is it conceptually and functionally distinct, useful, for example, under different circumstances than military power? To repeat the question posed by Susan Strange (1975): "What is economic power and who has it?"

The topic of power in the international political economy spans a variety of empirical issues, from the use of economic sanctions, to bargaining between host countries and multinationals, to the economic foundations of great power or "hegemonic" status. Our approach is necessarily a limited one: to examine the way the concept of power has been used as an *explanatory* or *causal* variable in international political economy. We explore several problems that have plagued power analysis more generally but are germane to our more limited inquiry as well. We argue that four approaches to power can be distinguished in the international political economy literature; we call these the decisional, structural, conversion-process, and locational approaches. The approaches are not mutually exclusive. Each has developed in part out of the limitations of the others, and we explore their strengths and weaknesses.

Our analysis suggests that a general theory of power in the international political economy is unlikely. For some important, but restricted, range of outcomes, a broad, homogeneous conception of power may be useful. This is true, for example, in discussions of hegemonic states that can link issues and wield influence over the entire framework within which international economic relations take place (Keohane, 1984; Russett, 1985; Snidal, 1985). For explaining most phenomena, such as discrete influence attempts or negotiations, "power" must be disaggregated if it is to be useful. Such disaggregation must include particular attention to the domestic political and institutional foundations of international strength and weakness.

Power: Prevalent and Problematic

Among realists, power is both motive and means, simultaneously defining one goal of states and the means to achieve virtually all possible objectives. Despite the claim that theorists of interdependence have been unmindful of power, it is in fact central to much current writing in international political economy. Theorists of interdependence have argued that power is transformed in economically integrated international systems and that the utility of force relative to economic instruments has declined. Economic interdependence alters states' goals, raises the costs of unilateral action in some issue areas, and results in a close interweaving of domestic and international politics. But interdependence has by no means reduced the importance of power in the international system. That there is broad agreement on this should be clear from the title of the seminal book by Robert Keohane and Joseph Nye, *Power and Interdependence* (1977), and the earlier classics on which the field has drawn, such as Albert O. Hirschman's study on *National Power and the Structure of Foreign Trade* (1945).

While power is hard to avoid in the literature on international political economy, it has not provided the core of a growing base of knowledge. Disaffection with the concept is not new in the social sciences. Some theorists have suggested that power is ultimately not a useful analytic concept. A recent edited collection of prominent articles in the rational choice tradition does not list the word "power" in the index (Barry and Hardin, 1982). James G. March (1966, p. 70) has argued that "On the whole . . . power is a disappointing concept. It gives us surprisingly little purchase in reasonable models of complex systems of social choice."

If we assume that the international arena is not such a choice system, and that power is here to stay, the failure of the power concept to explain important international relations phenomena demands explication. Power theories may be defective because they are based on inadequate conceptualization and measurement, because they incorrectly specify the linkages between power and outcomes, or because they fail to take into account extraneous factors that may also be theoretically relevant. We refer to these problems as those of measurement, theory, and extraneous variance.

The problem of measurement should be understood broadly to include the rules of concept formation, criteria for inclusion and exclusion, as well as quantitative and qualitative bases for distinguishing the forms and magnitudes of power. How do we know that some actor "has" power or that some relationship is characterized by the exercise of power? Is the phenomenon of power properly viewed in a choice theoretic context or are physical models based on analogues of relative mass and mechanical advantage more appropriate? How should the concept of cost be incorporated into discussions of power? Is success in achieving one's goals a definitional requirement of power or simply a prediction generated by theories of power?

A central conceptual debate is whether power should be conceived and measured as a relatively enduring and fungible attribute, or whether it is situational and relational. The first conception makes measurement easier and enables the analyst to make statements about the relative power of two states without specifying the exact context and issues at stake. If power were enduring and stable across a number of different contexts, it would facilitate the construction of general explanatory theory. The second approach, by contrast, demands careful specification of the context within which power is exercised. This no doubt increases explanatory power, but at some price in terms of lost parsimony and theoretical generalization. If context is overemphasized, variables can be added indefinitely, measurement and generalization become impossible, and explanation gives way to description.

The work of David A. Baldwin (1979, 1985) suggests that this debate can be resolved in part by viewing power in a choice-theoretic framework. It follows that the idea of relative costs is central to power analysis. As we shall demonstrate later in more detail, this conception allows for a marriage between power analysis and existing game-theoretic and rational choice models (Alt et al., 1988, p. 448). As we shall also show, Baldwin's seemingly obvious points are frequently ignored. Power is normally viewed in terms of the probability of winning, alternatives are usually expressed dichotomously as exercising power versus doing nothing, and the cost of exercising power is overlooked altogether (Baldwin, 1985, chap. 7).

Reliable and valid measures are a prerequisite to explanatory success, not a guarantee. Even if measures of power are sound, explanations may still fail because of faulty theory. The function of conceptualization and measurement is to generate sound concepts with internal integrity, either homogeneous or explicitly multi-dimensional. The function of theory is to formulate statements that relate concepts. To the extent that there has been any explicit modeling of international power relationships—and such modeling has been limited—power usually appears as an independent variable used to explain the outcomes of negotiation or influence attempts. In the last decade, there has also been an increasing interest in the relationship between power and the creation and maintenance of systems of international rule or "regimes" (Haggard and Simmons, 1987). The separation of power into independent and dependent variables is not always clear, however. Is power the achievement of the desired outcome itself, as when *a* complies with *b*'s wishes, or is this outcome not logically entailed, but an independent fact to be explained by the *exercise* of power? Some broad, relational notions of power, such as those embedded in "structural" theories of imperialism and dependency, are maddening in their conflation of dependent and independent variables and come perilously close to equating power with the attainment of goals.

Finally, even where measures and theory are sound, extraneous variables may obscure the ability to assess the independent effect of power on the outcome being explained. Though this is one of the central and recurrent problems in power analysis, it is generally overlooked. Some attempts to use power as an explanatory variable assume that a measure of power should incorporate everything relevant to explaining the outcome at hand. Yet if power analysis is to be useful, a distinction must be drawn between power and other variables that might produce an outcome. Even if power were perfectly measured and a power theory correctly specified, different variables would still operate either to offset or reinforce the effect of power per se; power is but one determinant in a field of different causal forces. If offsetting forces were strong, we might mistakenly deny power to agents who possess it. If reinforcing forces were strong, we might attribute power to those who had none.

An example of these two types of spurious inference can be drawn from research on the effectiveness of economic sanctions. Powerful states do not always succeed in achieving their objectives in sanction attempts. To call the United States "weak" as a result of its failure to dislodge Panamanian General Noriega is an example of the first type of faulty inference. Yet even where sanctions *appear* to be successful, the second type of faulty inference is possible if the outcome is not, in fact, the result of the sanctions. A target state may ultimately pursue a set of policies that is in line with the objectives of the sanctioning state for reasons unrelated to the sanctioning effort.

This discussion has an important methodological implication, namely, that strong controls are needed to provide a proper evaluation of power. Appropriate research design and data analytic procedures must be deployed to isolate the influence of power from other forces, which, in a power-theoretic context, should be treated as noise. This should be obvious, since if power is a species of cause it is not different from other members of its genus. Yet a kind of "exceptionalism of power" seems to reign, often placing power beyond acceptable methodological canons. These difficulties, and others, can be seen by examining several different lines of power theory that have appeared in the literature on international political economy.

Decisional Power

The classic definition of power in American political science is Robert A. Dahl's (1969): power is the ability of *a* to get *b* to do something he would not otherwise do. This conception of power assumes a setting in which an issue already exists; hence, separately identifiable parties, interests, conflict, and opposition of wills are all logically entailed. Power *analysis* involves examining how parties to the conflict utilize their resources and skills to achieve outcomes favorable to them. This approach has an intuitive appeal and is the way the term power is used in much descriptive empirical writing on international political economy. Powerful states are those that get their way; power is equated with outcome success.

Despite its appeal, there are serious problems with this conception of power that make it virtually useless for the purpose of constructing theory. The first concerns the issue being contested. There is frequently a prior "editing" of what constitutes a conflict in the first place, a process of agenda setting that itself involves power. This point was made in the community power debate by Peter Bachrach and Morton S. Baratz (1962), who noted that much of politics concerns "nondecisions." A similar point is relevant for understanding a number of issues in international political economy, in particular, explanations of state behavior that rest on the concept of deterrence. States may be deterred from acting in the way they wish, for example, in imposing tighter restrictions on multinational corporations, out of the fear of the consequences, whether explicitly threatened or merely anticipated. If a weak country faces protection from a stronger one and has little hope of reversing these policies or could only do so by expending substantial resources, quiescence and even deference are possible without any actual negotiation or conscious attempt on the part of the strong party to exercise influence.

Power may therefore be most in evidence when it is not "deployed" at all. This insight, and the paradoxes that flow from it, have been central to the long-standing debates over nuclear deterrence and has generated an interesting new literature in game theory on reputation (Alt et al., 1988). It is not well captured, however, by the traditional Dahlian notion of power.

But the decisional approach to power raises an even more fundamental and troubling question. At least in its barest statement—the ability of *a* to get *b* to do what he would not otherwise do—this concept of power comes dangerously close to tautology. Successful attempts to secure compliance from others against their wishes are the basic data of power—positive proof that power exists. But if the powerful must always get their way, if it is logically impossible for the powerful to lose, we are in a theoretically untenable position. Power is defined in terms of an "ability," but what predicts this ability? Surely there are other determinants of outcomes beside power, and if so, we can imagine circumstances under which these other determinants are operative. To say that the power of agents affects outcomes is not to say that nothing else does. Yet conceptions of decisional power have conspicuously lacked a measure of power independent of outcome success. To the extent that decisional power has theoretical leverage, it does so by reaching toward a conception of power as an asymmetrical distribution of resources.

Power as Structure

The dominant theoretical conception of power within international political economy, and in international relations more generally, is structural. The structural approach sees power as residing in the unequal distribution of various resources or interdependencies, with implications for the relative costs of undertaking certain actions. Those who hold more assets and have fewer dependencies win more often and engage in conflicts where the costs of losing are less than their opponents' costs. The theoretical aim of structural analysis is to identify the relevant assets and interdependencies that successfully predict the outcome in question. This approach, which March (1966) has labeled the "basic force model," has the advantage over the decisional one that it generate predictions that are subject to falsification. If no stable links exists between specified asymmetries in resources or dependencies and outcomes, then the theory is either wrong or misspecified (Keohane, 1984a, p. 20).

The resources that are of relevance to a structural explanation of outcomes may be broken down in a number of different ways. In *After Hegemony*, for example, Keohane (1984a, p. 32) argues that "hegemonic powers must have control over raw materials, control over sources of capital, control over markets and competitive advantages in the production of highly valued goods." This list could easily be extended. Analytically, however, it is more useful to distinguish two types of resources depending on whether they are an attribute or possession of the units in question, or a relationship between two units. If the property adheres to the unit, we speak of *attribute capabilities*. This is the most common form of theoretical power analysis in international politics and is central to balance of power theory in both its traditional and neorealist or Waltzian form (Singer et al., 1972; Waltz, 1979). Power resides in the aggregate capabilities of states relative to others and can be measured by some inventory of domestic attributes, such as weapons, the size of armies, population, GNP, or level of technology.

These attributes confer power because they can be "brought to bear" in specific situations. Basic force models presume the ability to "translate" underlying capabilities into effective influence or compliance through the imposition of costs or conferring of benefits on the opponent or the threat or promise to do so. As in the analysis of threats in standard bargaining theory, the stronger party improves its position by worsening the position of the weaker party if it fails to comply. Such basic force models are prone to the criticism that they frequently fail to show *how* a given resource base is relevant for actually achieving compliance, particularly if opponents have a high tolerance for pain. We return to this problem in more detail below.

A second type of resource is particularly important under conditions of economic interdependence and therefore deserves more extended discussion. Resources are not limited to properties that inhere in the units but include resources that emerge from *asymmetries in the exchanges that occur between units*. These resources may be called *exchange capabilities*. In the case of nation-states, these exchanges include trade, technology transfer, direct investment, and other financial flows, including foreign aid. The analysis of exchange capabilities can be extended to nonstate actors, whether multinational corporations and banks or multilateral institutions such as the IMF or World Bank.

What are these asymmetries and how can they be theoretically tied to the exercise of power? The answers to these questions are not obvious. Ricardian models of trade that rest on comparative advantage see exchange as mutually beneficial, since it expands the consumption possibilities of both countries. However, countries can and do bargain over the terms of trade or the distribution of the gains from trade, and this is the subject of a strand of theory on the optimal tariff. States with *market power* have the capability of unilaterally changing the terms of trade in their favor.

Standard trade theory says nothing about the relative *vulnerability* of the two parties to a *disruption* of the exchange relationship, however, and it is this form of vulnerability that has formed the basis for most structural analyses of economic power. Hirschman (1945) observed over four decades ago that country A's power over country B is inversely related to A's benefits from trade and directly related to the degree of reliance of B on A. Hirschman's insight was that the asymmetry in dependence generates power through the ability on the part of the more powerful, or less dependent, to extract concessions by interrupting or threatening to interrupt the exchange at *relatively* low cost. Building on Hirschman, James A. Caporaso (1978), Baldwin (1985), Bruno S. Frey (1984, chap. 6), and others (but see Wagner, 1988) have specified more exactly the conditions under which such asymmetries are more likely to generate influence.[1] These include most importantly the extent of reliance of the weaker party on the exchange, the ability to diversify sources of supply, and the ability to adjust domestically to a supply interruption by substituting for the good or service in question or going without it altogether. It should be noted that this last condition goes beyond the structural asymmetry per se and rests on the *domestic* capabilities of governments to absorb costs.

Because it is formulated explicitly in terms of the manipulation of resources in order to confer benefits and impose costs, the structural approach to power can be linked to formal choice and cost-based views of power, such as those developed by John C. Harsanyi (1969) and Hayward R. Alker Jr. (1973), and to bargaining theory (Wagner, 1988). Extending Harsanyi's original insight, Alker (1973, p. 308) argued that we can "summarize power in terms of a schedule or graph or function linking opportunity costs to desirable performance possibilities." The first step is to assign utilities to i and j for all alternatives and costs coefficients for the use of varying amounts of resources, whether of the attribute or exchange sort. In Harsanyi's words (1969, p. 232), power becomes a kind of

> "production function" describing how a given individual can transform different amounts of his resources . . . into social power of various dimensions (of strengths, scopes, amounts and extensions). The commonsense notion of social power makes it an *ability* to achieve certain things—an ability that the person concerned is free to use or to leave unused.

In contrast to the decisional conception of power, which reduces to the frequency of times that outcomes favor i versus j, power in this model is a generalized function of i's utility for various actions of j and the resource costs to i of attempting to influence j and j's costs of resisting or complying, both of which are affected by exchange capabilities. This formulation is of policy as well as theoretical interest since, as Baldwin (1985, p. 118) points out, "assessing the utility of a technique of statecraft is essentially a matter of estimating and comparing the costs and benefits associated with alternative ways to pursue a given set of foreign policy goals."

Recent literature on economic sanctions, the political economy of foreign direct investment, and international regimes suggests both the utility of, and limits on, structural conceptions of power. Economic sanctions are important because they clearly invoke the threat or actuality of economic punishment as part of a strategy of achieving a political result; this is as close to the attempted exercise of power as one can come. In general, the sanctions literature has focused on the question of whether sanctions "work," with the received wisdom being that they do not (e.g., see Paarlberg, 1980; Kaempfer et al., 1987). As Baldwin has pointed out, the question of success has exercised a deleterious influence on the study of sanctions, since it ignores the question of costs. Economic sanctions are often held to higher standards for judging success than other means of exercising influence. Diplomatic and military attempts at influence also frequently fall short of reaching their objectives, but neither has ever been branded as *generally* ineffective. The analysis of the effectiveness of sanctions must begin with an examination of the difficulty of the goals being pursued, a crucial factor that goes beyond the structural setting within which bargaining takes place. Attention must also be paid to the costs imposed on the target state even where the sanction effort fails and to the costs of alternative means of attempting to exercise influence. By ignoring costs and limiting the examination of alternatives to doing nothing versus carrying out the sanction, critics of sanctions have made it extremely difficult for sanctions to work. As Baldwin (1985, p. 115) puts it, "the tendency to denigrate the effectiveness of economic instruments is caused by concepts that make it *definitionally* difficult for them to succeed."

Against the received wisdom that sanctions are generally ineffective, a number of recent studies have suggested the conditions under which sanctions are more likely to succeed; most confirm the intuition and the broad line of theory on exchange capabilities developed by Hirschman and his successors. Gary Hufbauer and Jeffrey Schott (1985) have attempted one of the few studies of a large number of sanction cases and have distinguished among the various goals of sanction efforts. Their findings suggest that sanction efforts are more likely to succeed where policy goals are modest, where trade dependence of the target is high, and where the costs imposed as a result of the sanction effort are high. In a somewhat different vein, Lipson (1985) shows that large commercial banks wield effective power to sanction because of their ability to overcome collective action problems and effectively isolate borrowers. This confirms the expectation that the availability of alternative sources of supply for the needed good will weaken sanction efforts. Similar observations have been made about the relative success of the American freeze of Iranian assets (Carswell, 1981) and the effectiveness of South African sanctions against Rhodesia (Cross, 1981).

The fact that sanctions frequently fail to achieve their objectives does not necessarily disconfirm structural theories so much as suggest that the structural conditions required to exercise influence are rare. Such cases as the American failure in Panama do raise questions about the utility of a structural approach, however, since the structural conditions could hardly have been more propitious; Panama even lacked its own currency. The literature on the political economy of the multinational corporation reveals some of these broader limitations to the structural approach.

Unlike older dependency writing that was concerned with the broad constraints in "the international system," a "new wave" of dependency writing (Evans, 1979; Gereffi, 1983; Bennett and Sharpe 1985; Haggard, 1989) has been concerned with host–firm bargaining on issues such as the terms of entry, incentives, regulation, local equity participation, taxation, and trade behavior. Though any bargaining approach presumes the possibility of joint gains, the central contention of the new dependency literature is that

MNCs possess assets that skew bargaining outcomes in their favor. The oligopolistic advantages that give firms an incentive to invest abroad in the first place—access to finance, technology, product differentiation, marketing capabilities, and managerial skills (Kindleberger, 1969; Hymer, 1976)—also translate into bargaining power with the host. A structural perspective would also expect the power of foreign firms to increase with their relative weight in the economy as a whole.

A practical application of structural power analysis is seen in the efforts of the "new wave" writers to explain why host bargaining power may be weaker in the manufacturing sector than it is in extractive industries. Raymond Vernon (1971), Theodore H. Moran (1974), and Franklin Tugwell (1975) noted that "traditional" investments had several characteristics that weakened the host at the point of entry. Investments were extremely large and demanded that the firm adopt a long time horizon. The high dependence of the developing country on the assets held by the MNC allowed the investor to extract substantial guarantees and support for the project prior to committing resources. Once the investment was sunk, however, the dependency of the host government was partly reversed. Costly investments became easy targets for contract renegotiation, regulation, indigenization, and even nationalization. Bargains "obsolesced" and contracts were rewritten.

The host–firm relationship is quite different in import-substituting manufacturing industries. The ability of the state to hold out the promise of access to the local market allows the host to exercise selectivity in accepting new entrants, particularly where the degree of competition among firms is high, the domestic market is large, and overall economic performance promising. At the point of entry therefore, the investor is *weakest*. The bargaining relationship changes once manufacturing firms are established. Networks of suppliers, distributors, joint-venture partners, and consumers become dependent on the MNCs (Gereffi and Newfarmer, 1985, p. 432). Manufacturing industries are also more likely to be characterized by ongoing technological change than are extractive industries. As Constantine Vaitsos (1974) noted in a classic study, technology markets are characterized by fundamental information asymmetries and paradoxes. To bargain intelligently demands knowledge of the technology which is being sought, but such knowledge is precisely the commodity being sold. Any move to increase national control "will run the risk of severing the lifeline of new innovations" (Gereffi and Newfarmer, 1985, p. 431; see also Kobrin, 1988). Again the "terms of trade" favor the firm.

As bargaining school critics of the dependency approach, such as Joseph Grieco (1984), have pointed out, the foregoing picture suggests that structural models of MNC power are incomplete unless they include reference to the assets of the host countries. Some elements of LDC bargaining power are likely to be structural, such as market size and level of income; large, wealthy countries do better than small poor ones (Goodman, 1987). Market conditions may also favor the host countries. Whether oligopolistic competition can increase national bargaining power is a major point of contention between dependency theorists and their bargaining school interlocutors. In their study of the Mexican automobile industry, Douglas C. Bennett and Kenneth E. Sharpe (1985) argue that foreign firms exercised strong influence over the bargaining agenda, while Grieco's study of India shows how the government exploited competition among foreign firms to enhance its position.

A point that emerges from both studies, however, is that bargaining power is not simply a function of structural conditions; facing a similar external setting, states respond differently. This is a fundamental weakness of structural approaches, which the "conversion process" approach to power has attempted to address.

The literature on sanctions and host–MNC bargaining concern themselves, respectively, with securing policy changes in a target country and the outcome of bilateral negotiations. These fairly discrete outcomes are not the only ones addressed by structural power analysis, however. One of the central debates in the field of international political economy in recent years concerns the theory of hegemonic stability (Keohane, 1984a; Snidal, 1985; Gilpin, 1987; Haggard and Simmons, 1987; Strange, 1987). This theory holds that strong, liberal international regimes are likely to exist only when a dominant or "hegemonic" state supports and sustains them; conversely, the decline of hegemonic power will be associated with the erosion of international regimes. Two theoretical underpinnings have been provided for this theory. One, based on the theory of collective action, suggests that international regimes constitute public goods which will be underprovided in the absence of leadership. Such leadership, it was argued, was more likely in systems where a single state dominated (but see Snidal, 1985).

The other, more traditional, conception of hegemony argues that dominant states write rules that conform to their interests and guarantee compliance through the exercise of power. The stability of regimes can thus be reduced to a problem of effective policing by the powerful. It is beyond the scope of this chapter to review this debate in detail; other reviews exist (Snidal, 1985; Haggard and Simmons, 1987). It is only important to note that power resources may be turned to the object of structuring the rules and institutions within which international economic transactions take place. In the international economy, these rules and institutions fall far short of a comprehensive set of property rights. Nonetheless, they can become a source of power, a point to which we return in our discussion of "locational" approaches to power.

The Conversion Process Approach

One line of criticism of the structural approach to power, even in its relational or exchange form, results from the "paradox of unrealized power" (Baldwin, 1979, p. 163). It is a long-standing observation that apparently weak states, the "Davids" of international politics, do better than expected in the international economy and can even prevail over substantially more powerful "Goliaths" (see Mack, 1975; Organski and Kugler, 1978). Apparently "structural" constraints are less restrictive or, put differently, predict outcomes less well than they should. There are several ways out of this predicament. One is to attempt to specify more precisely what the relevant power resources are in a particular context. The debate between dependency and bargaining approaches to host–MNC relations is partly along these lines. Here, the "paradox" is resolved by noting that resources assumed relevant in the bargaining or influence attempt were not relevant, or by showing that assets held by the "weaker" party were overlooked. Unless an efforts is made to move back and forth between empirical observation, generalization, and the construction of theory, this strategy runs the risk of incorporating virtually all elements relevant to the explanation of outcomes under the rubric of power. Some scholars move in this direction when they note that virtually anything might be a power resource in the right context, and that what constitutes power is difficult to know ex ante. Context is important, but to advance theoretically we need to specify classes of "contexts" across which generalization might be made.

A second way to address the paradox of unrealized power, however, is to focus on the process by which resources are converted into influence, the efficiency with which resources are used, and the effectiveness of different tactics and strategies. While underlying material resources may remain unchanged over time or across cases, the willingness to deploy them or the ability to organize and exploit assets effectively varies. The line between this approach and what we call a structural one is somewhat artificial, since asymmetries in such conversion processes can themselves be interpreted as a "structure" that yields power; Thomas J. Biersteker (1980), for example, suggests this in his discussion of how multinationals can devise tactics to evade compliance with host country regulations. Nonetheless, there is an intuitive appeal in drawing a distinction between resources and the capacity to deploy them effectively to achieve goals.

Keohane has argued that such conversion process models, or what March calls "force activation" models, "are essentially *post hoc* rather than *a priori*, since one can always 'save' such a theory after the fact by thinking of reasons why an actor would have wanted to use all of its available potential power" (Keohane, 1984, p. 35). Keohane points out that such approaches dilute the determinacy of basic force models, such as the theory of hegemonic stability.

Once conversion processes are introduced, "whether a given configuration of power will lead the potential hegemon to maintain a set of rules remains indeterminate unless we know a great deal about its domestic politics" (Keohane, 1984, p. 35).

These objections can be addressed, however, and are partly misguided. The charge that conversion process models are post hoc can be overcome by specifying in advance the institutional conditions, or range of tactics, which are most likely to result in a successful conversion of assets into increased influence. Structural theories can also become post hoc if new resources are uncovered to account for anomalies. Similarly, the exclusive focus on system structure in most contemporary international relations theory is misguided. A fear exists that the "second image" of international relations is a Pandora's box filled with country-specific parameters. The fact that knowledge of domestic politics is required to make predictions is not a block to the formation of a good theory, nor even to parsimony. The belief that each domestic society offers its own laws is unfounded, as the work of Organski (1965), Organski and Kugler (1980), Kugler and Domke (1986), and Lewis W. Snider (1987, 1988) demonstrates. New empirical work on American foreign economic policy makes the same point (Ikenberry et al., 1988). Explanations that rest on domestic political capabilities may be quite parsimonious if the components of the domestic political system relevant to the exercise of power, such as the ability to extract resources or make coherent decisions, can be dimensionalized. The above writers have noted, for example, that the state's capacity to extract resources is a crucial intermediate variable between societal resources and the exercise of state power. Measures of extractive capacity can overcome erroneous predictions of the outcomes of war based on indicators of societal resources alone.

One area in which there have been theoretically informed efforts to incorporate conversion processes into power analysis is in studies that directly address the "paradox of unrealized power" by looking at bargaining between "weak" countries and "stronger" states or multinationals. David B. Yoffie (1983), for example, has attempted to understand why the outcomes of bilateral trade bargaining between the United States and the Third World are more favorable toward the LDCs than one would otherwise expect (see also Odell, 1985). Yoffie outlines an ideal-typical strategy for an LDC facing trade restraints and then seeks to measure the performance of the East Asian newly industrializing countries against it. All the countries in the study confronted high asymmetrical power situations: all were heavily dependent on the United States market and as a result the agenda of trade negotiations was set wholly by the United States. The United States sought to impose restrictions via the mechanism of "voluntary" export restraints. But states varied in their success in pursuing tactics and strategies that would reduce the costs associated with these structural asymmetries. Within the context of the negotiation itself, the exporting countries could negotiate for ambiguity and flexibility in the terms of the signed agreements that would leave them larger opportunities for expanding their exports in response to market changes. Bargaining tactics also included mobilizing transgovernmental and transnational allies with the aim of reinforcing bureaucratic splits in the United States (Moon, 1988). Somewhat less successfully, countries could attempt to link issues, for example, by demanding compensation for losses associated with protection on the grounds that the country, such as Korea, was providing other defense-related services.

The strategies proposed by Yoffie ultimately included shifting economic resources in order to adjust to the imposition of trade restraints where they were inevitable. This, in turn, rested on the flexibility of the economy and the decisionmaking structure. While these may not constitute power resources as we normally think about them, they did lessen the cost associated with an asymmetrical bargaining situation.

As these examples suggest, the discussion of power cannot be divorced from domestic political and organizational capabilities, a point also frequently noted in discussions of military power. One of the most important factors in determining bargaining outcomes in international economic negotiations is simply the sophistication and administrative capability of the state. Gereffi (1983), for example, concludes his excellent case study of host–firm bargaining in the Mexican steroid hormone industry by arguing that the MNCs limited Mexico's bargaining power, but he also notes the importance of government inaction caused by "conflicting priorities within the state bureaucracy, inadequate administrative capabilities for monitoring and regulating the activities of the TNCs, and corruption" (Gereffi, 1983, p. 155). This suggests that MNC "power" is not a given but is contingent on the institutional capabilities of the host, a point developed by Emanuel Adler (1987) in his study of the Argentine and Brazilian computer industries.

Dependency theorists have countered that the entry of a MNC itself serves to undercut the power of the state (Biersteker, 1980). But as Hirschman (1981) pointed out in a reflection on his early work, the very asymmetries in exchange that generate power relationships are also likely to generate an asymmetry in *attention* and *stakes* that favor the more dependent party. Peter Evans (1985) argues that the penetration of transnational actors and linkages provides an incentive to the development of state capabilities designed to regulate them. The next stage of this research is to develop more clear hypotheses linking governmental structure to such regulative capacity.

The conversion process approach raises a final question, however. Should we consider domestic structures, and even variables such as know-ledge, tactics, "will," and bargaining skill, as elements of power, or extraneous variables that reinforce or offset underlying power considerations? One could certainly discuss asymmetries in knowledge and skill as constituting a power structure, as Vaitsos (1974) does. To do this in a theoretically useful way, however, these variables must be dimensionalized and operationalized in such a way as to permit generalization; otherwise, they will appear as ad hoc amendments rather than as components of a refined theory.

Locational Power

Decisional, structural, and conversion-process approaches all assume that power is exercised self-consciously in situations of conflict; all three views are predicated on strong conceptions of agency, intentionality, and strategic behavior (Giddens, 1979). Actors pursue their goals in competitive environments, using resources and strategies to overcome resistance.

The idea that power is tied to conscious agents exerting their will runs deep in American social science and can be traced from Max Weber to pluralists in the community power structure debate, such as Dahl and Polsby, to modelers such as Simon (1953) who see power as "preferred causation." There are, however, quite different traditions of power analysis in which agency and intent play a less central role. Karl Marx's idea that exploitation and the extraction of surplus value under capitalism occurs through the routine operation of the system of wage labor and the competitive strategies of individual capitalists is a key example. Gramscian conceptions of power start from the observation that workers voluntarily comply with systems that exploit them because of hegemonic ideologies that redefine perceptions of self-interest (Lukes, 1974).

Giddens (1979, p. 88) points out that power has a twofold meaning: as involved institutionally in processes of interaction and as used to accomplish outcomes in strategic interaction. Decisional power, structural power (as used here), and power as a conversion process are all connected to strategic behavior. All are concerned with how capabilities are used, processed, or transformed in the service of exercising influence. Giddens' first category of power, by contrast, rests on very different foundations. The core claim is that power is best seen as a pure structure, as a set of interlocking roles and institutional complexes that directly allocate scarce values. To the extent that power is personal at all, it goes to those occupying particular structural locations. Individuals are simply the "bearers" of the power seated in institutions. The "real" subjects are the roles and structural locations themselves. Individuals cannot walk away with structural power; it is not portable. The results of the normal workings of institutions deserve to be called power, however, because resources, income, status, and other goods are allocated by them.

It is important to differentiate this view from what we have called a "structural" one. Institutions and rules can provide the setting for strategic conduct and can create capabilities that empower and limit agents; Krasner

(1985) has advanced this argument most cogently in his discussion of the debates about a new international economic order. Such a view is broadly in line with what we call a "structural" approach, with the institutional setting viewed as an additional resource that unit-level actors tap to achieve objectives. This is *not* the view advanced by the "locational" view of power; instead, the claim is that institutions represent value-allocating processes *quite apart from and even in contradiction to the intentions of agents* (Caporaso, 1978, p. 29).

For want of a better term, we label this conception of power locational. While far from a homogeneous group, theorists of locational power are tied together by the assumption that power and powerlessness flow directly from position or location in the international economic hierarchy. This view is common to a number of interpretations of the global division of labor and world inequality that rest on noncoerced transfers of wealth (Prebisch, 1950; Singer, 1950; Lewis, 1978) and can be seen most clearly in the work of Immanuel Wallerstein, Johan Galtung, and theorists of unequal exchange.

For Wallerstein (1974, 1979), economic life is organized into a single world economy with various political subdivisions (nation-states). The world economy is not simply an aggregation of national economies; it is best seen rather as a hierarchy of "zones" or "regions" differentiated by level of technical sophistication, processing, and forms of labor control, and held together by commodity exchange, capital flows, and labor migration. A static view of Wallerstein's world system is compatible either with the neoclassical interpretation of specialization based on comparative costs or a radical emphasis on the coercive structuring of center–periphery relations. Regardless of how this system came into being, it operates (noncoercively) in such a way as to benefit the core to the disadvantage of the periphery. Wealth is created in different locations, surplus is extracted, and then transferred from one region to another through trade, repatriation of profit, licensing fees, and royalties. Wealth is transferred from some locations to others, the term "location" being interpreted here in geographical and class terms. Some locations systematically fare better than others. Yet there is no grand design and only a part of the transferred wealth occurs as a result of conscious bargaining attempts.

Johan Galtung's (1971) essay, "A Structural Theory of Imperialism," shares basic reference points with dependency theory (Frank, 1969; Cardoso, 1973; Cardoso and Faletto, 1978) and with Wallerstein and self-consciously attempts to develop an alternative to actor-oriented views of power. First, Galtung refers to *parties* or *social categories* rather than to actors, and to *conflicts of interest* rather than *conflicts of goals*, signaling a move away from conscious agents toward collectivities identified on the basis of shared or conflicting interests (Galtung, 1971, p. 82). Core and periphery for Galtung are not simply a way of drawing a distinction between poor and rich countries, but of identifying geographical and class locations between which there are *objective* conflicts of interest. Again, inequality results not from bargaining outcomes but from mechanisms embedded in the organization and routine operation of the hierarchy.

A problem with the work of Wallerstein, Galtung, and the dependency tradition more generally lies in the underspecification of the mechanisms through which inequality is presumably reproduced. If it is neither the result of conscious state action nor of the exploitation of market power by private agents, it must reside in other structural features of market exchanges among actors in different zones that confer benefits unequally.

Three approaches to such "unequal exchange" can be identified: an elasticity approach, the labor-supply approach, and the unequal exchange approach developed by Arghiri Emmanuel (1972). The elasticities approach centers on the structure of demand for the products of different country groupings. As incomes rise, the demand for manufactures outstrips the demand for raw materials, worsening the terms of trade of those countries specializing in raw materials. If the world economy is territorially specialized in the production of different products, it follows that rising income will lead to uneven price movements, worsening the terms of trade for those countries specializing in primary product exports.

The labor–supply approach, associated with Lewis (1978), argues that because of historical factors, demographics, and differential patterns of labor migration to the tropical and temperate zones, the price of labor came to vary sharply between these two zones. Lewis insisted that the poor terms of trade for some less developed countries were not the result of the product exported but of the supply of labor and the capital–labor ratio in the exporting countries; proof of this is provided by the fact that the terms of trade for agricultural products originating in the temperate zone—Canada, the United States, Australia—are not at all adverse.

Emmanuel's (1972) book, *Unequal Exchange*, is a variant of the labor–supply argument. Emmanuel relies more heavily on the historical struggles of labor, rather than labor as simply a productive factor. These historical struggles resulted in higher wages for workers in advanced capitalist countries, quite apart from productivity differences between rich and poor countries. While higher wages cut into the surplus, preventing higher levels of accumulation in the core, they also raise the price of goods in the export sector. If high-wage, high-price goods in the core exchange with low-wage, low-priced goods in the periphery, unequal exchange results. The claimed strength of Emmanuel's argument, as that of Lewis, is that unequal exchange results without superior bargaining power, market imperfections, differential elasticities, or productivity differences. Given the same level and rate of technical progress, the same intensity of demand, and no market power, unequal exchange will occur.

It is beyond the scope of this chapter to review the many criticisms that have been leveled against theories of unequal exchange; the main concern here is with the nature of the theoretical enterprise. None of these theorists are oblivious to the effects of political action, but the core of the approach is the hypothesis about the noncoerced transfer of wealth that results from the global organization of production into differentiated "zones." Location within this division of labor is a *determinant* of outcomes.

The key question is whether such arguments should be considered forms of power analysis. The argument for an expansive definition is that it acts as a corrective to purely intentionalist models by alerting the analyst to unintended consequences. There are many factors affecting welfare, some within the realm of conscious choice and others outside it. It can be argued that a theory of power should rightly encompass both. A similar argument might be developed for "location" with reference to some *rule* structure that confers benefits unequally through its "normal" operation; this was a major political objective of the New International Order proposals, which sought to change international regimes in a direction more advantageous to developing countries (Krasner, 1985).

There are, however, strong arguments for limiting the referential domain of power. As we have argued above, the risk of "conceptual stretching" and circular reasoning is high. For Wallerstein, for example, the characteristics that *define* the different zones in the world economy, and thus its structure, are also *outcomes* of the operation of the structure. Structure causes structure, and the distinction between unit attributes and systemic characteristics is hopelessly blurred (Waltz, 1979). The core–periphery distinction becomes an essentially descriptive, rather than theoretical, one. Severing the link between power and agency also disconnects the theory of power from theories of decisionmaking, choice, costs, and even alternatives. This has political, as well as theoretical, consequences.

Locational approaches also often slip into the language of agency. Thus, the advanced industrial states are "imperialist" according to Galtung, but quite apart from any conscious actions that they take. This adoption of the language of agency has a political function. Agency-oriented views of power limit responsibility to those actions where intent plays a role (Connolly, 1974); one cannot receive credit or blame for what is not willed. The concept of locational power, by contrast, provides a language of consequences, rather than intentions. This language is appealing to those at the bottom of a hierarchy, who see the consequences of the system as the product of structures at the top, structures that might have been otherwise.

Summary and Conclusion

The four approaches to power outlined here are in some ways competing theories that address the weaknesses of the others. The decisional approach appeals to the intuitive notion that power is getting one's way; the proof of power lies in the pattern of outcomes. This immediately begs the question of why certain actors get their way, however. The structural approach answers this question by pointing to asymmetries in the distribution of resources, whether seen as attributes of the actors or characteristics of exchange relations. These asymmetries are used to predict directly to outcomes. The strength and weakness of the structural approach are its falsifiability. If power can be measured relatively easily, these measures can be used to predict outcomes. Strong, falsifiable predictions can be made, but what happens when those with fewer resources prevail?

One answer is to turn to the processes through which resources are converted into capabilities. The central problem with the conversion process approach is that it lifts the lid on an extremely wide array of possible influences. The failure to use power resources effectively is not solely a function of organization and the strength or flexibility of institutions, which are difficult enough to measure; it also depends on a series of intangibles that can easily degenerate into ad hoc emendations: the "stake" an actor has in a conflict, the "will" one party brings to the bargaining table, and the skill of the protagonists. The key question for the conversion process approach is whether such intangibles can be given empirical referents that help us generate stronger theory.

The locational approach to power, by contrast, seeks to address a different weakness in the structural approach, its focus on intentional attempts at influence. Theorists of locational power address outcomes that may not result from influence or the exercise of power in this sense but that still reflect some underlying asymmetry in capabilities.

Thinking of the exercise of power in concrete situations suggests the metaphor of a funnel of causality. In this metaphor, power as the successful enactment of one's will is the end result of a long and complicated causal chain, from the more remote background factors such as underlying resources to the more proximal forces influencing the outcome. Figure 6.1 attempts in a schematic way to capture this causal chain and suggests a number of concluding observations.

First, the four types of power that we have outlined are not necessarily competing theoretical approaches as much as distinctive locations in the funnel, clusters of power variables that may be more or less relevant in the explanation of particular outcomes. The research task is to weight these clusters of variables. For example, decisional power focuses narrowly on the immediate environment of the contest of power, the bargaining skills

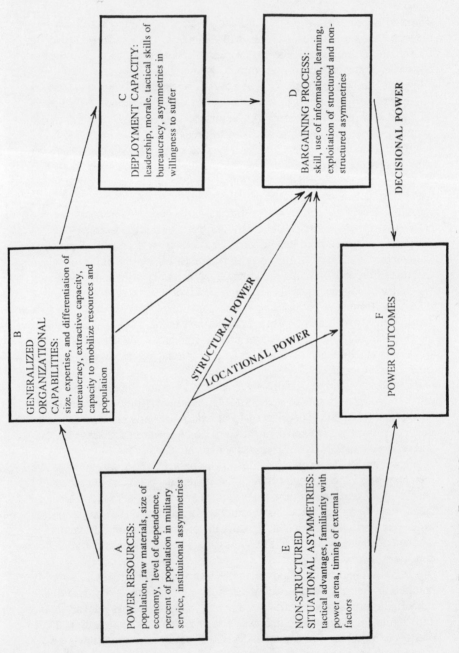

Figure 6.1 Power and the Funnel of Causality

employed, and the structured tactical advantages and limitations of the participants. Structural power, whether based on attributes or exchange capabilities, stresses the connections among underlying capabilities, the bargaining process, and outcomes. The bargaining process itself tends to be deemphasized. In contrast to locational power, however, such a bargaining process is still presumed to be important; capabilities work through agents to produce outcomes. Finally, the conversion process approach emphasizes the mechanisms that link the different boxes.

A second point that emerges from Figure 6.1 is that a sharp line must be drawn between determinants that are systematic and those that are not. Can the assets in question be *systematically* related to outcomes? Are the assets in question and the functional relations between them and outcomes stable or fickle? It may well be that the personal qualities of those engaged in economic bargaining and diplomacy "matter," while at the same time representing specific, nontransferable aspects of the conflict. On the other hand, factors such as information, will, and bargaining skill may not be idiosyncratic, but the result of some other stable structures and capabilities. Power theorists should not attempt to deal with everything that counts, but only with those variables that can be systematically related to outcomes.

Our review also points to an important weakness in current power studies that opens a new vista for research. Very little work has been done on the domestic organizational capabilities that link resources to their effective use. In part because of the dominance of systemic theory in the field of international relations, power is generally conceived as a relation between actors. Inadequate attention is paid to the internal characteristics of states that make them externally "strong" or "weak." Several strands of literature have begun to explore this lead, however. The work by Organski and Kugler (1978) and Kugler and Domke (1986) focuses on the extractive power of states as a key component of power. Barbara G. Haskel (1980) noted in a suggestive article that the openness of societies to external influences can affect the ability of governments to act coherently. And despite its difficulties, the literature on "state strength" has been suggestive in attempting to isolate more clearly the organizational and political factors that allow political elites to realize their objectives (Katzenstein 1978; Ikenberry et al. 1988). While this literature has been concentrated in political economy, a similar strand of theorizing about the importance of domestic organization has emerged in security studies, and even in the discussion of nuclear weapons (Blair 1985).

International political economy is still without a coherent theory of power. The thrust of this chapter is that a single theory is not only unlikely, but probably undesirable as well. A more coherent understanding of how different conceptions of power fit together may be the best that we can expect from power theory in the years ahead.

Notes

We would like to thank David Baldwin and Robert Keohane for comments on an earlier draft of this chapter.

1. As this book was going to press, R. Harrison Wagner (1988) published an interesting critique of Hirschman (1945). To simplify a complex argument, Wagner contends that asymmetric interdependence does not necessarily lead to increased bargaining power and political influence. Analysts have mistakenly assumed that this link holds because they fail to distinguish between two separate forms of power: market power and bargaining power. Market power is the ability to manipulate the terms of trade, which rests in turn on differential elasticities of demand in the respective countries. This type of power is distinct from bargaining power, which is a consequence of the relative evaluation by governments of the costs of severing trade links (p. 463). Wagner's paper contains a number of insights, but it also makes distinctions and analogies that are not relevant to an assessment of Hirschman's core argument. In particular, Wagner argues that Hirschman's thesis rests on the exercise of market power, which is not the case. Rather, it rests on asymmetries in total dependence on trade. We agree with Wagner, however, that these asymmetries are at best one base of power, and the conditions under which they can be translated into influence must be carefully specified. The article raises important issues that need to be addressed, but a thorough response is beyond the scope of this chapter.

7

Power in the International System: Behavioral Salience and Material Capabilities

Michael D. Ward

The notion of *power* has long endured in the study of political phenomena precisely because the notion of "political" implies some visible and tangible imposition of one's will upon another. Despite many varieties of meanings, intended and inferred, the term "power" in international relations has come to be synonymous with the ability to impose one's will on another in order to extract some perceived benefit. A broad survey of the relevant literature over the past 2000 years will convince most that power is an important concept in the history of ideas, but that it is an idea, like causality, that is hard to pin down. In fact, it may be that the term is exactly as salient as it is difficult to pin down; Paul Kennedy (1987) wrote a volume, *The Rise and Fall of the Great Powers*, that was on *The New York Times* best-seller list for over 20 weeks (at the time of writing, July 1988) without ever coming close to providing a definition of the term. At the extremes, power is easy to identify: virtually everyone can recognize, as M. Foucault puts it, the inherent role that power plays in both bureaucracies and concentration camps. Beyond the extremes, however, our examples and our understanding very often get away from our grasp. United States–Panamanian relations were thought to provide an exemplar of a dominant, powerful regime (i.e., the United States) directing with considerable accuracy the actions of a much weaker, subservient client regime, Panama. Our simplistic versions of power as determination of beneficial outcome and power as derived capabilities often conflict, as they have come to do in the case of contemporary United States–Panamanian relations. Is Noreiga's regime more powerful than the United States? Is the United States *powerless* in the face of a much "weaker" opponent? How is power exercised, and when is it impotent? If power is impotent on the ground in Central America, is there such a thing as power? Is God no longer on the side of the larger battalions?

Questions such as these immediately give rise to the contradictions of the commonsense meanings of power as outcome and power as capabilities. The tautology is not hard to follow. Power is derived in some straightforward fashion from material capabilities such as economic productivity, military weaponry, human capital, and the like. *Power is capability*. Furthermore, the more powerful party to a conflict or dispute will prevail, assuming that they show the requisite will in using their power. *Power is determinant of the outcome*. Under such a scenario, we might presume that if nations are able to accurately assess the power of their potential allies and adversaries, they would always be able to prevail in conflicts since they would not rationally undertake to wage a battle that they would be certain of losing. Somewhat more cynically, if all nations used the Correlates of War capability scores to gauge their power, war and conflict would be relegated to hypothetical studies. Obviously, power is at once more nuanced and incorrigible.

The main point of this chapter is to assert, amplify, and examine the notion that conflict outcome should *not* be our ultimate yardstick for gauging power in world affairs. In so doing, a new, synthetic definition of power is proposed and dissected. This definition and operationalization of power shares much with the main dominant tradition; namely, it builds on the notion of attributes such as Gross National (economic) Product and the six components of the Correlates of War measure (military personnel, military expenditures, population, urban population, energy consumption, and iron and steel production). However, it radically diverges from such approaches in insisting that the notion of power is not only contextually bound, but that it is inherently a relational property, one that does not simply emerge from attribute comparisons. Thus, the main goal of this short chapter is to develop and illustrate a theory of power that is more nuanced in taking into account not only capabilities but also actual behavior as well.

Behavioral Power and Salience[1]

In Michael D. Ward and Lewis House (1988) we developed the notion of behavioral power. In this research, I stepped back from the notion of power as outcome or attribute and argued for a weaker form of power relationships, based on somewhat stronger assumptions. Without looking for beneficial outcome or relying on possession of material capabilities, I conceptualized power as the ability to influence either directly or indirectly the behaviors of other nations. Simply, what I was looking for was a way to capture the ability to start trouble. Nations whose actions preceded a great burst of activity on the part of other nations were by inference said to be behaviorally powerful. Obviously, temporal precedence guarantees neither causation nor power, but it is a necessary component in each. And in ways conceptually similar to the recent simplification of economic notions of causality (*Granger causality*), I sought to provide a simplified definition of power relationships.

The basic premises of this approach, the behavioral power approach, are several. I assumed that the international system consists of a variety of agents that are characterized by varying degrees of autonomy. For the most part these are nations, but obvious to many scholars is the notion that supra-, trans-, and subnational actors are also crucial to a complete analysis of world affairs. I also assumed that these actors were purposeful in their actions and that one of their main purposes was to influence the actions of other agents in the world. The instruments through which such influence is attempted are widespread and vast, ranging from legal instruments through diplomatic maneuvering to informal, personal "walks in the woods." I assumed that the public record of world affairs, comprised of the reporting of many sets of journalists, contained the important traces of the actual influence attempts through which the ebb and flow of world affairs are conducted. Thus, I took event interactions to comprise the flow of influence attempts from one nation to another.

Since I believed that multilateral as well as bilateral networks of interaction and influence were important, but ignored by most attempts to gauge power in the international system, I felt that it was important to look not at each bilateral pair of nations, two at a time, but rather to construct a summary of the totality of interactions of all nations with one another. Furthermore, since much research had established the salience and ubiquitous character of reciprocity (see especially Axelrod, 1984, and Leng, 1984), I inferred that a basic underlying equilibrium level of conflict and cooperation existed among nations. Short-term fluctuations could be seen in terms of their deviations from this basic level of interaction (Engle and Granger, 1987).

Finally, I made an even spicier assumption; namely, that behavioral power in the international realm was constant at any given point in time. By this I argued that in the short run, what one nation may gain in behavioral power, can only come at the expense of other nations. In this sense, power is a private, not a public, good. If the Soviet Union is able to determine completely the foreign policy actions of North Korea, for example, no other actor can also have influence over the actions of the Pyongyang regime. Mathematically and conceptually, behavioral power is exactly, not over-, identified. However, it is clear that behavioral power can itself grow over time, and two nations, for example, may jointly act to increase their behavioral power. This increase will—under our simplifying assumptions—come at the expense of other agents in the system. Thus, I assert that, because of the reciprocity norm at the system level, behavioral power functions as an equilibrium system. Accordingly, nations with greater behavioral power will employ fewer influence attempts to generate responses on the part of others, while less behaviorally powerful nations will be required to employ a great many more influence attempts to gain similar results.

My way of systematizing these ideas is to argue that behavioral power is the metric that establishes a statistical balance in the flow of events among agents in the international system. In dynamic form this is given by the following set of N equations for N nations:

$$\frac{dB_{n,t}}{dt} = \sum_{\substack{m = 1 \\ m \neq n}}^{N} B_{m,t}F_{m,n,t} - \sum_{\substack{m = 1 \\ m \neq n}}^{N} B_{n,t}F_{n,m,t}, \quad N = 1, 2, ..., N - 1. \quad (1)$$

Herein, $B_{n,t}$ is the behavioral power of nation n at time t and $F_{m,n,t}$ is the flow of events from nation m toward nation n at time t. This approach was convolved with the event data taken from the COPDAB data set and the results described in Ward and House (1988). Results suggested that the top behaviorally powerful or salient nations in the world were the United States, Egypt, the Soviet Union, Israel, England, France, North and South Korea, the People's Republic of China, West Germany, India, Syria, and Italy. In terms of raw capability comparisons, few other compilations would reveal the importance of Egypt and Israel on the one hand and North and South Korea on the other. When looking at conflict interactions alone, we found over the period from 1948 to 1978 that the three nations whose actions brought about the greatest international response were North Korea, South Korea, and Israel, respectively (Ward and House, 1988; p. 21).

While this earlier work was undertaken to highlight the noncapability aspects of power in the world affairs—and indeed explicitly ignore capabilities—the bulk of extant theoretical and empirical work on this topic to date has started by examining *capabilities*. The next section turns to an incorporation of capabilities into the basic behavioral power framework.

Material Capabilities

Legion are attempts to measure power through assessing capabilities. In this book, it is fair to say that such an approach is the dominant one. Chapter 2 by Richard L. Merritt and Dina A. Zinnes provides a crystal clear overview of many of the so-called capability approaches. I assert here that both the capability approach and the behavioral approach are necessarily incomplete to the extent that they exclude each other. It is patently clear that capabilities such as economic productivity, military personnel, and human capital, for example, are important, necessary components not only of attempts to understand, but also efforts to employ, power in world affairs. But resources are not sufficient. Chapter 4, by Jacek Kugler and Marina Arbetman, comes from a recent tradition that asserts that the political capacity to extract extant resources from society is another relevant and necessary (though not sufficient) step along the way to the unraveling of the power puzzle. This step is the extraction of relevant resources for governmental use. Behavioral power was an attempt to define the actual use of those resources to influence world affairs.

It seems clear that nations that undertake certain actions are more or less credible, based in part not only on their past actions but also on their current capabilities. Thus, the weight of available resources would quite plausibly appear to have strong implications for specific actions. *The Mouse that Roared* notwithstanding, the more capabilities an actor has to back up and implement proposed actions, the greater weight will such actions have upon the responses they engender. The shooting down of a commercial airliner by the Soviet Union has greater implications than one can imagine if the same act had been undertaken by Kirubati. Accordingly, a simple approach is to suggest that not only are events weighted by their behavioral power [equation (1) above], but they are also weighted by the material capabilities of the actors that undertake them:

$$C_{n,t}\frac{dB_{n,t}}{dt} = \sum_{\substack{m=1 \\ m \neq n}}^{N} C_{m,t}B_{m,t}F_{m,n,t} - \sum_{\substack{m=1 \\ m \neq n}}^{N} C_{n,t}B_{n,t}F_{n,m,t} , \quad N = 1, 2, ..., N-1. \quad (2)$$

Notation is the same as in Equation (1) above, except that $C_{n,t}$ represents the *capabilities* of nation n at time t. Dividing through by $C_{n,t}$ yields a somewhat simpler equation that captures the behavioral power of a nation, once the impact of capabilities has been taken into account:

$$\frac{dB_{n,t}}{dt} = \sum_{\substack{m=1 \\ m \neq n}}^{N} \frac{C_{m,t}}{C_{n,t}}B_{m,t}F_{m,n,t} - \sum_{\substack{m=1 \\ m \neq n}}^{N} B_{n,t}F_{n,m,t} , \quad N = 1, 2, ..., N-1. \quad (3)$$

Given this, the net power of a nation would consist of a combination of its actions and those of others, the behavioral salience of each actor, and the material capabilities of each actor. Thus, the net power, $NP_{n,t}$ is given by the following definition:

$$NP_{n,t} = B_{n,t}C_{n,t}. \quad (4)$$

Such conceptualization and formalization have a number of distinct advantages. First and foremost, it combines behavior with capabilities. In so doing, it is possible to span the power process from capabilities, to political extraction, to usage. Second, like behavioral power, it is a systemic measure that emerges from a consideration of the entire set of players in world politics. Net power, like behavioral power, is inherently a relational, as opposed to attributional, property. One can only attribute power in the context of a set of actors; in the absence of other nations, a single nation can have no power.

The next section elaborates what theoretical implications may flow from this measure of power and conducts a brief test of those ideas.

Theoretical Expectations

Per Unit Behavioral Power

Strategically salient actors will have a larger amount of per unit behavioral power, while larger actors will tend to have smaller amounts of per unit power. Thus, the per unit behavioral power of "clients" may be large relative to the major powers.

Nations with a large per unit behavioral power will be more likely to get involved in conflictual and cooperative ventures since they are likely to engage a large number of other actors in the international system.

Net Power

Nations with a large amount of net power will be more able to avoid getting into conflicts with other nations because of two interrelated components. First, they will tend to have a large amount of capabilities that could be viewed as threatening enough to deter engagement. Second, they will also tend to have the ability to garner support from other "client" or allied nations.

In general, larger superpowers will have dominant amounts of total net power, owing to the large volume of their interactions with other nations.

Conflict Interactions

Nations with a large amount of behavioral power on the conflict dimension will be more risk prone, and more likely to become involved in conflict. Decisionmakers in these nations will be likely to gauge their probability of success as being very high owing to their past ability to garner support. This is consistent with Bruce Bueno de Mesquita's (1981) notion that some nations will be able to garner enough support to believe themselves capable of winning conflicts against stronger potential foes. Holding capability development constant, it would also appear that nations would "learn" to accurately gauge their behavioral power.

When combined with a nation's material capabilities to yield net conflictual power, we may expect that nations with larger amounts of net conflictual power will be more likely to succeed in prevailing in conflict situations. In this way, we begin to approximate the way in which beneficent outcomes may result from net power, while at the same time recognizing that not only desired consequences may result from actions involving others.

Cooperative Interactions

Nations that have a dominant amount of behavioral power in the cooperative realm will tend to be risk averse and will tend to concentrate their activities toward conflict avoidance, owing to their long-run success in engendering cooperative behaviors from other players in the international system. If this is combined with a large amount of material capabilities, yielding high levels of net cooperative power, we may hypothesize relative success in conflict avoidance.

Total Interactions

It seems obvious that some nations will be "powerful" by virtue of the cooperative abilities, while others may find "power" via their ability to use conflict. In addition, material capabilities will play a role in all this. While many have argued that on the one hand conflict and cooperation are polar opposites, others have suggested that they are part and parcel of the same underlying dimension. Nations that are able to employ effectively both cooperative and conflictual strategies will tend to be more successful (Leng and Wheeler, 1979; Leng, 1984). Thus, I look at the total mix of all types of purposive actions to ascertain the total behavioral (and net) power held by a nation.

It is expected that total behavioral power will increase neither risk proneness nor risk adversity. Rather, nations with a large degree of net power on the dimension of total interactions will be better able to avoid conflicts—especially conflicts with high stakes and/or those they might lose—and win conflicts they enjoin.

Empirical Results

In this section, I do not test the variety of theoretical speculations about behavioral and net power that were made above; rather, my goal is less ambitious. I simply generate the trajectories of these variables for "the most powerful" nations in the contemporary era and explore in detail the trajectories of two pairs of nations. Because of the overriding importance of the two superpowers for the ebb and flow of current world affairs, I look in detail at the behavioral and net power of the United States and the Soviet Union. Next, I explicate some aspects of the protracted Middle East conflict by focusing on Israel and Egypt. Instead of focusing on the conflictual and cooperative aspects of power in isolation from one another, total interactions are examined.[2]

My basic approach has been to employ two data sets: (1) the COPDAB data set of Edward E. Azar (1980), which served as the empirical materials for earlier work on behavioral power, and (2) the revised capability data from the Correlates of War Project. The first of these data sets established the $F_{m,n,t}$ terms in Equations (4), while the second was used to measure the $C_{n,t}$ terms. Note that these results should be cross-validated against other concepts (and data sets) of both behavioral interactions on the one hand and capabilities on the other.[3]

Superpower Behavioral Power

Figure 7.1 provides one portrayal of the changing power balance between the United States and the Soviet Union. These data are taken from the reworking of the Correlates of War data set by Kun Y. Park and Michael D. Ward (1988). These data suggest that there has been a relative decline (from about 25% to around 18%) in the overall share of global power capabilities (economic, military, and demographic) held by the United States, while the Soviet share has remained at roughly the same level. These data support the widely discussed notion of a declining "hegemon."

The behavioral power of these two powers, as reflected in Equations (4)—solved for total interactions—provides quite a different view of power relationships. These data are presented graphically in Figure 7.2. The relative balance in the behavioral, as opposed to the capability, power characteristics of the two major superpowers shows considerable fluctuation over the post-World War II era.

Several features of this graphic deserve mention. In general, the Soviet Union exhibits more behavioral salience than does the United States, for while both superpowers have a relatively small share of the total amount of global behavioral power, Soviet scores tend to be greater than those for the United States. There are two exceptions to this generalization. During the aftermath of the Cuban missile crisis, Soviet behavioral power falls significantly to a level less than that held by the United States. During the period of detente beginning in the late 1960s and continuing until the mid-1970s, the United States consciously followed a policy of some "linkage" in its relations around the world. The success of that policy in linking behaviors of others to U.S. behaviors is reflected in the growth of U.S. behavioral salience beyond the level held by the Soviet Union.

Note also that the behavioral power of the two superpowers exhibits an *increasing* rather than declining trend, despite the fact that the absolute levels

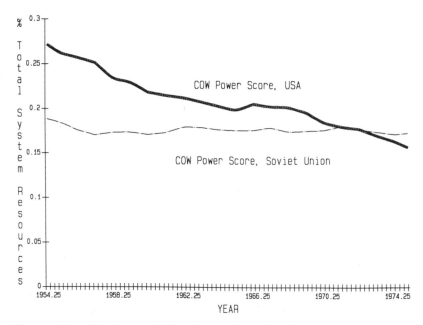

Figure 7.1   Correlates of War Power Capability Indices for the United States and the Soviet Union, 1954–1975.

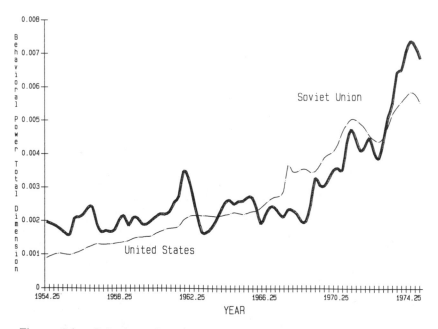

Figure 7.2   Behavioral Power of the United States and the Soviet Union, 1954–1975.

tend to be fairly low. Net power calculations are not significantly different and are presented in Figure 7.3. All in all, these presentations suggest a markedly more complex political situation vis-à-vis power in the international system than can plausibly be gleaned from capability calculations alone. And it might plausibly be argued that superpowers tend to rely more on capabilities than they do on the nuance of managing complex interdependence networks. In short, it may be that the superpowers are not behaviorally *super* powerful, if the evidence presented here is accurate.

Egypt and Israel and Behavioral Power

Turning to Egypt and Israel, one can see in Figure 7.4 what is well known; namely, that Egypt has a much larger share of the global military, economic, and demographic resources than does Israel. Egypt scores far above Israel throughout the entire post-1950 era. Furthermore, the absolute levels of capabilities for these two societies are obviously much lower than for the United States and the Soviet Union. Figure 7.5 details the *behavioral* power of these two Middle Eastern societies, after the impact of capabilities has been controlled for in Equations (4). One sees a dramatic reversal of the findings from Figure 7.4. Throughout the time period, the per unit behavioral power or salience of Israel's actions is almost twice that of Egypt. In a behavioral sense, Israel is much more powerful than Egypt, and one might expect it to be more successful, if behavioral power can reflect the kind of successful mixture of cooperation and conflict that Russell J. Leng's findings suggest lead to more effective foreign policies. Stated differently, these behavioral calculations illustrate the sensitivity and vulnerability of the range of actors in the international system to Israel's actions; and they represent the relative insensitivity and invulnerability of those same actors to Egypt's actions.

Finally, Figure 7.6 presents the net power scores for these two nations, combining both the capability components and the behavioral ones. These calculations do not allow one to *postdict* the outcome of each of the relevant wars in the Middle East (1956, 1967, and 1973), but it is the case that the behavioral and the net power scores show interesting fluctuations both prior and subsequent to these three conflicts. For the latter two wars, Israeli behavioral power shows considerable growth and acceleration *prior* to the outbreak of the war. Israel also evidences, along with some fluctuation, major growth in its behavioral power over the time period, as does Egypt. Egypt also shows considerable growth prior to each outbreak of violence in the Middle East during this era.

In comparison with the results for the conventional (i.e., capability based) *superpower* of the United States and the Soviet Union, it appears that the strategically important, smaller societies of Israel and Egypt are not only

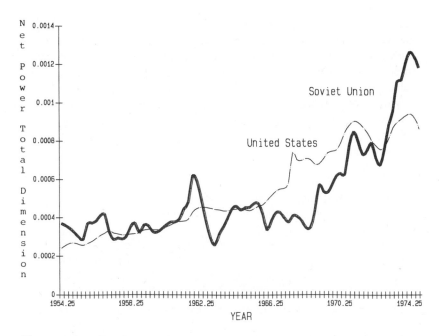

Figure   7.3   Net Power of the United States and the Soviet Union, 1954–1975.

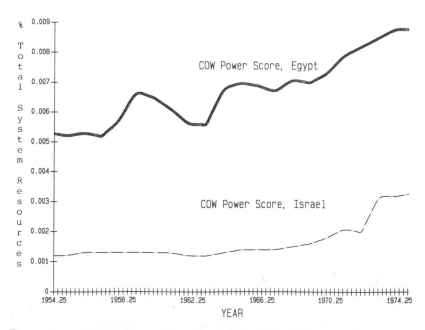

Figure   7.4   Correlates of War Power Capability Indices for Egypt and Israel,   1954–1974.

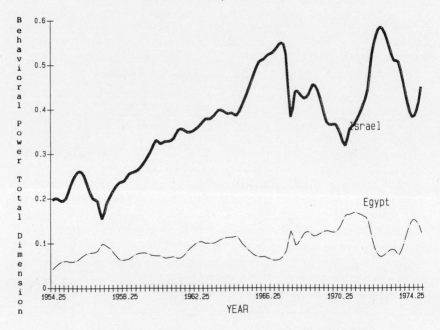

Figure 7.5   Behavioral Power of Egypt and Israel, 1954–1975.

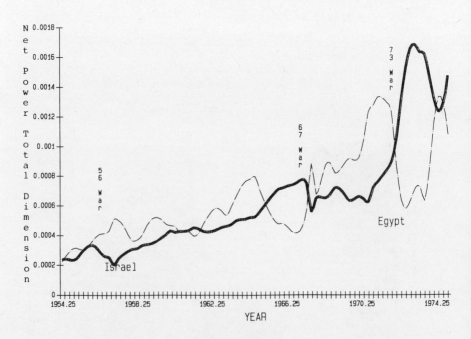

Figure 7.6   Net Power of Egypt and Israel, 1954–1975.

more behaviorally powerful but may even be behaviorally *superpowerful*. In spite of the obvious importance of material, and especially military, capabilities in the protracted conflict in the Middle East, the behavioral use of the entire range of diplomacy appears to be additionally salient.

Conclusion

This chapter offers a way of integrating the behavioral and capability components thought to be important in understanding the ability of nations to wield power in the international system. This approach to thinking about power is a complex one that permits a great deal of nuance not afforded by attribute-based approaches. The basis of the approach is to tap the sensitivities and vulnerabilities that nations exhibit in regard to the actions of one another, and following in the tradition of Robert Keohane and Joseph Nye, to suggest that power in the international system may flow not so much from the barrel of a gun, but rather from the complex interdependencies among nations (Keohane and Nye, 1977).

Notes

1. I am indebted to Jacek Kugler for his interpretation of behavioral power as actor salience.

2. Although the specific conflict and cooperation results are available upon request from the author.

3. The former could be cross-validated against WEIS data, but current efforts to obtain a nonproprietary, publically available copy of this have been unsuccessful. In terms of the latter, it seems appropriate to investigate other measures of capabilities such as GNP or better still to build in (and on) the so-called Kugler–Organski–Domke (see Chapter 4 in this book for an overview) approach of measuring the amount of resources that the government is able to extract from domestic and foreign sources. Unfortunately, we were also unable to obtain RPC scores to employ for comparative purposes; doubtless this remains one important task for the agenda of future research.

8

State Power, World Views, and the Major Powers

Richard J. Stoll

> From the Treaty of Wesphalia to the present eight major states at most have sought to coexist peacefully or have contended for mastery . . . [international relations can be v]iewed as the politics of the powerful. (Waltz, 1979; p. 131)

Kenneth Waltz's statement expresses an opinion held by many international relations scholars: that the interstate system is hierarchically organized, with a small number of states possessing an extremely high amount of power and influence. Consequently, the rest of the actors in the system have their capacity for independent action limited both by their own lack of resources and the implicit threat of counteraction by one of the powerful states.

The member of this powerful oligarchy are most often called the major powers, and their actions have been the focus of much research in international relations. The vast literature on the balance of power comes immediately to mind, but even writers such as A. F. K. Organski (1968), who doubt the existence of a balance of power system, focus on the few and the powerful in their research efforts. But is the concept of "major power" still as useful in today's world? This question is implicitly raised by the variety of approaches to understanding international relations that developed in the post-World War II era.

If the concept of major power is no longer meaningful when describing the most influential actors in the world and their interactions, a great deal of what has been learned and written from studying the past has small relevance for understanding today's world. But before we discard these many accumulated studies, we should consider to what degree the world of today *is* different from earlier eras. In particular:

1. In terms of power capabilities, does the group of nation-states designated as major powers by M. Small and J. David Singer

(1982) in 1980 dominate the top ranks of the interstate system in the same manner as major powers of earlier eras?

2. In 1980, are there more dimensions of power capability in the 1980 time period than in earlier eras, and, as we shift across measures of power capability, do different groupings of states appear as major powers?

3. Across a diversity of power capability measures in 1980, do any nation-states *not* identified as major powers by Small and Singer present themselves as candidates for inclusion in the grouping?

At the conclusion of this investigation, the similarities and differences between the major powers of today and those of yesterday will be drawn more clearly; this should aid us in determining how much reliance we should place on insights from the past when trying to understand the world of the present.

I begin by contrasting the traditional world view in international relations with several alternatives that are used to describe today's world. Then the empirical investigation to answer the three questions posed above will be outlined and the results presented. Finally, I dwell a bit on the implications of the findings for the study of international relations in the contemporary world.

Alternative Views of the Major Powers in Today's World

Before contrasting the descriptions of major powers from various bodies of literature, we need a definition of that term which will allow us to make these comparisons. This is not as easy as it sounds. It may be true that "all students of world politics use, or appreciate the relevance of, the concept of 'major power'" (Small and Singer, 1982, p. 45), but this use and appreciation has failed to lead to either a single definition accepted by the field or a series of contrasting characterizations, each with its own adherents.[1] Knowing full well that one reason for the lack of definitions is the difficulty with constructing an acceptable one, I use the following: *a major power is a state that has interests, and the power to influence actors in pursuit of these interests, in other regions of the world as well as its own.*

Explicit definitions of interest and power are not included to allow for the composition of both to vary through time, since these two issues are ones on which the variety of "modern" views of international relations disagree.

The Classical World View and the Major Powers

The essence of "classical" international relations (work written during or about the pre-World War II era) is the study of a small group of actors who were very powerful and whose actions and interactions dominated not only their own regional system but often areas beyond it. These few actors, be they city-states or nation-states, have most of the "action" and have their fates heavily intertwined with the status of the entire system.

Most typically, writings about this group of actors fall under the general rubric of balance of power theory. This term means many things to many people (Haas, 1953; Claude, 1962), but even those who argue that balance of power does not account for international behavior in the industrial era make use of a number of similar assumptions in their frameworks (Organski, 1968). Despite the great variety of approaches and writings on the subject, some common elements emerge in this body of thought and literature:

1. A small group of actors contains a large proportion of the total power capability of the system.
2. Members of this small group seek to influence one another and the rest of the actors in the system by using these power capabilities to pursue their interests.
3. These interests are defined in terms of national security concerns.
4. The most useful kind of power for influencing actors is military power. Other forms of power capability are useful to the extent that they can be converted into or are supportive of military power.

This stark picture implies that power (at least *useful* power) is a one-dimensional attribute and that only a small number of actors possess the prerequisite amount of this attribute to exercise a high degree of influence. This "high politics" view dominated descriptions and analysis of the interstate system through the end of World War II, and even for a period of time afterward; evidence of this is the fact that the most well-known text in international relations (by Hans Morganthau) follows this approach.

But in the post-World War II era, some observers have detected significant changes in the world, and these changes have led them to promote alternative pictures of the most important elements of the (now global) system. I should caution that I have taken great liberties in synthesizing these alternative views, collapsing a great deal of diversity in the name of simplicity.

The Bipolarist World View and the Major Powers

One view begins with the observation that two nation-states—the United States and the Soviet Union—have an overwhelming share of global power capability. The most obvious indication of this dominance is the size of their nuclear arsenals, but a similar picture emerges if other indicators, such as conventional military capability, or some economic indicators, are examined (Waltz, 1979).

This view has certain similarities with the earlier balance of power view, but there are differences. The most obvious one is that only two states are considered to have the requisite level of power capabilities to influence actors across the globe. Furthermore, due to the presence of nuclear weapons, nation-states (especially the two superpowers) are more reluctant than "classical" major powers to resort to the large-scale use of military power. Some would go a bit further and say that possession of these weapons serves only to negate this type of power capability. Consequently, the key to exerting influence in the modern world lies with other types of power capability, the most important of which are conventional military and economic. Large amounts of these types of capability are in the hands of the United States and the Soviet Union.[2]

To summarize, the bipolarist view has the following elements:

1. Two actors, the United States and the Soviet Union, have a large proportion of the power capability of the system.
2. Both actors use their power capabilities to pursue their national interests on a global level.
3. These interests are defined to a large extent in national security terms, but other interests may predominate from time to time.
4. Nuclear weapons are used to influence other actors, but so are a variety of other means. These additional means are also concentrated in the hands of the United States and the Soviet Union.

The Interdependent World View and the Major Powers

There is another view of the post-World War II era, although it did not develop until some years after the war. It is associated with scholars that study interdependence (Keohane and Nye, 1977). Central to this view is the observation that a wide variety of actors possess significant amounts of economic capabilities and that these capabilities can be used to influence other actors. Furthermore, there are now a variety of issues that are important on an actor's agenda—not just national security problems—and the types of power capability appropriate for one issue may not be appropriate for other issues. The rise of Western Europe, Japan, OPEC, and multinational corporations are the most frequently cited examples of actors that have achieved a high level of influence without large amounts of military power. Of course, the United States and the Soviet Union are considerable economic powers, but they must share the world arena with the other powerful actors mentioned above.

Similar to the classical view, the interdependence view has a world with a number of powerful and influential actors, but none that can dominate in all regions and issue areas. This view can be summarized as follows:

1. Large numbers and varieties of actors—not necessarily just nation-states—contain a significant proportion of the power capability of the global system.
2. These actors seek to influence one another and the rest of the actors by using their power capabilities to pursue their interests.
3. These interests are defined in a variety of ways; national security concerns are not necessarily dominant.
4. A variety of kinds of power can be useful for influencing actors. The issue at stake and the actor over whom influence is sought will determine the kind of power capabilities that are most likely to lead to influence.

This picture is far more complicated than those of the classical and bipolarist views presented above. Power is not a single, fungible quantity viewed primarily in military terms. It has a number of different aspects that do not always appear together. Thus, power capabilities are multidimensional and diffused across a larger number of actors.

Summary of the Different Views

The three different world views, the number of major powers in each, the number of dimensions of power capabilities, and the similarity of distribution of power capabilities across the dimensions are shown in Table 8.1.[3]

Each world view has very different implications for the role of the major powers. In the classical view, the system revolves around this oligarchy; their behavior and interactions dominate the rest of the nation-states. And power in such a system flows from the barrel of a gun. All else is subordinate to national security considerations.

Table 8.1 Comparison of the Three World Views

World View	Number of Major Powers	Dimensions of Power	Distribution of Power Across Dimensions
Classical	Small, but >2	One (military)	N/A
Bipolarist	2	Several	Similar
Interdependent	Many	Several	Dissimilar

In the bipolarist view, the number of significant actors is reduced to just two, and while these two actors possess an extraordinary amount of destructive capability, additional dimensions of important power capability can be discerned. However, the dual dominance of the United States and the Soviet Union across all these dimensions eliminates the possibility of extensive interactions between as large a group of nation-states as in the previous era, so the importance of focusing on a group of states (as opposed to just two) is diminished.

Finally, in the interdependent view, the concept of major power has even less utility. Although there are more important actors than in the bipolarist view, there are a number of distinct dimensions of power capability and little overlap in the most influential actors across these dimensions.

In the next section, I turn to a description of the empirical analysis to be conducted to ascertain which of these three views is a more accurate description of the distribution of global power capabilities in the current era.

Data, Operationalizations, and Methods of Analysis

Four basic analysis issues are dealt with here: the points in time to be analyzed, the identity of the states and the major powers at each of these points in time, the measures of power capability to be used at each point in time, and the techniques of analysis to be used to measure the differences between major powers and nonmajor powers.

Time Points

Four time points are examined: 1850, 1900, 1950, and 1980. The first two points are during the period of time that most observers believe a balance of power system existed. The third point is in the post-World War II era, but it is unlikely that the full impact of the bipolar and interdependent worlds had yet occurred. It is only 1 year after the Soviet Union first exploded a nuclear weapon, and it would be several years before it possessed an ability to deliver these weapons globally. It is also before many of the world's economies recovered from the effects of the war, making it unlikely that the multiple kinds of connections between states that are assumed in the interdependence world view existed. Thus, 1950 serves as a bridge between the old world of classical international elations and the possible new worlds of bipolarity and interdependence.

Finally, 1980 is a year in which the nuclear arsenals of the superpowers are clearly dominant over the rest of the world, and the world economy is developed enough to show a high degree of interdependence.

Identity of States and Major Powers

The Small–Singer (1982) definitions of states and major powers are used to identify the cases for analysis. To be considered as a state, Small and Singer have the following requirements:

1. A minimum population of 500,000.
2. For the 1816–1919 time period, receipt of diplomatic missions at or above the rank of chargé d'affaires from both Great Britain and France.
3. For the 1920–1980 time period, membership in the League of Nations or the United Nations, or receipt of diplomatic missions from any two major powers.

Small and Singer arrive at their judgment as to which states were major powers by interpreting the scholarly consensus on the matter. As they note (1982, p. 45), they are less confident of their major power classification after 1965, but they are still able to enumerate the membership of this group.[4] Table 8.2 displays the states that Small and Singer identify as major powers in each of the years to be analyzed, along with the total number of states in the world.

Power Capability Data

The next matter to be considered is the measurement of nation-state power capability. Of course, scholars have different views on how to measure power capabilities, and that problem is compounded in this study by the long time span under consideration. What we seek are measurements of the relatively concrete components that either can be used by the state in pursuit of its national interests or represent significant national constraints on its ability to pursue these interests.

It is not unreasonable to expect that these building blocks have changed through this time period. Maintaining a single set of indicators for the entire period risks having some or all of them being invalid for portions of the time period under study. But simply changing the indicators does not automatically mean that a more valid set of measures has been obtained. Furthermore, if the results vary across a changing set of indicators, we cannot be sure that this is due to a substantive change or just the change in the composition of indicators. These are important concerns with no easy answers, and the problems of data availability have not even been mentioned!

In this chapter, power capability data from the Correlates of War Project are used for the 1850, 1900, and 1950 time points, and a much wider variety of indicators, primarily from Ruth Leger Sivard (1983), are used for the 1980 data.

Table 8.2   Major Powers and Number of States in the Globe

1850	1900	1950	1980
Great Britain	United States	United States	United States
France	Great Britain	Great Britain	Great Britain
Prussia	France	France	France
Austria–Hungary	Germany	Soviet Union	Soviet Union
Russia	Austria–Hungary	China	China
	Italy		
	Russia		
	Japan		
40	42	75	155

Source: Small and Singer (1982, pp. 44–45, 118–122). Number at bottom of column is number of states in the globe.

There are few alternatives to using the Correlates of War data for the earliest two time periods, when data from all the countries of the world are required. Using the same indicator set for the 1950 period allows us to make some assessment of how these indicators fare in the early postwar period as measurement of power capability. But use of a much wider array of power capability indicators is justified for 1980. It allows for a better assessment of which of the three world views (classical, bipolarist, or interdependent) is a more accurate description of the world; if Correlates of War data were used, it would be difficult to find evidence confirming the interdependent world view.

The variables in the Correlates of War power capability data set are familiar to many. A total of six indicators are used: total population, urban population, iron or (after 1895) steel production, commercial energy consumption (after 1885 for nonmajor powers), military expenditures, and military personnel. These indicators tap three aspects of a state's power capability (population, industrial capability, and military capability) that are frequently mentioned in the classical international relations literature.

The indicators of power capability for 1980 total 22. They were selected to reflect a wide variety of power capabilities that are mentioned in the classical, the bipolarist, and the interdependent literature. Most of the data were taken from Sivard (1983), with a few additions to make up for some gaps that I perceive in her collection. Table 8.3 gives a brief description of each variable that was included, along with the source if it was not taken from Sivard.

The increase in numbers and the change in composition of indicators make it more likely that in 1980 power capability appears to be multidimensional. This suspicion is increased when one notes that the

Table 8.3 Power Capability Indicators for 1980 Analysis

1. Total population (POP)	14. Percentage of population with with safe water (WATER)
2. Percentage of population in urban areas (PCTURB)	15. Gross National Product per capita (GNPPC)
3. Area in square kilometers (AREA)	16. Number of embassies, high commissions, legations accredited to the state (EMBASSY)
4. Gross National Product (GNP)	
5. Military budget (MILEXP)	17. Number of international organization HQs and secretariats located in state (HQIO)
6. Education Budget (EDUC)	
7. Health budget (HLTH)	18. Food as a percentage of all manufactured imports (PCTFUL)
8. Amount of foreign economic aid given (ECOAID)	19. Fuel as a percentage of all manufactured imports (PCTFOD)
9. Armed force personnel (ARMFOR)	20. Concentration index of exports received (CONEXP)
10. Number of physicians (PHYS)	21. Total Imports (IMP)
11. Literacy rate (LITERACY)	22. Number of strategic nuclear delivery vehicles (NUKE)
12. Infant mortality rate (INFMOR)	
13. Life expectancy (LIFE)	

Note: Source for all variables is Sivard (1983), except EMBASSY (*Europa Yearbook, 1982*), HQIO (*Handbook of International Organizations, 1981*), PCTFOD, PCTFUL (*World Tables*), CONEXP(*World Handbook of Political and Social Indicators*), IMP (*1981 Yearbook of International Trade Statistics*), and NUKE (*Military Balance, 1981–1982*).

Correlates of War data have an underlying theoretical unity, while the 1980 data do not. Thus, these data are biased to show that today's world is multidimensional, and previous eras are unidimensional. But the composition of the dimensions in 1980 and the factor scores for the various states will still be of interest despite this possible bias. Furthermore, the alternative of a uniform set of indicators for all time periods, with the consequent validity and data availability problems, seems far less attractive.

Methods of Analysis

Two statistical techniques are used to analyze these data: *t*-tests and factor analysis. The *t*-tests are used to compare those states designated as major powers with the rest of the states across the power capability indicators. This is a simple way of determining just how preponderant the major powers are as a group.

Factor analysis is used to determine the number of dimensions of power

capability at a time point. Scores produced from the factor analysis are used
to determine which are the most powerful states in each year.

The unweighted least-squares method is used, and a pairwise correlation
matrix is used as input. The squared multiple correlation of each variable
with the rest of the indicators is used as the initial communality estimate. In
several cases, variables achieved comunality estimates of greater than 1.00;
these were dropped from the factor analysis. All factors with an eigenvalue of
1.00 or greater are retained. If more than one factor emerges using these
criteria, varimax rotation is used.

Summary

I have outlined an exploratory investigation to ascertain the degree to which
global power capabilities are concentrated in the hands of those states
designated as major powers by Small and Singer at selected points in time
from 1850 to 1980. At the same time, using a shifting set of power
capability indicators, the dimensionality of power capability at each point in
time is measured. Finally, the analysis also shows whether other states
appear to possess higher levels of power capability than the major powers.

Let me be very clear. A major power is more than a state with a great
deal of power capability. But while possession of large amounts of this asset
is not sufficient for being a major power, it is a necessity. Thus, when
examining the concept of major power, an inquiry centering around power
capabilities is a good starting point.

Results

Analyses are presented separately for each time point. Since the main focus
of this inquiry is the 1980 results, my discussion of the earlier analysis is
brief.

Analysis of 1850 Data

The t-tests of the individual power capability indicators are shown in Table
8.4. In each case, the major powers show a higher mean value than the
nonmajor powers; in fact, for all but total population, the major powers are
larger by a power of 10. Only the t-tests for the two military indicators are
statistically significant, although urban population is very close (.07).

Turning to the factor analysis for these data, a communality estimate
greater than 1.00 forced the deletion of the military personnel data from the
analysis. The remaining four variables fall into a single dimension. The
eigenvalue for the first factor in the analysis was 2.60, while the second

Table 8.4 *t*-Tests of Power Capability Data, 1850: Major Powers Versus Non-major Powers

Variable	Group	N	t Value	Probability
Total population	Major	5	0.92*	.36
	Nonmajor	27		
Urban population	Major	5	1.91	.07
	Nonmajor	27		
Military personnel	Major	5	3.04*	.04
	Nonmajor	23		
Military expenditures	Major	5	4.22*	.01
	Nonmajor	14		
Iron production	Major	5	1.39*	.24
	Nonmajor	12		

Note: Degrees of freedom for *t* values with an asterisk have been adjusted due to unequal variances between the two groups.

factor is only 0.36; about 65% of the variance is accounted for by the first factor. Both population variables and military expenditures load heavily on the factor (the lowest loading was the 0.84 for urban population), but iron production is not as closely tied (its loading is 0.37). Considering that the industrial revolution had not worked its way through all of Europe by that point, this should not be too surprising. Table 8.5 displays these results.

The states with the ten largest factor scores are shown in Table 8.6. As a group, the major powers clearly dominate the rankings. The only "intruder" is the United States, a nation with large amounts of power capability, but a low level of participation in the world system. The low loading of iron production on the factor is the cause of the low ranking of Great Britain (fourth). As an alternative measure, I calculated *z* scores for each state on each variable and then took the average.[5] These are also displayed in Table 8.6. Although this does not change the dominance of the major power over the

Table 8.5 Factor Analysis, 1850

Variable	Loading
Total population	0.947
Military expenditures	0.923
Urban population	0.843
Iron production	0.374
Eigenvalue	2.599
Percentage of variance accounted by factor	0.65

Table 8.6 Factor Scores and Average z Scores for Ten Highest Scoring States, 1850

State	Factor Score	State	z Score
Russia*	0.991	Great Britain*	3.311
France*	0.620	Russia*	1.727
Austria–Hungary*	0.410	France*	1.465
Great Britain*	0.339	Austria–Hungary*	0.784
United States	0.014	United States	0.407
Prussia*	-0.082	Prussia*	-0.020
Spain	-0.086	Spain	-0.067
Italy (Sardinia)	-0.266	Belgium	-0.386
Belgium	-0.290	Italy (Sardinia)	-0.426
Netherlands	-0.295	Netherlands	-0.465

Note: An asterisk indicates state was a major power.

rest of the states, Great Britain does rank a clear first. Note that the same ten states appear in both sets of scores.

This analysis illustrates a possible problem with the use of factor analysis to create these power capability scores. Great Britain's dominance in the early 1800s was based on its large industrial base, and the key to this was the fact that no other nation-state was even close until later in the century. Unfortunately, this same circumstance (iron production scores do not correlate well with the other variables) means that this variable will not load that highly on the factor.

Analysis of 1900 Data

In the 1900 data (see Table 8.7) five of the six t-tests show the major powers dominant over the rest of the system. For the insignificant t-test (steel production), data are available for only nine nation states.[6]

Urban population had a communality of greater than 1.00, so it was dropped from the factor analysis. As with the 1850 data, only a single factor emerges from the analysis (the eigenvalue of the first factor is 2.87; the eigenvalue of the second is 0.45). The effects of the industrial revolution are very evident in the factor loadings for the variables (see Table 8.8): the two industrial indicators have the heaviest loadings, while total population shows the lowest loading. About 57% of the variance is accounted for by this factor.

As with the 1850 data, the major powers cluster at the top of the rankings of factor scores (see Table 8.9). The former "intruder," the United States, is now a major power and scores just behind Great Britain. The two intruders into the major power grouping are China and Belgium. China's score is due to its large population (total and urban) and large army. To illustrate, China's z score on total population is 6.85. This totally swamps its minimal economic resources. Belgium achieves its score in precisely the opposite manner—by means of its industrial resources. The ranking of

Table 8.7 *t*-Tests of Power Capability Data, 1900: Major Powers Versus Nonmajor Powers

Variable	Group	N	t Value	Probability
Total population	Major	8	2.01	.05
	Nonmajor	31		
Urban population	Major	8	3.90*	.01
	Nonmajor	21		
Military personnel	Major	8	4.18*	.01
	Nonmajor	34		
Military expenditures	Major	8	3.29*	.01
	Nonmajor	34		
Steel production	Major	2	1.27*	.24
	Nonmajor	7		
Energy consumption	Major	8	2.47*	.04
	Nonmajor	10		

Note: Degrees of freedom for *t* values with an asterisk have been adjusted due to unequal variances between the two groups.

Table 8.8 Factor Analysis, 1900

Variable	Loading
Total population	0.267
Military expenditures	0.876
Military personnel	0.623
Steel production	0.889
Energy consumption	0.920
Eigenvalue	2.865
Percentage of variance accounted by factor	0.57

average z scores drops Belgium from intruding into the ranks of the major powers (and out of the top ten altogether), but China still remains. Again, the top ten group on both scores is almost identical.

Analysis of 1950 Data

For 1950, only one of the *t*-tests is statistically significant, although most are close. In all cases, the major powers as a group score higher than the nonmajor powers. This lessened dominance by the major powers is due to the effects of World War II, particularly on France and Great Britain (see Table 8.10).

Table 8.9 Factor Scores and Average z Scores for Ten Highest Scoring States, 1900

State	Factor Score	State	z Score
Great Britain*	3.677	United States*	3.514
United States*	3.532	Great Britain*	3.364
Germany*	2.051	Germany*	2.566
Russia*	1.220	Russia*	2.105
France*	1.146	China	1.869
Austria–Hungary*	0.400	France*	1.458
China	0.276	Austria–Hungary*	0.703
Italy*	0.016	Italy*	0.372
Japan*	-0.042	Japan*	0.339
Belgium	-0.081	Turkey	0.092

Note: An asterisk indicates state was a major power.

Table 8.10 t-Tests of Power Capability Data, 1950: Major Powers Versus Nonmajor Powers

Variable	Group	N	t Value	Probability
Total population	Major	5	2.00*	.12
	Nonmajor	60		
Urban population	Major	5	3.68*	.02
	Nonmajor	64		
Military personnel	Major	5	1.97*	.12
	Nonmajor	61		
Military expenditures	Major	5	2.27*	.09
	Nonmajor	53		
Steel production	Major	5	1.76*	.15
	Nonmajor	29		
Energy consumption	Major	5	1.68*	.17
	Nonmajor	70		

Note: Degrees of freedom for *t* values with an asterisk have been adjusted due to unequal variances between the two groups.

All six capability variables were retained for the factor analysis. The power capability data fall into a single dimension even more strongly than in 1850 and 1900. The eigenvalue for the first factor is 4.02 (accounting for 67% of the variance in the variables), and the eigenvalue for the second factor is 0.56. As with the 1900 analysis, total population has the lowest loading on the factor. The next lowest loading is military personnel; urban population, steel production, and energy consumption all load about equally on the factor. The highest loading (.98) on the factor is military expenditures. This is the highest loading of either military indicator in any of the three factor analyses discussed so far; clearly, there is little evidence of an interdependent world in the scores of the six indicators used here. Table 8.11 displays the results of the factor analysis for 1950.

The factor scores for the ten largest states are shown in Table 8.12, along with the ten largest average z scores. The z score rankings show the overall dominance of the Singer–Small major powers, but not so the factor scores. The largest three scores (the United States, the Soviet Union, and China) seem reasonable, but there are a few surprises. First, France appears nowhere in the top ten. In fact, France ranks 43rd overall. Second, some of the nonmajor powers in the top ten are unexpected. This is purely a subjective judgment of course, but the appearance of India, Argentina, and Egypt is surprising. Two different kinds of explanation can be advanced for these apparent anomalies. First, 1950 is not long after the end of World War II, and a number of the nation-states that would typically be regarded as powerful (i.e., the industrialized states of Western Europe) were devastated in that war. Considering that France was first occupied and then the site of numerous battles after the invasion of Europe, it is not surprising that it is not ranked in the top ten (although a ranking of 43rd seems too low even when this is taken into consideration).

Another reason for these results stems from the manner in which the factor scores are computed. The set of scoring coefficients for the variables is produced by premultiplying the matrix of factor loadings by the inverse of the matrix of correlations among the variables. If there is high collinearity among some or all of the variables (as is the case here), this can create problems in computing the scores (Cooley and Lohnes, 1971, pp. 151-158). On several occasions, the factor scores are *negative* even though the corresponding factor loading is *positive*.

Despite these problems, these results are consistent with the previous time points. In all cases power capability falls into a single dimension, and with a few exceptions, those states designated as major powers by Small and Singer score at the very high end of the scale. The results so far do not contradict the basic tenets of the classical world view in international relations. But bear in mind that the power capability data used so far appear to have a built-in bias in favor of supporting such a view. Finally, as before, the group of top ten z scores has considerable overlap with the group of top ten factor scores.

Analysis of 1980 Data

We now turn to the primary focus of our investigation: the 1980 data. On all variables, the major powers score higher than the nonmajor powers, and for most of the t-tests this difference is statistically significant. These results are displayed in Table 8.13.

The results of the factor analysis are interesting (always an ominous

Table 8.11   Factor Analysis, 1950

Variable	Loading
Total population	0.535
Urban population	0.868
Military expenditures	0.976
Military personnel	0.735
Steel production	0.872
Energy consumption	0.852
Eigenvalue	4.019
Percentage of variance accounted by factor	0.67

Table 8.12   Factor Scores and Average z Scores for Ten Highest Scoring States, 1950

State	Factor Score	State	z Score
United States*	3.748	United States*	5.303
Soviet Union*	2.452	Soviet Union*	4.032
China*	1.853	China*	2.188
India	1.398	Great Britain*	1.114
Italy	0.938	France*	0.496
Japan	0.897	India	0.333
Argentina	0.419	Japan	0.281
Great Britain*	0.085	Italy	0.119
Sweden	-0.045	Spain	0.094
Egypt	-0.056	Brazil	0.048

Note: An asterisk indicates state was a major power.

word). Power capabilities are clearly multidimensional; three factors emerge with eigenvalues of greater than 1.00; they are 5.84, 5.31, and 4.48, respectively. These three factors together account for 74% of the variance in the data, indicating that this does a good job of fitting the data. The similar size of all three eigenvalues indicates that the three factors are equally important in accounting for the data.

Table 8.14 displays the factor loadings for the rotated factor matrix. All the loadings with an absolute value of .4 or greater are underlined; empirical evidence indicates that variables with loadings this large make meaningful contributions to defining factors, while those with lesser values usually do not (Lindeman et al., 1980, p. 273).

Nine variables have large loadings on the first factor: GNP, military expenditures, education expenditures, health expenditures, economic aid given, number of embassies accredited to the country, number of IO headquarters, imports, and number of nuclear weapons. Given these variables, we would expect that large, advanced, internationally active nation-states

Table 8.13 t-Tests of Power Capability Data, 1980: Major Powers Versus Nonmajor Powers

Variable	Group	N	t Value	Probability
POP	Major	5	1.69*	.17
	Nonmajor	136		
PCTURB	Major	5	1.83	.07
	Nonmajor	136		
AREA	Major	5	1.92*	.13
	Nonmajor	136		
GNP	Major	5	2.55*	.06
	Nonmajor	134		
MILEXP	Major	5	2.64*	.05
	Nonmajor	135		
EDUC	Major	5	2.08*	.11
	Nonmajor	132		
HLTH	Major	5	2.38*	.08
	NonMajor	130		
ECOAID	Major	5	2.78*	.05
	Nonmajor	136		
ARMFOR	Major	5	2.55*	.06
	Nonmajor	135		
PHYS	Major	5	2.39*	.08
	Nonmajor	136		
LITERACY	Major	5	2.37	.02
	Nonmajor	136		
INFMOR	Major	5	6.18*	.01
	Nonmajor	136		
LIFE	Major	5	2.35	.02
	Nonmajor	136		
WATER	Major	5	1.71	.09
	Nonmajor	126		
GNPPC	Major	5	2.05	.04
	Nonmajor	126		
EMBASSY	Najor	5	4.74	.01
	Nonmajor	135		
PCTFOD	Major	5	0.01	.99
	Nonmajor	118		
PCTFUL	Major	5	0.93*	.35
	Nonmajor	118		
CONEXP	Major	5	3.39*	.01
	Nonmajor	116		
HQIO	Major	5	2.14*	.09
	Nonmajor	133		
IMP	Major	5	2.48*	.06
	Nonmajor	133		
NUKE	Major	5	—	—
	Nonmajor	136	—	

Note: Degrees of freedom for t values with an asterisk have been adjusted due to unqual variances between the two groups. See Table 8.3 for variable abbreviations. No nonmajor power has strategic nuclear delivery vehicles.

Table 8.14 Factor Analysis, 1980

Variable	Factor 1 Loadings	Factor 2 Loadings	Factor 3 Loadings
POP	.035	.014	.629
PCTURB	.246	.781	.012
AREA	.182	.046	.823
GNP	.828	.166	.497
MILEXP	.635	.069	.728
EDUC	.854	.147	.430
HLTH	.906	.211	.284
ECOAID	.877	.254	.148
ARMFOR	.160	.065	.929
PHYS	.305	.112	.924
LITERACY	.108	.910	.130
INFMOR	-.128	-.927	-.091
LIFE	.132	.973	.101
WATER	.215	.823	-.020
GNPPC	.393	.605	-.067
EMBASSY	.431	.581	.180
PCTFOD	.023	-.442	-.010
PCTFUL	.159	.367	.008
CONEXP	-.134	-.124	-.060
HQIO	.808	.245	.090
IMP	.914	.312	.188
NUKE	.502	-.003	.708
Eigenvalues	5.838	5.310	4.477
Percentage of variance accounted by three factors		0.74	

Note: See Table 8.3 for variable abbreviations.

would rank high on this factor, and this is true to a degree (the top five ranking states on this factor are the United States, West Germany, France, Japan, and Great Britain).

Eight variables have large loadings on the second factor: percent urban, literacy, infant mortality (a negative loading), life expectancy, percent population with safe water, GNP per capita, number of accredited embassies, and food as a percentage of all manufactured imports (a negative loading). The profile implied by these variables suggests an advanced industrial nation-state, but not necessarily a large one (note the small loadings for population and area). Governments that load heavily on this factor have opted for policies that emphasize butter over guns (note the small loadings for military expenditures, armed force size, and nuclear weapons). The top five ranking states on this factor are reasonably congruent with this description: The Netherlands, Australia, Belgium, Norway, and Switzerland.

The third factor has eight variables with high loadings: population, area, GNP, military expenditures, education expenditures, armed forces size, number of physicians, and number of nuclear weapons. The profile suggested here is that of a large nation, but not necessarily a highly developed one (note the low loadings of giving economic aid, literacy, and GNP per capita). The top five ranking nations on this factor do not fall quite so cleanly into this profile: the Soviet Union, China, Italy, the United States, and Saudia Arabia.

Referring back to the characterization of each factor, it appears that although three orthogonal factors capture most of the variance in the power capability variables, there is some overlap in the characterization of the dimensions. *Economic development* is a part of both the first and second factor, while *size* is a component of both the first and third factor. These two characteristics are ones with which those scholars who take the classical world view would be comfortable, despite the fact that the power capability variables used here are multidimensional. And the factor scores are totaled across the three factors; the top ten ranked states have one or both of these two characteristics (see Table 8.15).

As can be seen, the major powers are all in the top ten. Three nations "intrude" within the group of major powers. The presence of West Germany and Japan is not surprising. Both are large and highly industrial nations, and although supposedly underarmed, both rank in the global top ten in military expenditures. Perhaps the lack of nuclear weaponry gives rise to this misleading expectation. The presence of Italy, Belgium, and Canada is a bit more surprising. Maybe we should interpret this as showing how the "traditional" major powers of Western Europe, Great Britain and France, have simply been slipping back in to the "pack," rather than indicating the great advances of these three "intruders." I should also note that in an earlier paper that experimented with various weights on the Correlates of War power capability data in the post-World War II years (Stoll, 1984), Italy also surpasses France by 1970, so the results in Table 8.15 are not strictly due to the data or analysis of this chapter. As with the earlier analysis, the z-score approach produces an almost identical group at the top of the heap (with Italy

Table 8.15 Factor Scores and Average z Scores for Ten Highest Scoring States, 1980

State	Factor Score	State	z Score
United States*	9.301	United States*	4.007
Soviet Union*	7.809	Soviet Union*	2.871
China*	4.337	West Germany	1.558
Japan	3.812	France*	1.495
West Germany	3.663	China*	1.364
Great Britain*	3.322	Japan	1.224
Italy	2.965	Great Britain*	1.168
Belgium	2.661	Belgium	0.776
Canada	2.283	Canada	0.769
France*	2.186	The Netherlands	0.765

Note: An asterisk indicates state was a major power.

replaced by The Netherlands). Regardless of the scoring technique, the United States and the Soviet Union dominate the rankings.

Discussion

What are we to make of these results? They clearly show that Correlates of War Project power capability data form a single dimension for each of the three time points examined. Furthermore, the states designated by Singer and Small as major powers rank at the top on the factor scores produced by the analysis. This result is not totally unanticipated; the Singer–Small selection of indicators was influence by a classical IR world view. Bearing in mind that the data for the 1950 time point contain the aftereffects of the war, note that the single factor for 1950 accounts for more variance in the power capability variables than the single factor for either of the two earlier time points (albeit by a slight margin). In 1950 power capability appears to be no less unidimensional than in 1850 or 1900.

The 1980 analysis is of the most interest. It represents a "fairer" test of the alternative world views, since sufficient time for changes to a bipolarist or an interdependent world view have had time to take hold. And, sure enough, three dimensions of power capability emerge, rather than the single dimension found with the COW data. As was noted previously, this too is not that surprising, given the larger number of indicators and the lack of a single rationale for their selection.

The dimensions that emerged were interesting. Although statistically independent (an orthogonal rotation was used), inspection of the variables that have high loadings on each factor reveals that there is a degree of theoretical overlap among them. In spite of rotation technique (varimax) that is designed to produce a clear separation of factors, economic development and size are each part of two factors. When total scores are calculated, the top ranks are dominated by large, industrialized states, and particularly the major powers; the United States and the Soviet Union are the top two states.

A Digression on Factor Scores Versus z Scores

Before discussing the implication of these results for the three world views, let me consider the value of the factor analysis. As far as determining the dimensionality of the power capability data, it was helpful. The technique provided a clear assessment of both the number of dimensions and the degree to which the dimensions account for variance in the variables.

But factor analysis was less satisfactory as a technique for producing the scores representing the composite power capability of the states. As noted above, due to collinearity among indicators, the factor scoring coefficients of a variable can be negative, even when its factor loading is positive. This is a slightly paradoxical state of affairs. In precisely those situations that factor analysis will produce the strongest results (a dimension or series of dimensions that fit the data very well), the factor scores are likely to be unreliable due to collinearity among the variables. The equally weighted z scores produced a composite index whose face validity was at least as high as that of the factor scores. Table 8.16 shows the correlation between the z-score scales and the factor scores for each year analyzed. As you can see, the correlations between the two scoring methods are quite high. Given the greater simplicity of the z scores, these circumstances argue for their use, rather than the factor scores.

Which World View Prevails?

When we turn to interpreting the results in terms of the three world views presented earlier, we are faced with a good deal of ambiguity. Consider the 1980 analysis from the perspective of each world view.

In support of the interdependence world view, the 1980 power capability data form three statistically independent dimensions, and taken together, these three dimensions account for the majority of variance in the data. In support of the bipolarist world view, the United States and the Soviet Union have the two largest composite scores with both scoring methods, and in each case, the score of the third ranked state is only about 55% of the second ranked state's score. Finally, in support of the classical world view and the continued importance of the major powers, all those nation-states designated as major powers by Small and Singer in 1980 rank in the top ten on both sets of scores.

From the standpoint of the distribution of global power capability, all three views have some validity. But no one view dominates. What then should a scholar do? On what basis should a choice be made? No simple answer suffices. Instead of pursing one particular viewpoint, it seems best to ask which view is more appropriate for the question to be investigated. Furthermore, there may also be value in applying a variety of world views to the same question, even when that appears to be inappropriate. Such an application may produce insights that have eluded studies that have used the "correct" world view.

Table 8.16   Correlations Between Factor Scores and z Scores

Time Point	N	Correlation
1850	19	.84
1900	40	.96
1950	50	.82
1980	106	.96

Aside from showing that each of the three world views has some validity today, this investigation points strongly to the conclusion that both Japan and West Germany are worthy of consideration as major powers. Their total power capability, as measured either by factor scores of z scores, places them in the first rank of the powerful. As noted above, even in the military sphere, they rank in the top ten in terms of spending. The lack of nuclear weapons, and perhaps the memory of their defeats in World War II, has served to downgrade their status. But it no longer seems appropriate to withhold great power recognition from them.

Conclusion

For much of scholarly history, the major powers have been at the center of inquiry in international relations. In fact, one could argue that we have devoted too much attention to this small group of states, Waltz's comment not withstanding. But in the current era, other perspectives that downplay or ignore the role of the major powers have achieved prominence. There is nothing wrong with using these additional perspectives; they may well shed new light on a variety of old questions and concerns. But have we thrown out the baby with the bath water? Is the concept of major power still a useful and important one? This chapter seeks to shed light on these matters by determining the degree to which the distribution and complexity of power capabilities is different in today's world from the pre-World War II era. Once again, I caution that there is more to being a major power than simply possessing large amounts of power capability, but certainly it seems that this is a necessary condition for being a major power.

The results of the investigation show that each of the three world views presented (the classical, the bipolarist, and the interdependent) is to some extent present in the distribution of power capabilities in the current era. But regardless of the world view, the analysis of this chapter shows that nation-state capabilities still remain concentrated in the hands of a small number of states. And most of these powerful states are from the group most commonly called the major powers. The concept of major power is still useful in the study of international relations.

Notes

1. The reader is invited to glance through several introductory textbooks to confirm that the term is rarely defined explicitly.

2. At the risk of blatantly misrepresenting the ideas of others, I would argue that there are some similarities between this bipolarist concept of the world and that presented by dependency theorists. The great common element

is the picture of a world in which a small number of powers (usually just one—the United States) possess a vast preponderance of power over the rest of the actors in the system (the Americas), and this power, intentionally or not, creates a high degree of influence over the rest of the actors.

3. As with other broad syntheses, while the general form of the contrasts between views is well defined, the specifics are not. For example, how many major powers need be present to apply the traditional view? Although most would argue that it must be more than two (Kaplan, 1957, specifies a minimum of five), Waltz (1979) sees this as an unnecessary and arbitrary limitation. Similar questions can be asked about both the number of dimensions of power in the bipolarist and interdependence views, and the classical view. Conceptual clarity can still give rise to operational fuzziness.

4. Their lessened confidence in the identity of the major powers in the post-1965 time period (stemming from the reduced scholarly consensus on the matter) may in itself be an indication that the classical world view in international relations has been replaced by the bipolarist and/or interdependent views.

5. The scores are used on the Correlates of War data rather than the more typical percentage capability scores because the metric of the z scores is comparable to that of the factor scores. The scores can be rescaled into percentage capability scores using a linear transformation.

6. This time point is only 5 years after the industrial indicator shifts from iron to steel production. The small number of data points is a reflection of the worldwide lack of steel production at that time.

9

Power, Political Capacity, and Security in the Global System

William K. Domke

Power is a core concept in world politics that every student must come to terms with in some way. Almost every theoretical argument includes a notion of power as a way of delineating relationships or explaining behavioral outcomes. The role of power in theories of world politics is ancient. Its long standing, however, has not led to much clarification in meaning. Instead, it has found a central place in the lore of power politics, a body of reasoning about world politics that combines historical record with generalizations about the actions and motivations of governments in dealing with international issues.[1] As a tradition, the lore of power politics serves both to guide contemporary theorizing about world politics and arguably has been the main source of lessons for the education of politicians through the centuries.

While the central role of power in theories of world politics is obvious, it also remains a problem.[2] As a concept, it is too vague to provide clarity to theory. There is no common definition for power, although most would agree that it represents the means to produce change in behavior. Because the sources of changing behaviors are complex, such a simple definition of power provides little explanation on its own. For this reason, theories of world politics must carefully define power to match the theoretical question at hand, or the class of behaviors under examination. Therefore, definitions of power are, and perhaps should be, very theory specific. The concept of power contributes most to theory when it is carefully defined and operationalized to suit the needs of particular theoretical argument and research. To date, its utility as a concept does not come from a consensus or common view of its meaning and role in world politics. Its value lies in the way specific theoretical arguments develop the concept and apply it in answering important questions.

Schools of thought on the meaning of power are interchangeable with complementary theoretical arguments on research questions. In other words, in the absence of a common meaning of power, there usually is conceptual consistency within bodies of theory and research on particular topics. For example, research on the causes of war tends to associate power with military capability (force). Research on North–South relations tends to emphasize wealth as the basis of power. One would get a different ranking of powerful nations from each.

In the end, power is used in too many different ways to stand on its own as a useful concept. Nevertheless, it is a vital concept to theory and research. Much can be done to tidy up confusion across and within theoretical and research topics. Clarity is needed in two dimensions. First, the problem with the concept of power is most often a weak or absent definition. Care must be taken to define explicitly what it is in relation to the theoretical question at issue. Second, the problem is also empirical. Once it is defined, how can it be measured, or at least recognized as an attribute or basis of specific behavioral outcome.

Conceputal clarity cannot easily be achieved. Sophisticated theory and research are the only paths to provide the concept of power a consistent and valuable general meaning. Until and unless a generalized concept of power is achieved, theory-specific definitions and operationalizations must suffice. At least concepts will have value to a particular theoretical argument, if not to world politics as a whole. If world politics possessed a dominant theory, then a single concept of power could assume a more general and core role. Many fields of economics can be observed to have such dominant theories, which greatly enhances the clarity, commonality, consistency, operationalization, and value of key concepts. In the absence of a dominant theory of world politics that defines and operationalizes power as a concept, a theory that explains many kinds of behaviors and guides the research of the majority of scholars in the field, we must be satisfied with more limited concepts, known to be related to power, but more easily defined and measured.

The diversity of theoretical approaches to world politics leads to interesting contradictions in arguments related to power. For example, the distribution of power is important to many theoretical arguments, especially those that address the consequences of hegemony, defined as a global system with a dominant nation of preponderant power. In Hans Morgenthau's (1948) balance of power perspective, hegemony is the greatest danger, the international development that all governments must be vigilant to act against. A hegemonic nation is potentially able to achieve world empire, the end of the balance of power, diplomacy, and international relations. Governments act on the basis of their relation to any potential hegemon and a set of principles of action can be derived form the logic of balance of power generally to fit the actions of European nations prior to the 20th century.

Partly in response to the inadequacies of balance of power arguments, especially when applied to the 20th century, the consequences of hegemony and dominant nations take on a new meaning in other theoretical arguments. A. F. K. Organski (1968) observes that the differential rates of socioeconomic change will tend to produce a dominant nation, which due to its capabilities is able to influence without force until a rising challenger produces conflict and war. Along the same lines, George Modelski (1987) and Robert Gilpin (1981) note that dominant nations provide important leadership to the global system, supplying certain authority and public goods as the basis of international cooperation. Conflict arises when the benefits of these cooperative policies are overtaken by the costs of defending them by challengers who gain wealth and power by themselves benefiting from cooperation.

From both perspectives, hegemony can be defined and recognized much the same, although one encounters some interesting divergences in which nation was dominant and when. Balance of power is unambiguous in defining hegemony as leading to conflict. Contrasting theories, like Organski's power transition and Modelski's long cycle, identify a cooperative or leadership role for dominance, before degenerating into conflict to resolve the contested role of system leadership. How can one decide which is the more correct theoretical argument? In the absence of data, one is hard pressed to draw a conclusion, which points out the critical role of definitions and operationalization of power. The question can only really be answered with data that capture the dynamic changes produced by real or alleged hegemons over the centuries.

The concept of power and its role in theory spawn many related concepts. Many theories prominently feature a concept of great power, generally meaning one of a group of nations, the power of which is superior to the majority of nations. The lore of power politics provides rules of thumb: a dominant nation can take on all other great powers in war, a great power can fight only one other great power at a time, and a small power does very poorly in fighting a great power (Wight, 1946). Traditionally, standing as a great power stems from a nation's record in war. One becomes a great power through military conflict with great powers. It should become apparent that the status of great power does not rest on attributes, which most theories presume. Instead, it is important to note that great power is a behavior. To be a great power is to act like a great power. Nations with more resources have not been great powers and nations with fewer resources have demonstrated considerable talent in great powering.

There are three general policy tendencies, not rules, associated with great powers. First, when another nation makes uncompromising demands, great powers do not concede; if force is used, they resist with force. Second, great powers maintain global interests; there is no corner of the earth that is not important, and this tends to produce colonial empires. Third and finally, great powers pick on small powers when expedient. Since the 17th century, great powers contested each other throughout the global system and found many smaller powers compliant to their influence. Failure to follow any one of these policy rules defines a small power. National attributes are obviously and directly related to the status of great power, but in the end, it is behavior that defines a great power.

The United States is the outstanding example of a large and rich nation that did not assume the mantle of great power until much after it became the most wealthy nation.[3] Clearly, socioeconomic or military attributes are not all there is to great power status. Before World War II, the United States maintained another status by following (with only a little exception) three elements of isolationism: (1) do not form alliances, (2) do not acquire colonies, and (3) do not maintain a large standing army in peacetime. In following these guidelines, however, the United States did not act as a small power, and many observers have difficulty fitting American diplomacy into the lore of power politics—not a great power, not a small power. In order not to mislead, it it important to note that the United States has always resisted great power challenges (since the XYZ Affair), had global interests (the war in Tripoli), and interfered in the affairs of small nations, especially Latin American neighbors. Taken together, the combination of American isolationist tradition with great power behaviors makes it difficult to include the United States in otherwise robust theories of world politics derived from the lore of power politics. "Colossus" is not a concept easily adapted to existing theories. That great power behavior existed together with isolationism points out additional limits to the role of power and the need to focus on the elements of foreign and security policy that can be defined and examined more clearly.

What Was the Most Powerful Nation in 1890?

The basic problems with the concept of power are revealed in attempting to answer the question of what nation was most powerful in 1890? This year is somewhat arbitrarily chosen because it was pre-airplane and especially pre-nuclear. It marks a time of relative peace in the international system, at the end of Bismarck's era. It is also prior to the modern era of systematic statistics gathering, yet workable pre-modern concepts of society and economy make data reasonably comparable and plentiful. It is possible to try to answer this question using the conceptual and information tools available to an enterprising political economist of that era. Such an exercise can show the problems with power as a concept, but it also points out how research can be profitably guided by narrower concepts of key attributes.

The leading indicators of power should be the obvious ones. If power is or was ever to be a useful concept, it must be recognizable. Table 9.1

Table 9.1 Which Nation Was Most Powerful in 1890?

	Army Peace (thousands)	Army War (thousands)	Total Cannon	Navy Ships (Ironclads)	Population (millions)	Wealth U.K. Sterling (millions)
Great Britain	210	606	5,789	455 (66)	38.0	9,400
France	555	1,315	7,694	280 (52)	38.5	8,598
Germany	492	1,492	5,380	92 (27)	48.0	6,437
Russia	800	1,720	4,424	221 (40)	92.0	5,089
Austria	323	1,150	2,170	72 (10)	40.0	3,855
Italy	255	940	1,680	136 (14)	30.0	2,963
Spain	145	400	1,241	120 (13)	18.0	2,516
Portugal	26	150	420	40 (1)	4.7	408
Belgium	48	148	324	—	6.1	1,007
Holland	29	55	900	108 (24)	4.5	980
Denmark	17	60	535	40 (8)	2.0	404
Sweden and Norway	57	230	1,072	93 (19)	6.8	880
Switzerland	126	207	42	—	3.0	494
Greece	26	105	300	31 (4)	2.0	300
Roumania	36	118	442	—	5.5	593
Servia	18	100	144	—	2.0	217
Bulgaria	29	100	96	—	3.0	205
Turkey	160	470	3,762	101 (15)	4.7	593
United States	26	—	4,155	89 (13)	62.5	12,824
Mexico	27	—	—	—	10.5	638
Brazil	16	—	416	42 (12)	12.4	—
Argentina	7	—	75	29 (3)	3.6	509
China	—	—	—	58 (9)	320.0	—
Japan	60	307	369	53 (1)	38.0	—
India	145	—	—	—	215.0	—
Australia	—	—	—	—	3.7	1,373
Canada	—	—	—	—	5.1	980
South Africa	—	—	—	—	1.9	135

All data (and spelling) are from Michael G. Mulhall, *The Dictionary of Statistics* (London: George Routledge and Sons, 1892). Columns 2–4: "Army," p. 66; peacetime footing, wartime footing, and total cannon in army, navy forts, and so on (except Servia and Switzerland, army artillery guns). "In the war footing of European armies as given above only the first line of reserves is included. If all reserves were included the numbers might be safely doubled." Column 5: "Navy," p. 612 for the number of ships, which "includes some vessels that are building," and ironclads from "Navy," p. 415. Column 6 and 7: "Nations," p. 414. The estimates of "wealth" are ill defined on p. 589 and are the sum of valuations for lands, cattle, houses, furniture, railways, ships, merchandise, buillion, and sundries ("It is well to observe that the subjoined table may serve for comparison, but cannot be considered mathematically correct. . . .")

displays Michael G. Mulhall's data for the year closest to 1890 for the sizes of armies, navies, and population and a concept of "wealth" (Mulhall, 1892). Although other data might be useful in answering the question, this short list comprises the leading candidate indicators of power.

Turning first to the size of land armies, which is generally associated with continental power instead of far reaching global power, Russia had the largest peacetime and wartime army, although its lead diminished after the mobilization of reserves into the wartime force. France had the second largest peacetime force, but Germany had a larger army when on a war footing, which is a testament to the conscription and reserve system that performed so well in the wars of German unification and was to produce a massive Germany army in the opening days of World War I. The five largest armies are of nations that had borders with at least two of the other four.

Great Britain had only the sixth largest army. Mulhall reports that the total land force of the British Empire, upon the mobilization of reserves, numbered around one million, which moves Britain past Italy for fifth place. On the other hand, perhaps Britain should be penalized in a continental comparison, because of the large portion of the regular service that served abroad and the large contribution of colonial forces. In 1889, only 78,000 officers and men served in Great Britain, with the rest in Ireland, India, Egypt, and the colonies. *Pax Britannica* obviously was not based on the size of the serving army, which is clearly too small to weigh in continental matters in a timely way. Russia, France, Germany, Austria, and Italy could quickly deploy large and ready land forces that the British could not. Likewise, the United States possessed only the skeleton of a standing army, and no reserve system, since the army was intended to expand only to fit wartime needs.

In the age of steel, the total number of cannon is an important feature of the destructive power of military forces. Column 4 in Table 9.1 shows the total cannon in army artillery, naval guns, guns deployed in fortifications, and so on. France had, by far, the largest number of total cannon, followed by Great Britain and Germany. Despite having the largest army, Russia had the fourth largest number of cannons. Austria and Italy drop out of the top six ranks, since the United States and Turkey possessed many more cannons than these European nations with far larger armies. Because France maintained both a large land and sea force, it should not be surprising that it possessed the most cannon.

Great Britain had the largest navy, 22% of all naval ships. France had 13% and Russia had 11% of all ships. The size of the British navy matches the global role of British forces and the maintenance of the British Empire. Such dominance is easy to associate with *Pax Britannica* and a prominent role for Britain in world affairs. But does 22% of all naval ships resemble hegemony? Probably not, especially when the distribution of ironclads is also weighed.[4] Ironclads represent the strategic weapons of the late 19th century. They were the vessels around which global power projection and gunboat diplomacy were based. In this category, however, the British have 20% of the total and France a close second with 16%. While 66/52 is a large margin, it is not a blowout, especially if allies are recruited. A British perception of naval supremacy is worth noting:

In ships we are well ahead of any competitor. It is in the matter of guns that our weakness lies. We have afloat or ready to go afloat 1065 modern heavy guns; France has 1447, Russia has 423, Italy has 180, and Germany 508. When all our war-ships are armed, we shall have afloat of guns that can pierce 15 in. of armour and upwards 104, while France will have 124, Russia 38, Italy 40 and Germany 61.[5]

The British had the largest navy, but it is difficult to judge the 1890 fleet as unambiguously dominant.

Population size is only rarely argued to be an indicator of national power in and of itself, although it is an important element of the pool of societal resources available for government use. As today, non-European nations had the largest populations in 1890. China and India possessed comparatively huge populations. Russia's 92 million people make it the largest of the Europeans and the United States' 62.5 million was already much larger than the rest of the European nations. The other nations that are usually considered great powers of the day had populations between 50 and 30 million: Germany (48), Austria (40), Japan (38), France (38), Great Britain (38), and Italy (30). It is also important to note that the French population, and therefore its economy, grew much more slowly than other nations in the 19th century.

Finally, a strong case can be made for the overall wealth of a nation constituting the basis of power in the global system. As such, a concept of wealth serves to summarize the comparative size of the societies' resources, which in turn can be translated into economic assets important to influence other governments and military capabilities to use as force. Table 9.1 shows that Mulhall's estimates of wealth in 1890 place the United States 36% richer than the United Kingdom (Great Britain plus Ireland). Since the valuation of land is a larger component of wealth, the United States and France benefit from higher valuations of farm land.

Whatever the difficulties of estimation, Mulhall's calculation shows the United States as that nation with the greatest pool of resources to draw upon. The U.S. governments of the late 19th century did not choose to tap this resource pool for a large standing army and navy, but such figures show the economic importance of the United States and the unambiguous potential for military capability that was revealed in the Civil War, and later in the world wars of the 20th century. Even though the United States did not behave like a great power, let alone a hegemon, it did possess the largest economy in 1890. Few, however, would judge the United States to be the most powerful nation in 1890. Despite the largest resource base, the United States was fourth in population size, fifth in the number of cannon, ninth in the number of navy ships, and tied with Portugal and Greece for the eighteenth largest standing army.

The lesson from the examination of Table 9.1 is important. One cannot answer the question of who was most powerful with this selection of indicators. No nation is ranked first in more than one category. Any concept of power is more complicated than the analysis of the obvious indicators. With that in mind, it might be reasonable to conclude that the concept of power has little utility for theory in world politics. If it cannot be made obvious, a concept of power should not serve as the basis for theory.

The alternatives to the obvious do not provide a good solution. First, it can easily be suggested that power drives from a combination of elements, which can be combined into a composite index of national strength. There is a major drawback to composite indicators, however, since there is no intuitive way to combine elements. Put differently, because a concept of power is vague, there is no theoretically derived basis for an algorithm used to produce a single indicator of power. More data can be used, but the results are determined by a weighting scheme that must be justified as a theoretically meaningful depiction of power.

A second solution to the deficiencies of obvious indicators of power is the reliance on the nonobvious. Factors such as national morale, organization, or social cohesion are often argued to be essential elements of national power, but they are necessarily intangible. To add even more vagueness to an already troublesome concept of power detracts considerably from theory. If the basis of power is to include elements so vague and intangible, then the concept of power is seriously hindered by inconsistency and guesswork.

It is apparent that no consensus can exist on the answer to the question of what nation was most powerful in 1890. For a concept of power to contribute meaningfully to theory, its definition and identification must be kept simple enough for all to recognize. For this reason, theory in world politics should not rely on a concept of power. Instead, it is far better to focus and rely on things we know about. The important and valuable concepts are those that can be defined fully and recognized easily.

To follow this prescription, concepts of power should be replaced by two categories of concepts. First, it is possible to make useful concepts surrounding military capability. This stems mostly from knowledge of war-fighting and the performance of armed forces in various eras and circumstances. For theory, the performance of armed forces is a ready validation of indicators of military capability. Taken further, however, elements of military capability should be kept specific. For example, Modelski's work on long cycles relies explicitly on naval capability (Modelski, 1987; Modelski and Thompson, 1987). Such specificity enables Modelski to provide empirical support for his theoretical arguments, which are far more consistent and applicable to explanations of developments in the global system. Explorations of deterrence also frequently make clear that nuclear capabilities are the appropriate concept.

Second, other important concepts derive from assessments of the societal resource pool, from where come military capabilities. The value of these concepts is the ability to recognize and integrate knowledge of domestic structure. Put differently, broader knowledge of the functioning of political institutions allow theoretical arguments in world politics to be enlivened by the variation of government–population relationships in each nation. It is not a profound conclusion to observe that each society is unique in many ways. Yet, without concepts describing the domestic structure of nations, theoretical arguments in world politics must make assumptions and simplifications that limit the generality. Because of this, concepts relating to the size of and governmental access to societal resources can be very important to the development of more sophisticated theoretical arguments in world politics.

Political Capacity and Societal Resources

The concepts required to develop theoretical arguments and empirical studies about governmental utilization of societal resources are not many and they are easy to define and operationalize. Moreover, the following concepts are robust, in the sense that they can be modified and refined to suit somewhat different research questions. Government–population relationships are the core of the issue. This linkage is most often referred to as state–society relationships, but the concept of state is used differently in various social science contexts and each takes on meanings that can be troublesome to analyses of the relationship of ruling elites and institutions of a governed population.

The concept of government needs to be kept as broad as possible in order to ensure that theoretical arguments take into account the constellation of authorities capable of extracting resources in the name of a political system. Central governments most often coexist with regional and local governments with their own taxing authority and perhaps complicated divisions of revenues. For example, the Imperial German government of 1890 was allowed only indirect taxation (customs, salt, sugar, tobacco, liquor, and stamps), whereas the several German states could undertake direct taxation (income, house, land, and trade taxes). Even within central governments, extraction authority can be outside finance ministries. This is especially true of the large and autonomous social security pension funds of the 20th century. In addition, a broad concept of government that recognizes all public institutions able to tax permits the analysis of less than fully independent nations. In 1890, Norway, Canada, and Australia could not be called fully independent, since their defense and foreign policies were subsumed by another government, yet each extracted taxes independently of any outside government and expended these resources in important national programs, including the maintenance of armed forces for territorial defense. Great

Britain, in particular, relied on "colonial" forces to provide self-defense and ease the burden on the Royal Army and Navy.

The vastly complicated network of human interactions that take place in any population is impossible to easily summarize or depict with a comprehensive model of dynamic socioeconomic structures. Too many factors are important—for example, demography, cultural values, ethnicity, economic distributions—to make any one of them especially meaningful as the basis of ordering and classifying domestic structures. Accordingly, for the purposes of analyzing governmental extraction of resources, it is best to treat a population as an undifferentiated whole. This is an important simplification that is necessary for comparative purposes. Conceptual simplifications of domestic structure, both the governmental and population dimensions, must be dropped when it comes time to root out the explanations of differences in extractive capabilities. It is only in dealing head-on with the differences of domestic structure that government–population relationships take on theoretical meaning.

A rather simple model of government–population relationships serves as the basis of an evaluation of resource extraction. The pool of societal resources, defined as the total productive output of the population, is another necessary concept. Here, it is possible to rely on well-developed economic concepts surrounding national income accounting. Not surprisingly, Gross National Product is the best indicator of the size of a societal resource pool. In this chapter, Mulhall's late-19th century measures of national income are used to illustrate resource extraction based on data existing in 1890.

Finally, extraction of material resources is best revealed through taxation of the population: the portion of the societal resource pool tapped by governmental authorities. Concepts and measures of taxation are the oldest elements of economic theories. For the student of world politics, taxation represents a continuous and conceptually consistent knowledge base on which to build. The role of taxation in the creation and modernization of governmental structures is prominent and, through the translation of tax revenues into armed forces, has direct bearing on international relations (Ardant, 1975). Although governments can raise large amounts of nontax revenue (e.g., the profits of publicly owned petroleum companies), it is only through taxation that governmental authorities call on citizens to allocate personal income to public use. The distribution among types of tax, direct taxes (income and property) versus indirect taxes (customs and excise taxes), is far less important than the total amount, because any population will maintain somewhat unique obstacles to some forms of tax. In addition, fiscal policies vary considerably in providing incentives for particular economic decisions. In short, even though it is composed of many types of tax, total taxation as an undifferentiated whole serves as the consequence of governmental extraction capability.

With a simple model of government–population relations and the concepts of societal resource pool and taxation, comparative analyses of extractive capabilities can lead to insights into the distribution of governmental resources in the global system. Total taxation as a share of national output offers a first approximation, but this ratio neglects the important socioeconomic conditions that have direct bearing on the ability of a government to penetrate the population and extract resources. The method that has been developed in earlier research provides a baseline expectation of a level of taxation, given salient socioeconomic factors (Kugler, 1983; Organski and Kugler, 1980; Kugler and Domke, 1986). In other words, a measure of the relative political capacity of nations can be derived by comparing actual taxation with what would be expected based on structural characteristics of the society.

Table 9.2 shows the results of ordinary least-squares estimation of a model of taxation applied to 18 nations in 1890. Overall, the model is a good predictor of taxes as a percentage of GNP, since almost two-thirds of the variance is accounted for in the model. The results of estimation also show that, among the nations included, there are five significant predictors of taxation. Income per capita is negatively related to taxation. There is a pattern, other things being equal, for the poorer, really less industrialized, nations in this study to generate higher tax ratios. This is also reflected in the positive relationship with agriculture as a percentage of GNP. These patterns change in the 20th century, because tax systems of 1890 emphasized excise taxes and the ability to tax land values and fixed property. Taxation of property is important here since local taxation is included, which tended to concentrate on property taxes. The higher incomes of the more industrialized nations were not well integrated into taxation, through corporate or income taxes.

Table 9.2 also shows that greater wealth is associated with higher proportional levels of taxation. Mulhall's measure of wealth emphasizes fixed assets, which are conducive to taxation. However, this relationship is conditioned by the size of population. The larger the population, the lower the level of taxation. The nations with the largest populations are also those

Table 9.2 Ordinary Least-Squares Estimation of Taxation, 1890

Variable	Coefficient	Standard Error	T-Stat
Intercept	2.22	7.53	0.29
Income per capita	-.39	.13	-2.88
Agriculture % income	.30	.13	2.34
Wealth	.16	.05	3.23
Population	-.16	.06	-2.47
Exports % income	.12	.05	2.25
	$N = 18$	$R^2 = .62$	$F = 3.86$

with the largest geographic area, Russia and the United States, which is consistent with the ability to reach citizens and tax.

Finally, the estimated model also reveals that a heavy reliance on customs revenue in 1890 makes exports as a share of income positively related to taxation. This is to be expected since commercial activity is more easily monitored by governmental tax and customs authorities. In the end, the higher levels of taxes as a percentage of income are predicted to be possessed by the smaller more agricultural active trading nations: Holland and Portugal, and less so Spain and Italy. The lower levels of taxation are predicted to be maintained by the more industrialized and richer nations: Belgium and Great Britain.

It is perhaps important to note that the model used here for the nations of 1890 is in many ways different from those used in previous research. Earlier models were estimated for thirty-eight third world nations from 1950 to 1975 and for fourteen industrialized nations in the period 1900–1960.[6] Because those two studies concentrated on nations of a particular type, Third World or industrialized, the group of nations in 1890 is more heterogeneous, containing nations with much more diverse socioeconomic characteristics. Likewise, this model is a cross-national estimation and not a pooled time-series estimation used in the earlier studies. The other two studies directed their primary attention to years of war, whereas this study of the year 1890 does not contain a nation seeking to maximize its extraction for a war effort. Finally, the results of this estimation are probably biased by the standardization of monetary indicators to British currency. Mulhall is not explicit as to his choice of exchange rates and it is likely that the conversion to pound sterling produces a margin of error. The most important element of this method of estimating political capability is that a model of taxation can be constructed that performs well in predicting taxation as a percentage of income with indicators that can be understood and justified as theoretically meaningful predictors.

By dividing the actual percentage of taxation by that predicted by the estimated model in Table 9.2, it is possible to obtain a ratio of relative political capacity that separates nations according to their government's ability to extract resources from the population. Table 9.3 shows the resulting index of political capacity in column 3. The highest index of political capacity is achieved by Australia, whose small population bore a comparatively high tax burden but also possessed the highest per capita income. Italy shows a remarkably high ratio of predicted to actual taxes, which is partly indicative of the mobilization of resources in the recently unified nation. Belgium and Great Britain, two very industrialized nations, also have a high value for political capacity, as does Argentina.

The lowest value of relative political capacity is that of the United States. Since general government taxation (consolidated state, local, and

Table 9.3 National Political Capacity and Resources in 1890

	Taxes as Percentage of Income	Political Capacity	Income Weighted by Political Capacity	Wealth Weighted by Political Capacity	GNP 1960 U.S. $ (billions)	GNP Weighted by Political Capacity
Great Britain	9.3	1.33	1,709	12,502	30.5	40.6
France	13.7	1.03	1,077	8,856	20.1	20.7
Germany	10.1	1.09	1,173	6,945	26.6	29.0
Russia	7.4	0.92	897	4,682	24.4	20.6
Austria	9.0	0.78	480	3,007	15.8	12.3
Italy	22.3	1.60	580	4,741	9.5	15.2
Spain	12.6	0.87	255	2,189	5.8	5.0
Portugal	13.8	0.92	51	375	1.5	1.4
Sweden	6.7	0.79	82	503	1.9	1.5
Norway	5.8	0.86	35	209	0.8	0.7
Denmark	5.3	0.77	51	311	1.1	0.9
Holland	14.3	0.94	96	921	2.6	2.4
Belgium	6.4	1.37	229	1,382	3.3	4.5
Switzerland	6.5	0.74	41	366	1.9	1.4
United States	5.3	0.64	1,509	8,207	54.9	35.1
Canada	4.6	0.72	94	705	3.8	2.7
Australia	7.4	1.76	253	2,416	2.9	5.1
Argentina	11.1	1.22	97	565	—	—

Data for Columns 2–5 are from Michael G. Mulhall, *Dictionary of Statistics* (London: George Routledge and Sons, 1892). General government (central and local/state authorities) taxes as a percentage of income is derived from "Taxes," p. 557 and "Finance," p. 259 (for Canada, Australia, and Argentina), and "Income," p. 320. The index of political capacity is the ratio of actual taxation to what would be expected given socioeconomic characteristics of the nation. Column 4 shows income, in million of U.K. Sterling, multiplied by the index of political capacity, and column 5 shows the same for "Wealth," p. 589. Column 6 is the estimated GNP in billions of 1960 U.S. dollars based on research described in Paul Bairoch, "Europe's Gross National Product: 1800–1975," *Journal of European Economic History* 5 (1976) and supplemented by additional data supplied by Professor Bairoch, Department of Economic History, University of Geneva, 1982. Column 7 is GNP multiplied by the index of political capacity.

federal taxation) is the basis of estimation, this result is not produced by the absence of many American taxing authorities. Instead, the very low ratio of actual to predicted taxation reveals the dominant tendency to extract very few resources in peacetime. One cost of low levels of extraction is the peacetime military, which we have seen to be at a very modest standing in 1890.

When the index of relative political capacity is used to weight Mulhall's data on income and wealth, the comparative access to resources of the governments of 1890 can be examined. Assuming that Mulhall's concepts and data on income and wealth are adequate measures of the size of societal resource pools, then the values of each multiplied by the ratio of actual to predicted taxation gives an indication of the resource base available to each government. Table 9.3 also displays Paul Bairoch's estimates of GNP for these nations as a modern indicator of national output in 1890. It is important to emphasize that the weighted estimates of income, wealth, and

GNP are only comparative indexes of the extractive capabilities of governments and have no real meaning outside their use in comparisons.

Although Great Britain was not the wealthiest or most productive nation in 1890, a high level of relative political capacity shows that the British government was able to use a larger portion of its societal resource base than most other nations. In contrast to the United States, which had the largest resource base but the smallest level of relative political capacity, the British government has access to the most resources. Compared to analyses that search for indicators of British dominance in the global system, and find that in most areas the British were surpassed by either Germany or the United States, the use of a concept of political capacity supports the conventional perception of Great Britain as the leading, if perhaps not dominant, nation of the era. It is not necessary to rely on intangible estimations of societal cohesion or national will to support the position of Great Britain as the leading nation at the end of the 19th century. Instead, a notion of political capacity can be used to demonstrate that a comparatively smaller share of societal resources was used more effectively than in other nations.

The potential resources of the United States are clearly revealed in Table 9.3, though the relative political capacity of the United States was small. The size of the U.S. economy in 1890 was large enough to provide the government ample resources without a heavy burden of taxation.

Of the other great powers of the day, German national output was larger than that of France, as was relative political capacity. Mulhall's measure of national wealth provides France a higher valuation of agricultural land, which places France second behind the British on this dimension. The financial resources of Paris in 1890 were very large, and this ranking may more closely resemble perceptions of 1890. Russia possessed a large economy, but a taxation rate below what would be expected based on socioeconomic characteristics. Austria's actual taxation level is even farther below expectations, which is indicative of the steady decline of the empire. Finally, the calculated index of relative political capacity for Italy is unusually high and suggests that the Italian government had greater access to resources than the Austrians. Though this is a plausible result, the Italian tax rate may be overestimated through Mulhall's exchange rate or another factor.

Based on the weighting of national output generated by relative political capacity, a ranking of the nations would produce the following order of nations: United Kingdom, United States, Germany, France, Russia, Italy, and Austria. Regrettably, Japan is excluded from the analysis, but since Bairoch estimates the Japanese economy to be the same size as Italy, it should rank ahead of Austria. A second group of nations with far smaller resources consists of Spain, Belgium, and Australia. The remainder of the nations have very few resources in comparison to the rest.

Security Policy and Consensus

Whereas power as a concept has proved difficult to define and operationalize, other concepts related to broader notions of power can be defined specifically enough to permit measurement and analysis. Concepts of military capability are more easy to develop and use in analysis, but measures of political capacity and societal resources are possible and can serve as key concepts in world politics theory.

The concept of political capacity leads in the direction of domestic structure and away from theoretical arguments based on the distribution of power. Since system structure arguments cannot deal with issues of motivation behind governmental behaviors, development of theory based on domestic structure stands to provide a much richer source of theoretical argument.

Domestic structure becomes more important if the concept of power is demoted in importance. Instead, it can be argued that security is the key concept promoted by the lore of power politics. Degrees of security are directly related to the motivations behind government behavior, whereas the connection between power and motivations is ambiguous. Powerful nations can be insecure, while nations with little power can be very secure. It is the perception of threat and the assessment of resources that serve as the basis of foreign and security policy.

Key aspects of domestic structure underpin national foreign and security policies. Political capacity is one such element and it is possible to offer a number of hypotheses as to its role in security policy. The most prominent relationship may be between levels of political capacity and the degree of national political consensus (Craig and George, 1983). Nations with higher relative political capacity are those with greater domestic political consensus, which enables the government to act more decisively. While such a relationship is merely a hypothesis, it is possible to support it with the knowledge that political capacity is highest during periods of war, when political cohesion is highest and dissent least tolerated. Likewise, it is interesting to note that of the nations examined above, the nations with the highest relative political capacity were those that were most active acquiring new lands through colonization, which is an active foreign policy based on political consensus.

Only further investigation can reveal the role of political capacity in foreign and security policy. Whatever the result, it leads in the direction of domestic structure and away from system structure. It promotes the concept of security at the expense of power. Moreover, a move to domestic structure allows theoretical arguments to be enlivened by a more explicit and usable set of concepts developed for the comparative study of national politics. Since the concept of power has so many drawbacks, it is best to leave it behind and look elsewhere for tools to understood the global system.

Notes

1. What I call the lore of power politics goes by many names, and its main tenets are described in may places. I find that the best concise description of power politics is found in Wight, 1946.

2. An excellent review of conceptual problems is given by David Baldwin (1979).

3. On the issue of great powers, Paul Kennedy (1987) has much of interest to say without defining the concept of power or great powers.

4. Modelski and Thompson (1987) argue the opposite and have carefully gathered data that show that the Royal Navy was dominant over the French, Russian, and U.S. navies.

5. *Daily News* (London), cited in Mulhall (1892, p. 145).

6. Organski and Kugler (1980) studied Third World nations and Kugler and Domke (1986) examined industrialized nations.

PART 3

Assessing the Role of Power

10

Dyadic Power, Expectations, and War

Bruce Bueno de Mesquita and David Lalman

Structural theories of the causes, or at least the correlates, of war dominate the literature in international relations. Confidence in seemingly contradictory structural perspectives perseveres despite theoretical and empirical weaknesses in the relevant hypotheses. Here we examine two structural approaches to war in light of insights from a more dyadic focus on national decisions to engage in violent or nonviolent behavior, given the presence of an articulated conflict of interest. We then test those insights using data on historical disputes from the Correlates of War Project.

Two prominent "rival" views of war emanate from balance of power and from power preponderance theories. These perspectives lead to alternative hypotheses about the factors leading to war (or peace) and the motives underlying the selection of allies. For instance, some balance of power theorists hypothesize that a balance of power tends to produce peace and an imbalance tends to produce war, and that alliances tend to be nonideological, power-seeking, and short-lived arrangements. Some power preponderance theorists claim that a balance of power tends to produce war and an imbalance tends to produce peace, and that alliances tend to be long-lived, ideological arrangements. Here we do not address the alliance arguments of these perspectives but focus only on the propositions related to conflict. For examples of the balance of power perspective, see Edward Gulick (1955), Hans Morgenthau (1978), and Kenneth Waltz (1979). Examples of theories of preponderant power include A. F. K. Organski (1968), George Modelski (1972), A. F. K. Organski and Jacek Kugler (1980), Robert Gilpin (1981), and Robert Keohane (1984).

This chapter also appears in *Prisoners of War? Nation-States in the Modern Era*, edited by Charles Gochman and Alan N. Sabrosky, forthcoming from Lexington Books.

The Balance of Power and War

The war and peace hypothesis from the balance of power is rooted in a reductionist view of national incentives that makes the derivation of meaningful results difficult. While a parsimonious axiomatic base is always a desirable feature of any theory, it is possible to reduce the assumptions to the point that no results are obtainable. In particular, balance of power theorists generally equate power (or security) with both the means to achieving national ends and with the ends themselves. As one observer astutely notes:

> It is dangerous to put in a key position a concept which is merely instrumental. Power is a means toward any of a large number of ends (including power itself). The quality and quantity of power used by men are determined by men's purposes. . . . The "realist" theory neglects all the factors that influence or define purposes. . . . The . . . beliefs and values which account in great measure for the nation's goals and for the statesmen's motivations, are either left out or brushed aside. (Hoffmann, 1960, p. 31)

Our approach to this issue is that power alone is an insufficient explanation of a nation's behavior. We share the belief that power may be only an instrument for achieving national goals. When balance of power theorists, for instance, treat power as both the means and ends of foreign policy, they assume that such considerations as ideology, domestic constraints, and international norms are either nonexistent or irrelevant to decisionmakers.

Even allowing this possibility, one must still distinguish instrumentally between power as the tool, or capacity, of achieving an end and the accumulation of power as the motivation behind behavior. Knowing a nation's level of power is not sufficient to determine the ways the power will be used. Suppose a national leader has two avenues for accumulating power. One avenue can lead to the accumulation of more power than the second, but going down the first path is less likely to be successful. How is the leader to choose between the alternatives? Balance of power theory gives us no answer to this question. To find an answer, we must account for both the desirability of the goal and the probability of actually attaining it. If enough extra power can be gained from the riskier path to compensate the nation for the risks, then that route is the one to follow. But, if the extra power is not large enough, then the avenue with the smaller, but more secure, reward is the one that will be pursued. In other words, national leaders seeking to improve their welfare must take account of the values of alternative outcomes and the probabilities of achieving them. They must calculate the expected utility associated with the alternatives available to them.

By specifying the necessary calculations of a decisionmaker acting in accordance with the precepts of balance of power theory, we demonstrate that the distribution of power does not, in itself, determine behavior. Furthermore, we can show that the hypothesis that a balance of power tends to lead to peace requires additional, restrictive assumptions not stated by balance of power theorists.

Balance of power theorists assume that nations prefer to gain additional power rather than maintain their current level, and that holding on to what they have is preferred to losing power. Morgenthau (1978, p. 215), for instance, notes that "the desire to attain a maximum of power is universal." We write the statement that all nations prefer greater power to lesser power as $U_g > U_m > U_l$, for all nations where U_g is the utility for gaining power, U_m is the utility for maintaining current levels of power, and U_l is the utility for losing power.

Let us postulate a hypothetical situation in which a nation faces the choice between holding its current power for sure or waging a war in which it has some probability of gaining and some probability of losing power. Then the decision to wage war can be preferred to not waging war only if:

$$[P(U_g) + (1 - P)(U_l) - C] > U_m, \tag{1}$$

where P is the probability of gaining power and C is the cost of war to that nation. Equation (1) states that for a power-seeking nation the expected improvement in power following war must exceed the current level of power. Solving for P, we rearrange (1), giving us,

$$P > \frac{U_m + C - U_l}{U_g - U_l}. \tag{2}$$

How large P must be to satisfy Equation (2) depends, of course, on the utility of the expected costs (C) and the shape of the utility function across the outcomes of gaining, maintaining, and losing power. Balance of power theorists seem to argue that nations will not initiate war if their chances of winning are only 50/50. Thus, for balance of power theorists war occurs only if P is strictly greater than .5, yet we can see analytically that Equation (2) can hold for any value of P between 0 and 1 while still satisfying the power maximization assumption. This is easily shown by selecting appropriate utility values and an appropriate magnitude of costs. The key balance of power hypothesis that peace follows when $P \leq .5$ holds only if

$$U_m \geq \frac{U_g + U_l}{2} - C \tag{3}$$

Equation (3) reveals an underlying assumption of balance of power theory. To our knowledge, however, this assumption has not been made explicit by any balance of power theorist. It is a restriction on the cardinal value of currently held power with important implications. The balance of power theory evidently includes the assumption that the value for maintaining power and the value of expected costs are inextricably linked. As costs approach zero, the utility for maintaining currently held power *must be* moving closer to the value attached to gaining power than to losing power if peace is to be preserved.

Additionally, according to Equation (3), as the expected costs from war rise, the value attached to acquiring power—the principal precept of balance of power theory—becomes inconsequential in comparison to maintaining current levels of power. That is, if the costs are large enough, they cannot be offset by the anticipated gains. This balance of power "result" merely indicates that as the costs of an action rise, holding all else constant, the desirability of the action diminishes.

What if a nation not engaged in warfare is uncertain, as assumed in Equations (1)–(3), of maintaining its power? Then, according to the precepts of the balance of power theory, such a nation must always be prepared to wage war regardless of how adverse the situation. Morgenthau (1978, p. 215) notes that "all nations must always be afraid that their own miscalculations and the power increases of other nations might add up to an inferiority for themselves which *they must at all costs* avoid" (emphasis added). The view that all costs are endurable is also a characteristic of Morton A. Kaplan's (1957, p. 23) rule 2, which states: "Fight rather than pass up an opportunity to increase capabilities." Of course, Kaplan, Morgenthau, and other balance of power theorists acknowledge that diplomacy is to be preferred to war whenever diplomacy will succeed in yielding new power or shoring up existing power. But, since shifts in the distribution of power are zero-sum, diplomacy cannot benefit both parties to a dispute over power. Therefore, since all costs are worth enduring in the pursuit of power—and war is surely a very costly foreign policy—balance of power theorists argue at once that a balance makes war unlikely and that a balance ensures war. Such a statement is the consequence of the assumption that power is both the means and ends of foreign policy.

National leaders may attach value to more ends than the acquisition of power. As S. Hoffmann and others have noted, a theoretical approach that recognizes a broader range of national goals can escape the limitations of treating power as both the objective and the instrument of foreign policy.

The Preponderance of Power and War

Unlike balance of power theorists, those who claim that hegemony promotes peace recognize that states may be motivated by a desire to fulfill goals beyond the acquisition of power. Indeed, in the past decade a large literature on hegemonic stability has grown up around the contention that the presence of a preponderant state ensures the security of weaker nations. In large part, a hegemon relieves smaller states of the burden of providing for their own defense. Less encumbered by the provision of defense expenditures and by the threat of war, these states are allowed greater opportunity to pursue economic and other goals. As long as a hegemon dominates the international system, peace can be enforced. But when a rival rises in power and challenges the international order established by the preponderant state, the ability of the hegemon to maintain peace is impaired. War among the major powers becomes likely.

Three conditions are required for hegemonic stability to give way to a power transition war:

1. The challenger must be approximately equal to the hegemon in power.
2. The challenger must be rising in power to overtake the hegemon.
3. The rate of growth of the challenger must be rapid enough to preclude the opportunity for a peaceful transition (Organski and Kugler, 1980; Gilpin, 1987; Kim, 1987).

According to power preponderance theorists, the goals of the major powers in the international system are not limited to the pursuit of power. Rather, they seek to control the formulation of the rules and norms governing international intercourse. Like balance of power theorists, students of preponderance are quickly moved to the view that the only way to ensure control over system rules and norms is to be stronger than any possible rival. Thus, power again becomes the central motivating force behind all international interactions, at least among the major powers.

The status of the empirical referents of this theory is itself a matter of some controversy. Gilpin (1987) maintains that the theory, though capable of providing an explanation of great power wars, is not susceptible to testing in a normal, scientific sense. In particular, he claims that the theory is not falsifiable. This stands in sharp contrast to Organski and Kugler (1980), who provide empirical tests that appear to corroborate the main claims of the power transition theory, or to W. Kim (1987), who purports to have tested the same theory. While Kim's analysis fails to yield support for the key hypotheses of the power preponderance perspective, he too believes that the theory is testable.

We share the view that the parts of the power preponderance argument that are relevant to war are subject to empirical investigation. We, however, do not examine all the aspects of this theory. Instead, our attention is restricted to the relationship between the distribution of power among rivals and the likelihood that they will engage each other in warfare. Our narrow focus seems appropriate in that an equality of power appears to be a necessary, if not sufficient, condition for war according to those who subscribe to the claim that power preponderance leads to peace. We are not able to test the claims linking the decline of hegemony to wars that altered the structure or rules of the international system. In our opinion, there simply are not enough such events to generate reliable evidence. But, we can test whether power preponderance provides an environment conducive to peaceful pursuits by members of the European community in general.

Expected Utility, Power, and War

In contrast to a balance of power or a hegemonic stability perspective, an expected utility approach to foreign policy decisionmaking does not restrict national goals to the quest for power or the pursuit of domination over the international system. Power is not ignored in an expected utility calculation; it is a critical aspect of any nation's prospects for success or failure in pursuit of its objectives. However, power is not thought to be synonymous with foreign policy objectives. Value, or utility, may be attached to any number of goals. Allowing for multiple sources of utility avoids the limitations implied by the preceding discussion.

What might motivate warlike behavior among expected utility maximizing decisionmakers? In answering this question we hope to highlight the differences in predictions from this and the balance of power or power preponderance perspective. To begin to answer this inquiry, it is necessary that we explicitly set out our assumptions. From these assumptions we derive hypotheses that can be tested against the predictions of balance of power and power preponderance theorists.

Assume that decisionmakers are rational in the sense that they do what they *believe* is in their best interest. Assume therefore that they calculate the expected utility associated with challenging and not challenging a putative adversary. For those in a threatening situation, assume the probability they will escalate their effort to achieve their objectives increases as a strictly monotonic function of their expected utility. More precisely, assume that decisionmakers face incomplete information, which leads them to feel uncertain about their expected utility estimates. Assume that they view errors as stochastic around some known mean. Then, the more their expected utility estimate deviates from zero, the more confident they can be that the sign of the estimate—indicating which strategy is preferred—is correct. This is equivalent to the assumption of monotonicity with respect to the selection of the strategy to use force or not to use force. That is, the more they believe they stand to gain, the more likely they are to use force in pursuit of their objectives.

Figure 10.1 depicts a coordinate space in which two decisionmakers' expected utilities are displayed. The point denoting the intersection of these two values is defined in terms of its distance from the origin (r) and its angle from the horizontal axis (θ)

The conjunction of choices to use or not to use force by two rival nations, i and j, defines four possible outcomes of a dispute: war, military intervention by i, military intervention by j, and the peaceful resolution of a dispute. As noted above, the probability that an actor will choose to use force in pursuit of national interests is assumed to be a monotonic function of its own expected utility. The ex ante probability that a conflict of interest will be resolved in each of the four identified ways is:

(i) $P(\text{war}) = P^i(F_i)P^j(F_j)$;
(ii) $P(\text{intervention by } i) = [P^i(F_i)(1-P^j(F_j))]$;
(iii) $P(\text{intervention by } j) = [P^j(F_j)(1-P^i(F_i))]$;
(iv) $P(\text{peaceful resolution}) = [1-P^i(F_i)][1-P^j(F_j)]$.

A fifth condition can be defined by combining all violent categories. The probability of this category is the sum of probabilities (i)–(iii):

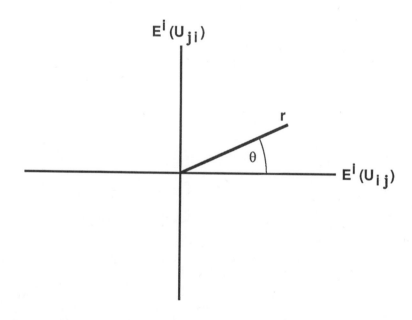

Figure 10.1

(v) P(violence) = 1 - P(peaceful resolution)

= P(war) + P(intervention by i) + P(intervention by j).

Condition (i) says that the probability of war, P(war), is equal to the product of the probability that i escalates its threat against j to the point of force, $P^i(F_i)$, and j also escalates its threat against i to the point of force, $P^j(F_j)$. The interpretations of the other equations are analogous.

The probability that nations i or j will use force may be restated in terms of polar coordinates as $P^i(F_i) = f(r \cos \theta)$ and $P^j(F_j) = g(r \sin \theta)$, respectively, where f and g are monotonic functions. Figure 10.2 displays the functional forms of the probability of the use of force by nations i and j for a fixed vector length r (Bueno de Mesquita and Lalman, 1986; Lalman, 1988).

It is evident from Figure 10.2 that two points exist in which expectations about the consequences of challenging an adversary (and its coalition of supporters) are balanced. From condition (i) we see that the probability of war is relatively high in the area that surrounds and includes the point marked A in Figure 10.2 because the probability of using force is

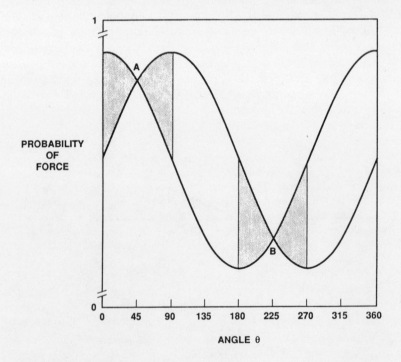

Figure 10.2

high for both nation i and nation j. In the area that surrounds and includes the point marked B, the probability of war is lower.

The shaded areas around points A and B also depict two "power transitions" in which one hegemon is surpassed by another. These two transitions are accompanied by a high and a low probability of war, respectively. The empirical attention of those supporting a balance of power perspective seems focused on situations typified by the area around point B. Power preponderance theorists draw attention to situations characterized by the shaded area surrounding point A, in which nation j equals and then overtakes nation i, while failing to note such circumstances in the neighborhood of point B in which balanced expectations lead to peace. Balance of power and power transition theorists do not differentiate between these two scenarios under which balance has different implications. The expected utility framework makes these distinctions, thereby differentiating between situations when "preponderance" or "balance" encourages peace or war.

An important insight provided by Figure 10.2 is that the probability of war does not follow from any particular distribution of power. Many "realist" theorists assume that if both sides have the same expectations, each side's probability of victory is .5, thereby confusing the probabilities of victory with the expectations of gain.

History is replete with examples of risky decisions made in a manner consistent with the requirements of expected utility theory, but not necessarily consonant with the expectations of power-centered theories. An example of the tendency for decisionmakers to pursue intensely held objectives even when their prospects of success are slim is found in the decisions leading to the outbreak of World War I. Charles Maier (1988, pp. 6–15), commenting on the Schlieffen Plan, writes:

> if the Schlieffen Plan were carried out . . . as a way of avoiding early defeat in a two-front war, then it was a risky but rational tactic. . . . Whether or not Moltke was sanguine about prospects in 1914, he certainly felt that the Schlieffen Plan was the only possible wager. . . . Why, it is sometimes asked, did [the Germans] not negotiate an end to the war and go home? . . . The Germans enjoyed present domination, which they were loath to sacrifice; the allies could hope for future recovery.

Here we have a succinct description of a series of choices, each rational, *given what was known to the decisionmakers at the time*, and yet leading to horrendous consequences. Why did negotiation fail for so long? Because, according to Maier's argument, the German's held significant gains (utility), which, despite the danger of eventual defeat, they could sustain in the short term. Similarly, the allies were loath to negotiate because they suffered significant losses which they believed could be reversed (high utility) in the long run because their prospects of eventual victory were high. Maier's evaluation is an informal expected utility analysis showing us how choices for war can be made rationally despite poor prospects of victory. We see here how the logic of power-based theories, in not accounting for the value of outcomes other than the quest for power, fail to explain the behavior of leaders faced with war or peace choices.

As these illustrations remind us, for any probability of success (and therefore for any level of relative power), there is a set of possible utility values such that waging war is preferred to not waging war *or* such that the opposite is true (Hussein, 1987). Power by itself is neither necessary nor sufficient for a rational, *realist* leader to choose war over peace. This insight, whether derived from expected utility theory or from historical analysis, helps make sense of many seemingly anomalous behaviors. Expected utility analysis always brings this feature to the investigator's attention by forcing the analyst to look at the situation, not with hindsight, but through the decisionmaker's eyes.

The discussion of Figure 10.2 suggests several possible empirical tests of the efficacy of a balance of power or power preponderance perspective compared to that of the expected utility framework. If, as suggested in Figure 10.2, "balance" can occur with either a high or a low probability of war, then the frequency with which disputes become wars should be high in the region for which the probability of war function [condition (i)] is high and should be low in the region where that function yields a low expectation of war. The actual power differential between adversaries in those same regions should be unrelated to the likelihood of war.

Operationalization

To test the empirical claims made here, it is necessary to estimate the balance of forces, the expected utilities of the adversaries, and the probability of war. We describe briefly the estimation procedure here, referring the reader to other studies for more detailed explications of the measurement approach (Bueno de Mesquita, 1981, 1985; Bueno de Mesquita and Lalman, 1986).

National power is measured as the annual composite capability score developed by the Correlates of War Project for each nation in a conflicting dyad (Singer et al., 1972). This variable is converted into an assessment of the degree of balance between the adversaries as follows: Balance = |(power of nation *i*) - (power of nation *j*)|. As the power of the two adversaries approaches equality, this variable approaches its minimum value of zero and as the difference gets larger, the variable indicates relative preponderance. This variable captures a balance of power perspective suggested by Henry Kissinger (1979, p. 195) when he wrote: "Throughout history the political influence of nations has been roughly correlative to their military power. . . .

In the final reckoning weakness has invariably tempted aggression and impotence brings abdication of policy in its train. . . . The balance of power . . . has in fact been the precondition of peace." Still, it is only one narrow slice of that complex theory. Elsewhere, we test other aspects of balance of power and other theories using a systemic and a coalitional, rather than dyadic, approach.

We construct one systemic variable, called preponderance, to test the argument that the existence of a hegemonic power provides insurance for lesser states against the threat of war. Preponderance is measured as the concentration of power among the major powers, with that group defined according to Singer and Small (1972). The concentration measure (Singer et al., 1972; Ray and Singer, 1973) is calculated using the Correlates of War Project's annual composite capabilities data.

As noted in condition (i), the probability of war is stipulated to be the product of monotonic functions of the expected utilities of rival states. To operationalize the probability of war then, it is first necessary to estimate the expected utilities.

Let us assume that the leader of nation i chooses between challenging some nation j, with the intention of convincing j to alter its policies to be more in line with those desired by i, and not challenging j, leaving j's policies to unfold in whatever manner they are expected to unfold in the absence of pressure from i.

If i chooses not to challenge j, then one of three contingencies may arise. First, i may anticipate that with some probability (Q^i), j will not alter its current policies over the time period of concern to i, and so i will derive whatever utility it receives from the preservation of the status quo between itself and j (U^i_{sq}). Alternatively, i may anticipate that j's policies will change, in which case there is some probability (T) that, from i's perspective, the policies of j are anticipated to improve (with U^i_{bi} being the associated utility) or to get worse (U^i_{wi}). When i contemplates challenging j, on the other hand, i must take into consideration the probability that j will not simply give in to i's policy demands (S_j), the likelihood that i will succeed in its efforts to enforce its demands (P_i), and the utility associated with success (U^i_{si}) and with failure (U^i_{fi}) in those efforts. The overall calculus of expected utility is then

$$E^i(U_{ij}) = E^i(U_{ij})_c - E^i(U_{ij})_{nc}, \qquad (5)$$

where the expected utility from challenging j equals

$$E^i(U_{ij})_c = S_j[P^i{}_i(U^i{}_{si}) + (1-P^i{}_i)(U^i{}_{fi})] + (1-S_j)(U^i{}_{si}) \qquad (6)$$

and the expected utility from not challenging j equals

$$E^i(U_{ij})_{nc} = Q(U^i{}_{sq}) + (1-Q)[T(U^i{}_{bi}) + (1-T)(U^i{}_{wi})]. \tag{7}$$

Of course, j calculates a comparable equation that reflects j's view of the relative merits of challenging or not challenging i.

The utility terms are estimated as a function of similarities in formal military alliance commitments (Small and Singer, 1969), so that nations whose portfolios of commitments are alike are viewed as having high utility for one another's policies, and those with sharply dissimilar alliance profiles are viewed as holding low utility for one another's policies. The exact method for estimating the utilities of success, failure, and the status quo is described fully by Bruce Bueno de Mesquita (1985). The utilities associated with anticipated changes in j's policies in the absence of a challenge by i are estimated in accordance with the method described in Bueno de Mesquita and Lalman (1986) and Lalman (1988).

The probability of success is estimated as a proportion of the capabilities expected to be available to side i relative to all the capabilities estimated to be available in the ensuing conflict. Nations i and j are assumed to be prepared to commit all of their capabilities to the dispute, while third parties are assumed to make their capabilities available proportionate to the intensity of their preference for victory by side i or side j. For a precise description of the estimation procedure see Bueno de Mesquita and Lalman (1986).

The likelihood of resistance to i's demands (S_j) is assumed, for convenience, to equal 1.0. In a subsequent study we hope to be able to relax this restriction. The probability that i anticipates the continuation of the status quo is assumed to equal .5, indicating that i is maximally uncertain about the future state of relations with j in the absence of a challenge from i.

When the expected utilities are estimated according to this method, the result lies in the range of -3 to +3. Recall that we have assumed that the probability that an actor chooses to use force is a monotonic function of its own expected utility. Therefore, the function must map expected utility values into the [0, +1] interval. We posit linear functions that are identical for both i and j and transform the respective expected utility values according to $P^i(F_i) = [3 + E^i(U_{ij})]/6$ and $P^j(F_j) = [3 + E^j(U_{ji})]/6$. From these two equations we can estimate directly the conditions specified by expressions (i)–(v). We define, for instance, the variable $P(\text{war})$ as the product of these two terms, $P(\text{war}) = P^i(F_i)P^j(F_j)$.

The dependent variable for our analysis, called WAR, is dichotomous. To specify this variable we use a modified version of the European conflict data set developed by Charles Gochman and Zeev Maoz (1984). The subset of their data that we use consists of all dyadic disputes in Europe between 1816 and 1965. The data include wars as specified by Singer and Small (1972), as well as a variety of other conflictual events. We modify the Gochman–Maoz coding slightly to bring it more in line with our theoretical purposes. We distinguish between nations engaging in warfare as initiators or opponents from those "jumping on the bandwagon" of one or the other side. Thus, we code the variable WAR as one for those nation dyads that Singer and Small (1972) specify as including an initiator and an opponent in war, subject to the constraint that to be such nations, the states must have entered the war within 1 week of its inception. Those disputes not meeting these conditions are coded as zero. The Singer–Small wars, combined with other Gochman–Maoz events yields 467 disputes in Europe.

Evidence

In our first test, we define the regions around which expectations are fairly balanced by selecting only those cases for which both nation i and nation j believed, according to our estimates, that they stood to gain from conflict, or that they both believed they stood to lose. Thus, we are selecting the subset of all cases that fall within quadrants 1 or 3 of Figure 10.1 in which the expected utility values for nations i and j are both positive or both negative. By doing so, we are focusing attention on the regions around points A and B from Figure 10.2 in which expectations are balanced, yet the probability of war is highly variable.

The first test is whether the likelihood of a dispute becoming a war is greater in quadrant 1, where both disputants expect to gain more than they anticipate losing, than it is in quadrant 3, where the disputants expect net losses. Eleven of the sixty-two events that satisfied the expected utility conditions of quadrant 1 became wars. And five of the fifty-seven disputes that fall in quadrant 3 became wars. The difference in these proportions is sufficiently large that it would have arisen by chance fewer than eight times in one hundred samples ($z = 1.43$). This first test examines our hypothesis in a weak manner since it does not take advantage of full information about how close each event is to point A or B in Figure 10.2. This weak test provides only partial support for our claim that situations in the area around point A of Figure 10.2 have a higher probability of war than do events occurring in the region surrounding point B.

The second test focuses on whether a balance of power or a balance of expectations is more successful at sorting out events that became wars from those that did not in quadrants 1 and 3. Here we take full advantage of all the information available to us regarding the precise location of events within quadrants 1 and 3. We undertake probit analysis with two independent variables—balance and $P(\text{war})$—and with WAR as the dependent variable. For this test there are 119 observations, consisting of the sixty-two events in quadrant 1 plus the fifty-seven disputes in quadrant 3. The estimated model results are

$$\text{war} = -1.96 + \quad 2.36\,P(\text{war}) + \quad 2.16\,\text{balance}$$
$$\phantom{\text{war} = } (.47) \quad (1.20) \qquad\quad (3.33)$$

As the standard errors indicated in parentheses show, the balance of power coefficient is *not* significantly different from zero. The $P(\text{war})$ coefficient compared to the standard error of its estimate indicates that the variable has a statistically significant effect at the .05 level and in the direction predicted by the theory.

To compare the performance of the two theoretical approaches of balance of power and expected utility in their ability to categorize correctly a broader set of past events, we include the events that fell into quadrants 2 and 4 as well. This test incorporates all 467 European disputes. Again probit analysis is applied to the same estimation model. The model and estimates are:

$$\text{war} = -1.66 + \quad 1.93\,P(\text{war}) - \quad 0.55\,\text{balance}$$
$$\phantom{\text{war} = } (.29) \quad (.94) \qquad\quad (1.37)$$

The inclusion of all events does not disturb either the direction or the significance of the effect of $P(\text{war})$, indicating its general usefulness. However, the balance variable is still statistically insignificant and the apparent direction of the relationship is reversed from the earlier test.

Now we turn to the test of the hypothesis that the presence of a power preponderance in the system reduces the likelihood of war for all states. For the 439 cases for which we have complete data on power concentration, the probit analysis of the model specification reveals that

$$\text{war} = -1.36 + \quad 2.63\,P(\text{war}) - \quad 1.66\,\text{preponderance}$$
$$\phantom{\text{war} = } (.40) \quad (1.03) \qquad\quad (1.28)$$

As with the previous analyses, $P(\text{war})$ is significantly associated with the dependent variable ($p < .01$) and in the direction predicted by the theory. Preponderance, however, is not significantly related to the likelihood of war, although the sign of the coefficient is in the direction expected by power preponderance theorists.

Conclusion

We set out a theoretical argument that shows that a balance of power or power preponderance can be accompanied by a high or a low probability of war. This claim stands in contrast to the many power-based theories that suggest that war is made less likely by one or another distribution of power. Our claim is that the probability of war is a monotonically increasing function of the expectation of gains by adversaries. Important characteristics of that function were derived theoretically, including when balance (or preponderance) of expectations heightens or diminishes the prospects for peace.

The theoretical discussion led to the specification of testable propositions that gave balance of power, power preponderance, and expected utility approaches an opportunity to distinguish situations likely to become wars from those likely to be resolved at a lesser level of violence. Each hypothesis was tested against a large number of European disputes in the post-Napoleonic era not previously used in investigations of an expected utility framework. Each test bore out the expectations from our theoretical perspective, while failing to corroborate the hypotheses of either the balance of power or power preponderance theories.

Our tests of power-based theories are limited, as are the tests of our own theory. Therefore, our empirical results should be viewed as tentative. The theoretical arguments, however, are less tentative and do lead to the conclusion that theories that rely exclusively on considerations of power are incomplete. On the basis of one set of empirical findings we are not prepared to reject power-based views. We are prepared to claim that an understanding of war and peace must include a decisionmaker oriented element based on a broader concept of national interests. Systemic or dyadic structures may constrain national behavior, but that behavior seems more firmly controlled by the states that engage in it than by the environmental circumstances within which nations exist. This observation should encourage caution among those who would formulate foreign policy on the basis of changes in the so-called balance of power. Our tentative conclusion is that policies intended to promote or restore peace should be grounded in considerations of individual national welfare and not merely considerations of structural change.

11

The Impact of Nuclear Weapons on Crisis Bargaining: Implications of a Spatial Model

T. Clifton Morgan and James Lee Ray

One of the unsolved debates in the international relations literature concerns whether modern weaponry has brought about a dramatic change in the power relationships among states by making war "unusable" as an instrument of policy or has brought about only an increase in the destructive power of states but no major changes in state behavior. Nuclear weapons, especially when joined to intercontinental ballistic missiles, constitute a military innovation with such destructive power that it might seem obvious that they make international war less likely. If there is even a modicum of rationality in the process leading to war, the destructive potential of modern weapons should make decisionmakers significantly less likely to become involved in war if there is any probability that nuclear weapons would be used. In fact, several theorists have argued that nuclear weapons reduce the probability that international conflicts will escalate to war. Michael Intriligator and Dagobert L. Brito (1984) have argued formally that the rapid accumulation of nuclear weapons has had a stabilizing impact on relationships between the superpowers and there have been a number of arguments suggesting that nuclear proliferation will make wars less likely in those Third World regions in which it occurs (Bueno de Mesquita and Riker, 1982; Feldman, 1982; Waltz, 1982). In addition, a number of empirical studies have provided evidence to support these contentions. Melvin Small and J. David Singer (1979) and Richard J. Stoll (1982) have noted that the percentage of conflicts between states possessing nuclear weapons that have escalated to war (that percentage has been zero) has been significantly smaller than might be expected on the basis of experience in the prenuclear age. Furthermore, Erich Weede (1983) has pointed out that even formal allies of the United States and the Soviet Union, presumably protected by the extended deterrence of the superpowers, have not become involved in wars or even low-level military conflicts, and James Lee Ray (1986) shows that no wars have occurred between the allies of any two nuclear weapons states not allied to each other.

On the other hand, A. F. K. Organski and Jacek Kugler (1980) and Kugler (1984) insist, and provide some supporting evidence, that nuclear weapons have had neither a sobering effect on their possessors nor a deterring effect on the enemies of their possessors. Charles S. Gochman and Zeev Maoz (1984) report that the introduction of nuclear weapons has not resulted in a reduction in the number of disputes, that major powers (possessing nuclear weapons) have been involved in a higher proportion of interstate disputes during the nuclear era than in any other time period since the Napoleonic Wars, and that "the increasing destructiveness of modern weapons" does not "seem to have altered the willingness of states to enter ongoing conflicts." Furthermore, Stoll (1988) suggests that while no disputes between states possessing nuclear weapons have escalated to war, this is well within the realm of statistical probability given the number of disputes that have occurred. Another relevant finding is presented in the work of Paul Huth and Bruce Russett (1984, 1988) who show that the impact nuclear weapons have on deterrence efforts is marginal, particularly when compared to that of other variables.

Thus, the impact of nuclear weapons on the occurrence of international conflict is not as obvious as it would first appear. There exists no theoretical consensus regarding whether the incidence of conflict should be lesser or greater than in the prenuclear era and the empirical results are contradictory. We cannot be certain whether or not modern weaponry has fundamentally altered the nature of power relationships in the international system by making their possessors essentially "equal" in military power, regardless of their other attributes. The possibility remains open that nuclear weapons have had relatively little impact on international politics and that their inhibiting effect on conflict behavior is, at most, minor.

There are many possible reasons for the apparently contradictory conclusions regarding the impact of nuclear weapons and a number of these have been discussed in some detail by James Lee Ray (1986) in a previous paper. One reason may be that most of these studies have tested hypotheses that have not been derived from a fully specified theory. It has often been assumed that the relationship between the existence of nuclear weapons and the occurrence of war should be simple and straightforward. This assumption has led to a body of empirical research that has sought to uncover simple, usually bivariate relationships,[1] and the results of these studies have generally been weak and ambiguous, as well as contradictory. As Benjamin A. Most and Harvey Starr (1984) have argued, a body of contradictory results may be reconciled by a fully specified theory that could lead us to expect that simple, bivariate relationships would be weak and/or context dependent. Since the empirical research to date has not considered a number of factors—such as the resolve of the parties in disputes or the major power status of most possessors of nuclear weapons—that could affect the relationship between nuclear weapons and the occurrence of war, it is possible that a theory including these variables would lead us to expect a context-dependent relationship that could account for the contradictory findings.

A Spatial Model of Crisis Bargaining

The spatial model of crisis bargaining recently proposed by T. Clifton Morgan (1984, 1986, 1987) may serve as the basis for such a theory. The model, which represents a synthesis of traditional utility-based bargaining theory (Nash, 1950; Pen, 1952; Zeuthen, 1968) and the spatial theory of voting (Enelow and Hinich, 1984), has been developed with a slightly different research question in mind; but it is generally applicable to a wide range of conflict processes. Thus, with only slight conceptual modifications, the model can be used to derive hypotheses linking the presence of nuclear weapons with the probability that a conflict will escalate to war. Although this is more of a "midrange theory" than a "grand theory" of international politics, it does incorporate a number of important variables, it does specify the relationships and complex interactions among these variables, and it does lead to some rather surprising, counterintuitive results. Because it leads us to expect that the nuclear weapons/war relationship should be dependent on other variables, it has the potential, at least, to account for the ambiguous and contradictory results provided by earlier research.

Since the model has been described in detail elsewhere (Morgan, 1984, 1986, 1987), this presentation is brief, highlighting only those features particularly important for the topic at hand and the necessary reconceptualizations. The two main components of the model are an issue space and a utility space. Conflict situations are represented in an m-dimensional space where each axis is associated with one of the issues under dispute and each point on a dimension represents a possible outcome on the relevant issue. Each participant is located in the issue space by an ideal point, the coordinates of which represent the participant's initial bargaining position on the issues at stake. An actor's preferences over the outcomes in the issue space are associated with the distances between each possible outcome and the actor's ideal point[2] and, by assuming the actors' preferences can be represented by von Neumann–Morgenstern utility functions, the utility space can be derived from the issue space. The issue space provides the basis for much of the analysis that can be done with this model (see Morgan, 1988a, 1988b) and serves as the linkage between the concrete issues over which disputes occur and the rather abstract utility space; however, the analysis that follows focuses exclusively on the utility space. Although actual bargaining occurs over the issues at stake, the decisions of whether to accept a proposal, begin a war, increase the costs imposed on the opponent, and so on will be made on the basis of how much benefit is expected from each option. These decisions are the focus of this chapter and the analysis of these decisions is much simpler in the utility space.

To simplify the presentation of the utility space, the discussion focuses on a specific example, depicted in Figure 11.1. Two assumptions that serve to facilitate the presentation of the model are adopted. First, we assume the situation regarding the issue(s) in dispute is zero-sum.[3] This involves some loss in generality, but the presentation is greatly simplified (e.g., without this assumption, the pictorial representation requires at least three dimensions). Note, however, that the model does not require this assumption (see Morgan, 1986, 1988a). Second, we assume a single substantive issue and that the possible outcomes on the issue map one-to-one to utility. This assumption imposes no further restrictions on the generality of the results and prevents us from totally ignoring the issue dimension aspect of the model. This will serve to clarify the presentation by allowing the use of a specific example that will facilitate an intuitive understanding of the ideas expressed. It should be kept in mind that the conclusions derived are in no way dependent on this assumption or on the specifics of the example.

Figure 11.1 depicts a dispute between two actors, i and j, that is represented on the single dimension, Π. Suppose that the issue involved concerns a region of territory that j wants to control. This may be a section of i that i wishes to retain or an independent area that i wants to keep from j. The points, π, on Π represent possible outcomes on the issue, ranging from j controls none of the territory in question to j controlling all of the territory. The actors' initial positions are denoted by O_i and O_j, and we assume that as j acquires a larger portion of the territory, j attains greater utility and i attains less. At any point in time, an actor can choose from a number of options: it can initiate a war; it can end the crisis by accepting the last proposal, π, offered by the opponent (perhaps the opponent's O); it can make concessions by offering a π closer to the opponent's O; or it can do nothing and wait for some movement by the opponent.

It is assumed that for any π the probability that both i and j would choose π over war can be determined and that a joint probability distribution of Π can be derived that can be used to determine the probability that war would occur. A participant's willingness to move toward its opponent in the issue space is assumed to be a function of (1) the loss of utility associated with such a move, which is characterized by the participant's loss function defined over the issue space and incorporates the actor's risk orientation; (2) the participant's resolve; (3) the probability of winning a war should one occur; and (4) the costs involved in failing to agree.[4]

In this example the utility loss function is assumed to be linear. This

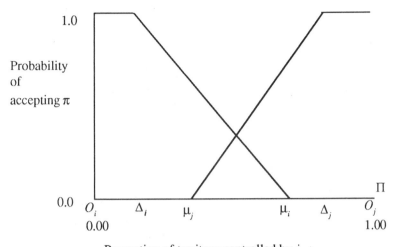

Figure 11.1 A Utility Space Representation of Crisis Bargaining

breaks somewhat from the fairly common practice of assuming a quadratic loss function (Hinich and Ordeshook, 1970; Enelow, 1984) but can be justified on the grounds that it facilitates this analysis with few costs. In fact, the loss function can take any monotonically decreasing shape and is usually taken to be quadratic in order to represent the actors as being risk averse. Linear loss functions make the calculations much simpler and will make it much easier to visualize the effects of the variables with which we are most concerned and are therefore used.

Two points on each actor's probability of acceptance function that are of particular importance are the upper and lower bounds for whether a π will be accepted. First, there exists some point up to which the utility loss is so minimal that π would be accepted with certainty. We can assume that a player's O would definitely be accepted and, since the prospect of nuclear war raises the fear of suffering horrible costs, it is further assumed that this upper bound might be adjusted downward to reflect a willingness to make some concessions to avoid the prospect of suffering these costs. The points providing i and j the least utility each would accept with certainty, represented by Δ_i and Δ_j, can be used to reflect changes in the players' ability to impose bargaining costs on one another—as j increases the costs it can impose on i, Δ_i will move farther from O_i. It is also assumed that there exists some point at which the utility loss is so great that the participant would definitely choose war over π. This reservation point (labeled μ_i or μ_j) establishes the lower bound of the probability that π will be accepted; any π

on or to the right of μ_i, for example, would be accepted by i with a probability of 0.0. We assume that a player's lower bound is limited at the proposal that has utility equal to the expected utility of war but that it may shift toward O as the player's resolve increases. That is, as a player's resolve increases, he will prefer war to an increasing number of proposals which, in purely strategic terms, would provide greater value than could be expected from war. Note also that when one of the μ or Δ parameters is altered, the entire probability of acceptance function is affected. If, for example, one actor's resolve increases and its μ shifts away from its O, the probability of acceptance is lowered for every π in $[\mu, \Delta)$.

Two points regarding this formulation should be made. First, note that the model is fully general with respect to the location of the μ's and Δ's. For example, setting $O_i = \Delta_i = \mu_i$ would indicate that i is irrevocably committed to either receiving O_i or going to war. Second, it is important to understand the assumption made here regarding the bargaining set (i.e., the interval $[\mu_j, \mu_i]$). In many bargaining theories it is assumed that a nonempty bargaining set (μ_j is to the left of μ_i) is necessary and sufficient to ensure a negotiated settlement. We have followed Frederick Zeuthen (1968) and assumed that a nonempty bargaining set is necessary for a settlement but that it is not sufficient. Obviously, if the set is empty, there is at least one party that prefers war to every π, so settlement requires a nonempty bargaining set. Since we do not assume that the parties are fully informed as to the location of each others' reservation points, a nonempty set does not guarantee a settlement. An actor may reject a proposal that is preferred to war in the hopes of achieving an even better deal. This may induce the opponent to believe that the bargaining set is empty and it may initiate a war, particularly if it believes there is some advantage to striking first.

The final factor that is assumed to determine the probability of a π being accepted by a player is the probability that it will win a war.[5] The justification for this is straightforward. Within a bargaining situation the party with the greatest power (here defined as likelihood of winning a war) should be less willing to make concessions, all other things being equal. Thus, the probability that i (or j) will accept some π is a function of i's utility for π; but the shape of this function is partially determined by i's chances of prevailing in war should negotiations fail. In the example shown in Figure 11.1 the linear probability of acceptance functions represent a case in which i and j are equally likely to win a war between them. The functions can take any shape that is monotonically decreasing (from Δ and μ) and other shapes are used to represent cases in which one party is more likely to win a war. In particular, an actor likely to win a war should be less likely to accept any given proposal, so its probability of acceptance function will be convex with respect to its O while the function for its opponent, who should be more willing to accept any given proposal, will be concave with respect to its O.

The bargaining model proposed here is constructed in such a way as to provide a probability distribution over all possible outcomes. We can thus determine the probability that any given proposal would be accepted by both parties and, more importantly for the purpose at hand, we can determine the probability that war will result. The most reasonable point to treat as the "solution" to the bargaining problem is that point within the range of possible negotiated outcomes that maximizes the joint probability of being accepted.[6] This is determined as follows: We have for each actor a function, $p_i(\pi)$, that provides the probability that each π would be accepted. The "solution" is the π' that maximizes the derivative of the product of these functions, evaluated within the interval $[\mu_j, \mu_i]$. Mathematically, μ' is the proposal that satisfies

$$\left(p_i(\pi)\,\frac{\partial p_{ij}(\pi)}{\partial \pi}\right) + \left(p_j(\pi)\,\frac{\partial p_i(\pi)}{\partial \pi}\right) = 0 \tag{1}$$

The second task of the model is to determine the probability that some negotiated settlement will be reached (i.e., that war will be avoided). For a given π, the value of $p_i(\pi)$ and $p_j(\pi)$ can be interpreted as being the probability that the lowest π that i or j would accept is π or some π that provides less utility. Thus, the probability functions can be seen as determining the cumulative probability distributions, which can be used to calculate the corresponding probability density functions. The probability that war will be avoided is determined by the product of the proportions. The probability that war will be avoided is determined by the product of the proportions of the p.d.f.s that are with the interval $[\mu_j, \mu_i]$. Mathematically,

$$p(\text{war}) = 1 - \left(\frac{\displaystyle\int_{\mu_i}^{\mu'} p_i{}'(\pi)}{\displaystyle\int_{\mu_i}^{\mu_i} p_i{}'(\pi)} \quad \frac{\displaystyle\int_{\mu_j}^{\mu'} p_j{}'(\pi)}{\displaystyle\int_{\mu_j}^{\mu_j} p_j{}'(\pi)} \right). \tag{2}$$

We can use Equations (1) and (2) to derive hypotheses relating the conditions in which a dispute occurs to the predicted outcome of the dispute. Equation (1) can be used to show how variations in the variables included in the model alter the most likely negotiated settlement, while Equation (2) can be used to show how these variations affect the probability that war will result. In order to use this model as the basis for a theory accounting for the impact of nuclear weapons on dispute outcomes, it is first necessary to determine which of the variables included in the model is dependent on the presence or absence of nuclear weapons.

Here, we associate nuclear weapons with the costs of engaging in conflict. When one party to a dispute possesses nuclear weapons, that is seen as increasing the potential costs for that party's opponent. Two important points must be made concerning this treatment. First, we are assuming it is not necessary for the weapons to be used for their impact to be felt. Rather, we are assuming that the potential costs of a war enter into each side's calculations regarding whether to fight or not and that the presence of nuclear weapons, by making a war potentially much more destructive, increase the likely costs for the opponent of their possessor.

Second, it is not necessary to assume that the variables included in this model are entirely independent. Thus, even though nuclear weapons may (and probably do) affect the actors' resolve and the probabilities of winning a war, and even though other factors affect the ability of the disputants to impose costs on one another, ignoring this will not seriously affect the theoretical results. All that is necessary to assume is that the majority of the impact of nuclear weapons will be felt through the cost factor. Obviously, the enormous destructive power of these weapons does increase the potential costs of any war in which they may be used. In addition, their impact on the other variables is not as strong or direct as it first appears. The resolve variable is not defined as a general willingness to go to war—it is intended to capture a party's unwillingness to lose on the issues at stake. This may be borne, for example, of a concern with losing face or of a concern with domestic politics. While an actor's resolve may be affected by military realities, these do not primarily determine it. Although a party's resolve may be overridden by some other consideration (such as the costs of war), this does not imply that the resolve was actually absent or weakened by the other factor.

It might seem also that nuclear weapons should have a strong effect on the probability of winning. In fact, this has probably not been the case. As Kugler (1984) points out, the states that have acquired nuclear weapons have been those already relatively powerful in terms of other types of capabilities. Thus, in those disputes in which nuclear-capable states were involved, the existence of the nuclear weapons probably affected the participants' probabilities of winning very little. At most, the effect would be to increase marginally the probability of winning for the side already superior.

Given this conceptualization, our concern with determining the effect nuclear weapons have on dispute outcomes can be approached theoretically by determining how changes in the costs of a dispute for an actor affect the probability distributions over dispute outcomes. Formally, we are interested in determining how changes in Δ_j and Δ_i (which will reflect the increased costs associated with the introduction of nuclear weapons) will alter the probability distribution of dispute outcomes. In particular, we are interested in using Equation (2) to show how changes in the Δ's affect the probability of war. Since a major presumption of this study is that the relationship between the presence of nuclear weapons and the occurrence of war is dependent on the values of other variables, we are also concerned with how the relationship is affected by changes in the μ's and the shapes of the probability of acceptance functions.

The formal, general derivations of these results are quite lengthy so we restrict this discussion to a brief outline of the logic behind the derivations and a presentation of the hypotheses derived. Readers interested in the formal derivations can refer to Morgan (1986, 1987). Since we are primarily interested in the effect of nuclear weapons on the probability of war, we focus on Equation (2) for a discussion of the general logic behind the derivation of the results. Keep in mind that the model provides a probability distribution over all possible outcomes to a dispute. This distribution is actually a joint probability distribution that, for any possible negotiated settlement, provides the probability that all actors would accept the outcome rather than resort to war. We can thus determine the total probability that some negotiated settlement will be reached and, by subtracting this from 1.0, we can determine the probability of war. Essentially, this is what Equation (2) does.

The term within the parentheses in Equation (2) is the probability that some negotiated settlement will be reached. Let us consider the components of this term. There is one component of the term for each actor involved in the dispute. For each actor we are determining the total probability that it would accept some settlement within the bargaining set. The denominator of an actor's component provides the total area under that actor's p.d.f., that is, the "unit" by which the actor's probability is measured. The numerator is the area under the actor's p.d.f. that is within the bargaining set. The ratio thus provides the probability that the actor would accept some possible negotiated agreement. The product of these ratios then represents the joint probability of avoiding war.

Our analytical task is to determine how changes in the parameters of the model affect this probability. Since the range and shape of the players' probability of acceptance functions are determined by these parameters, we can see how changes in our key variables should affect the likelihood of war. For example, if increases in the costs that j can impose on i cause (only) an increased proportion of i's p.d.f. to be within the bargaining set, we can conclude that j's having nuclear weapons would decrease the chances of war.

Before examining how nuclear weapons affect the probability that a dispute will escalate to war, we briefly discuss how they should affect π', the most likely negotiated settlement. For the purposes of this analysis, we can hold both players' resolve at any level, provided that the bargaining set is not empty, because variations in resolve do not affect the relationship between the costs of the dispute and the most likely negotiated settlement. First consider cases in which the parties are equally likely to win a war between them. It has been shown (Morgan, 1986) that increasing the costs to one or both actors does not affect π'. Thus, in disputes between equals, nuclear weapons should not be a factor in deciding who "wins" the dispute. Note that this is consistent with the empirical results provided by Stoll (1988) and Huth and Russett (1984, 1988) that were mentioned above. If one party, say j, is more likely to win a war should one occur, then this factor alone suggests that j should be likely to obtain a favorable negotiated settlement if one is reached. If i were to acquire nuclear weapons, increasing its ability to impose costs on j, this would be expected to reduce j's advantage somewhat—though not entirely provided that j continues to be more likely to win a war. Surprisingly, however, if j becomes able to impose increased costs on i, that too shifts π' in i's favor, though the shift is exceedingly slight. Since it is unlikely that there have been any cases in which a state possessing nuclear weapons has been otherwise much less likely to win a war than its dispute opponent, we would expect to find that, empirically, nuclear weapons have had very little impact on negotiated dispute settlements and that any impact there has been may be against the possessors of nuclear weapons. This implication of the model is particularly interesting in that it explains the Organski–Kugler (1980) empirical result suggesting that nuclear weapons have not provided their possessors a markedly greater ability to prevail in disputes.

Turning to the question of how nuclear weapons affect the probability that a dispute will escalate to war, we can see first that when we ignore the resolve of the parties and consider cases in which both are equally likely to win a war, the independent effect of increasing the ability of one party to impose costs on the other is to lower the probability of war. Since the shape of the actor's probability of acceptance function is unchanged, changes in the range of the function brought about by a shift in Δ are reflected in both the numerator and denominator. Thus, the only impact on the probability of war will be the result of the change in the interval over which the denominator is evaluated. When we increase the costs of the dispute of an actor, the interval between Δ and μ is decreased; therefore, the interval over which the numerator is evaluated constitutes a greater proportion of the actor's p.d.f. The ratio will increase, which will decrease the probability of war.

The general nature of this result holds whatever the value of the other variables, but some interesting comparisons can be made. Consider a situation in which j is much more likely than i to win a war between them. If i's ability to impose costs on j is increased, the probability of war drops precipitously. The straightforward, intuitive explanation for this is that, in such a situation, both parties have a strong incentive to avoid war—i is reluctant to fight because it would lose, and j is reluctant because its victory would be at a high price. Since few weak states have acquired a nuclear capability, however, this conclusion is not likely to be reflected empirically. Of greater empirical interest are situations in which j's ability to impose costs on i are increased. In this case, the probability of war declines with the introduction of nuclear weapons, but the decrease is exceedingly slight. Thus, we would expect the presence of nuclear weapons to decrease the frequency with which disputes between military unequals escalate to war very little. One explanation for this may be that a state willing to fight even when faced with highly unfavorable odds is not likely to be deterred when the situation becomes even worse. When the issues at stake are sufficiently valued to fight a hopeless war, increasing the costs of the war is not likely to make much difference. This result is consistent with Stoll's (1982, pp. 597–598) findings that major power–major power disputes have been somewhat less likely to escalate to war in the post-World War II period than in the prewar period while the probability of escalation in major power–minor power disputes has remained about constant.

Finally, we can consider the effect of resolve on the nuclear weapons–war relationship. We know that the independent effect of the presence of nuclear weapons serves to decrease the probability of dispute escalation and that the independent effect of increases in one (or more) of the actor's resolve serves to increase the probability of escalation to war (Morgan, 1986). The general nature of the interaction of these variables is straightforward (i.e., there are no true interaction effects), so we cannot determine precisely whether the probability of war will go up or down without knowing the specifics of the situation. We can draw an interesting observation regarding our likely empirical findings, however. Any statistical test we perform that does not include the resolve variable must contain either the assumption that resolve is not important or the assumption that resolve is distributed randomly across the sample of cases. The former assumption is contrary to the model; the latter will probably be violated. The variables used in this model of dispute escalation are also likely to be important in decisions regarding dispute initiation. Since an actor's decision to engage in a dispute would be affected by the opponent's ability to wage war and impose costs, we might assume that higher levels of these abilities on the part of an opponent would require higher resolve and/or importance of the issues for an actor to engage in a dispute. Thus, it may be the case that states facing nuclear-capable dispute adversaries would be, on average, more resolved than would states facing nonnuclear adversaries. This would be particularly true in cases in which a minor power faces a nuclear-capable major power. Since, on average, the war-inhibiting effect of nuclear weapons might be balanced somewhat by the war-inducing effect of increased resolve, we might expect to find the dichotomous relationship between the presence of nuclear weapons and escalation to war to be weak statistically.

We can draw a number of conclusions regarding the impact of nuclear weapons on the probability that disputes will escalate to war. In general, nuclear weapons should serve as an inhibiting factor. Under even the best of circumstances, however, this inhibition should not be expected to be complete. In disputes between military equals, both of whom have little resolve or concern for the issues at stake, the possession of nuclear weapons by one or both will have the greatest impact in deterring war—but note that in such cases the probability of escalation is already quite low. At the other extreme, in cases in which a militarily overpowered but highly resolved state is facing a superpower (a situation in which the probability of war is fairly high), the possession of nuclear weapons by the superpower should have very little impact on the probability of escalation. If, on the other hand, the minor power were to acquire a nuclear capability, the probability of war should go down significantly—but we have very little empirical basis for testing this hypothesis. In short, the model suggests that the war-inhibiting impact of nuclear weapons should be relatively modest and expected to vary, according to the other characteristics of the disputing parties, and, depending on the distribution of the values of these other variables, the empirical observation of this war-inhibiting character may be masked by other factors.

Data Analysis

Thus far we have outlined the spatial model of crisis bargaining and have used this model to derive implications relating nuclear weapons to the likelihood of war. We have also pointed out that the results of a number of empirical studies are consistent with these implications. In this section we conduct a fairly simple test designed to provide further evidence regarding the expectations derived from the model. The cases to be analyzed are "militarized interstate disputes" that have occurred in the international system between 1816 and 1976. The data on these disputes have been generated by the Correlates of War Project and have been described in some detail by Gochman and Maoz (1984). A "militarized interstate dispute" is defined as a "set of interactions between or among states involving threats to use military force, displays of military force, or actual uses of military force. To be included, these acts, must be explicit, overt, nonaccidental, and government sanctioned" (Gochman and Maoz, 1984, p. 587).

We describe the hypotheses to be tested by referring to Table 11.1. We are basically interested in determining the impact of nuclear weapons on the probability that a dispute will escalate to war. The table is set up to display the impact of two factors on that probability. The first is the relative war-fighting ability of the parties. In this preliminary analysis, our index of those relative abilities is admittedly crude. We sort disputes into three categories,

Table 11.1 The Hypothesized Relationship Between Nuclear Weapons
and Dispute Escalation

Power Status	Number of Actors with Nuclear Weapons		
of Actors	None	One	Two
Major–major	#1	#2	#3
Major–minor	#4	#5	#6
Minor–minor	#7	#8	#9

that is, those between major powers, those between major powers and minor powers, and finally those between minor powers. The second factor is the degree of nuclear involvement in the dispute. Ray (1986) shows that there are a surprisingly large number of categories into which one might logically sort disputes according to the involvement of nuclear weapons, depending on whether one or both of the principal belligerents (the initiator and the target) possess nuclear weapons, whether one or both of the principal belligerents are allied to states with nuclear weapons, whether those are allied to each other, and so on. But again, for the preliminary analysis in this chapter, we rely on a simple trichotomous categorization of disputes, depending on whether none, only one, or both of the principal belligerents possess nuclear weapons. There are nine cells in Table 11.1, but since there have been no minor–minor disputes in which each belligerent possesses nuclear weapons, cell 9 is empty. (Cells 6 and 8 are almost empty, but India does provide one case for each of those cells.)

Our hypotheses regarding the impact of nuclear weapons essentially involve comparing the cells displayed in Table 11.1 according to the proportion of militarized interstate disputes falling into each that have escalated into war. The model suggests that nuclear weapons should have some inhibiting effect on war, so the proportion of cases escalating to war should decline as we move from left to right in the table; but since the inhibition is not total, there should be some crises involving nuclear powers that escalate to war. Furthermore, the model suggests that the impact of nuclear weapons should be less in crises between states unequal in military capabilities; thus, the decline should be less as we move from cell 4 to cell 5 than as we move from cell 1 to cell 2.

The results of our analyses are presented in Table 11.2. All the militarized interstate disputes were sorted into the categories depicted in Table 11.1. The cell in the upper left corner of the table, for example, contains all those disputes in which both principal belligerents were major powers, and neither possessed nuclear weapons. That cell indicates that 21.9% of those disputes, in the years from 1816 to 1976, escalated to war. The other cells contain the analogous percentage figures for the additional categories of disputes.

These results provide somewhat mixed support for the hypotheses. First,

Table 11.2   Proportion of Militarized Disputes Escalating to War, 1816–1976

Power Status of Actors	Number of Actors with Nuclear Weapons		
	None	One	Two
Major–major	.219 (73)	.200 (5)	.000 (11)
Major–minor	.107 (298)	.034 (58)	.000 (1)
Minor–minor	.078 (513)	.000 (1)	—
	(N = 960)		

Note: Cell n's are shown in parentheses.

the hypothesis that nuclear weapons should reduce the probability that a dispute will escalate to war is supported. For each row in Table 11.2, as the level of nuclear involvement increases, the proportion of cases ending in war declines. The additional hypothesis that this decline should be more modest for major–minor disputes than for major–major disputes is not supported, but the number of cases in which only one side in a major–major dispute possessed nuclear weapons is so small that the significance of the contrary evidence is debatable. In more specific terms, there are only five cases of disputes between major powers in which only one has nuclear weapons. The implication of our model is that the proportion of cases in cell 2 that escalated to war should be greater than 0.0 but significantly less than 0.22 (the proportion of cases in cell 1 that escalated to war) and that the difference between 0.22 and this proportion should be greater than the difference between the proportions in cells 4 and 5. This expectation cannot be borne out, however, with only five cases in cell 2. The empirical result would have been "closer" to our expectation had none of the cases in cell 2 escalated to war but this divergence from the hypothesized result may well be accounted for by the nature of the case that did end in war—the United States–Chinese dispute resulting in the Chinese involvement in the Korean War. Recall that we are using the major–major/major–minor distinction as a crude indicator of relative war-fighting abilities. Since the United States had much greater capabilities than did the Chinese, the classification of this case as one in which there existed power parity is probably misleading.

Conclusion

Previous research on the impact of nuclear weapons on the probability that international disputes will escalate to war has produced apparently contradictory results. Some of these apparent contradictions may have been associated with the lack of a fully specified theory on which to base the analyses. A spatial model of crisis bargaining proposed by Morgan focuses on several factors that might have a significant impact on the relationship between the presence of nuclear weapons and the likelihood of war. In this chapter, we have derived several hypotheses regarding that impact from Morgan's crisis bargaining model, we have shown how the implications of the model are consistent with a number of the earlier empirical studies, and we have tested the hypotheses in an analysis of militarized interstate disputes that occurred between 1816 and 1976.

The analyses reveal somewhat limited support for the hypotheses. However, the full potential of the model to account for the impact of nuclear weapons on conflict escalation may only be revealed if the data used in the test of the hypotheses are tailored to fit the stipulations of the model more closely. For example, our indicator of power parity is extremely crude. While the major-minor category should guarantee power disparity, the major-major and minor-minor categories do not assure power parity. In addition, the results here may suggest a need for modifications in the model, or, at least, in the way nuclear weapons have been incorporated into it. In this chapter nuclear weapons are assumed to affect crisis bargaining through their impact on the ability of the belligerents to impose costs on opponents. That impact has been measured, in effect, with a dichotomous scale. States were classified as nuclear or nonnuclear. Perhaps it will ultimately be necessary to incorporate data on the size and the range of nuclear forces. Similarly, nuclear weapons were assumed to increase a state's ability to impose costs, but no attempt was made to estimate the extent of that increase. Furthermore, it is possible that nuclear weapons had an impact on some of the disputes analyzed here because the belligerents were allied to states possessing nuclear weapons or were actively supported by states with nuclear weapons even though no alliance ties were involved. No attempt was made here to deal with such indirect nuclear involvement in serious disputes.

With these caveats in mind, we may now consider the implications of this study in regard to whether or not nuclear weapons have fundamentally altered the nature of power relationships in the international system. The model suggests that nuclear weapons should have an inhibiting effect on the occurrence of war but that this effect should not be total and that under certain conditions the effect would be exceedingly slight. These conclusions do seem to receive some empirical support and, in fact, can account for some apparent contradictions in the empirical literature. For example, the results of the test conducted here, indicating that the likelihood of a dispute escalating to war decreases as nuclear involvement increases, and of the tests conducted by Stoll (1988) and Huth and Russett (1984, 1988), which indicate that nuclear weapons are relatively unimportant in determining the effectiveness of the use of force by the United States and in assuring the success of extended deterrence, are all consistent with the implications of the model. This would seem to suggest that nuclear weapons represent a change in degree, not a change in kind. Power relationships in the international system function much the same as they did in the prenuclear era. States remain willing to use war as an instrument of policy and remain prepared to risk devastation to protect perceived vital interests. The fact that the potential costs of war have increased dramatically does not seem to have altered this aspect of state behavior, although it does seem to have reduced somewhat the number of issues that are sufficiently "valuable" for which to fight.

Notes

1. Bueno de Mesquita and Riker (1982) do develop a theory on the impact of proliferation, but they do not test the impact of proliferation per se. They could not, since the number of cases of proliferation is so small. The studies by Stoll (1988) and Huth and Russett (1984, 1988) do include multivariate analyses that compare the impact of nuclear weapons to that of other variables, but these tests were not guided by a fully specified theory.

2. Since all issues may not be equally salient for every actor, the preference rule is based on distances that are weighted by issue for each actor.

3. Note the situation is not entirely zero or even constant-sum. Should a war occur, for example, both sides would incur costs that would lower the total amount of benefit. We only assume that the division of the values under dispute is zero-sum.

4. We must acknowledge that there exists no consensus regarding the definitions of these concepts. Space does not permit a lengthy discussion of these matters at this time. To an extent, the conceptualizations adopted here are inherent in the way these variables are incorporated into the model. Those interested in further clarification are referred to Morgan (1986).

5. We do not wish to imply that determining the victor in a war is a simple task. Of the several methods of defining "victory", the one most relevant for our purpose is that the victor is the side achieving most of its political aims. Even this poses problems because, in the language of the model, the outcome of a war will not necessarily be either O_i or O_j: war, like negotiations, may lead to any result. We assume that the expected outcome of war can be expressed as a probability distribution over the range of possible outcomes. Thus, the relative power of the disputants will be reflected in the shape of this distribution.

6. This should not be interpreted as a "solution" in the standard game-theoretic sense; rather, it is the negotiated settlement most likely to be reached (keeping in mind that war may be more likely than *any* negotiated settlement). This is equivalent to the Nash (1950) solution, however.

12

The Management of Power in a Warring State System: An Evaluation of Balancing, Collective Security, and Laissez-Faire Policies

Thomas R. Cusack

This chapter examines whether different rules for power management within multistate systems enhance the survival of their practitioners. Drawing on debates within the international politics literature, three distinct rules of behavior are isolated. Each is argued by its advocates to afford an optimal return to those who employ them and are also said to assure the diversity of the system. The rules are incorporated within an abstract representation of a multistate system, which itself is formalized within a large-scale computer simulation model. Using an experimental design and controlling for a variety of system conditions and policy factors, the relative efficacy of these rules is assessed.

Power Management Styles

One of the hallmarks of the international political system is the absence of any central coordinating agent or regime. In effect, a form of anarchy can be said to characterize international political relations. In such a situation, the principal actors, states in this particular case, are left to their own devices to settle disputes among themselves. Each must rely on no one but itself to safeguard its existence and advance its interests. Needless to say, this poses a critical problem for such actors. How can each guarantee its survival in such a setting? More generally, what will prevent some other actor from achieving a preponderance of power that will permit it to dictate others' terms of existence—or indeed destroy all other independent concentrations of power?

A crucial element in the dynamics of social systems is the set of rules that actors use in determining their response to circumstances in their environment. Examples abound in economics and politics. Within the sphere of international relations concern for this runs deep. In a loosely joined system, the creation and maintenance of mutually acceptable rules have always been troublesome tasks—and ones that have significant consequences. In the modern era, the globalization of international relations has compounded the problem as ever more heterogeneous elements join what is loosely called the "community of states." During the 20 century two major efforts, both arising out of major calamities—World Wars I and II—have been made to fashion a set of principles that should guide nations in their behavior. While employing different institutional arrangements, both sets had in common the central principle of "collective security." The core of this principle is the notion that states must foreswear aggression themselves and act in unison to oppose the aggression of others.

Clearly, the tenets of collective security are a radical departure from previous rules that governed states in their dealing with one another. These tenets embody a rejection of less altruistic rules, which were held to be sufficient to provide for both national survival and prosperity on the one hand and system stability and preservation on the other. In going against the grain, the collective security principle embodied a denial of the value of short- and medium-sighted self-interest as bases for state behavior and facilitation of system welfare.

Previous to the Development of Collective Security

A near consensus prevailed to the effect that selfishly based behavior could serve as the bulwark against the ravages of international anarchy. In its pure form, this tradition maintained that, as within economic markets, behavior motivated by short-sighted gain was not only conducive to the national interest but also maximized the welfare of the system as a whole. By disregarding values and objectives that stood outside narrow selfish interest, not only would the individual actor prosper, but so would the system.

Some advocated and practiced an approach to international relations less tinged by the spirit of laissez faire. This approach starts from the assumption that the workings of the international system are as prone to failure as any economic market. Under such conditions, neither short-term national interests nor those that benefit from the long-term stability of the international system can be guaranteed by singularly selfish behavior. The unseen hand that works the balance of power machinery must be assisted to contract and extend its muscles so as to provide optimal performance. Automatic stabilization, and the individual gains that derive therefrom, cannot be guaranteed. Either the lender or lenders "of last resort" need to intervene and act in ways that might not prove directly beneficial in the short term but would enhance long-term interests. A more complete discussion of these three sets of rules begins with simple national interest.

Laissez Faire

One of the dominant interpretations of traditional realpolitik logics and the workings of the balance of power is the "automatic stabilization" model (Claude, 1962). Here an equilibrating process works in the fashion of an "invisible hand," directing the shape and flow of international politics. Conscious intervention on the part of particular states or decisionmakers is assumed to be unnecessary. Rather, the logics of competition are argued to compel state behavior that is both beneficial to the practitioner and to its fellows. In this "natural law" version of international politics state survival and system preservation are guaranteed by the "self-neutralizing tendency of power; thrust engenders counterthrust, power drives cancel each other" (Claude, 1962; p. 47).

One of the starkest descriptions of this image is contained in a passage from Arnold Wolfers (1962, p. 123):

> While it makes little sense to use the term "automatic" literally, as if human choices and errors were irrelevant to the establishment, preservation, or destruction of a state of equilibrium, there nevertheless is a significant element of truth in the theory of "automatism" which is valid even today. If one may assume that any government in its senses will be deeply concerned with the relative power position of hostile countries, then one may conclude that efforts to keep in step in the competition for power with such opponents, or even to outdo them, will almost certainly be forthcoming. If most nations react in this way, a tendency towards equilibrium will follow; it will come into play whether both sides aim at equilibrium or whether the more aggressive side strives for superiority. In the latter case, the opposite side is likely to be provoked into matching these aggressive moves. Forces appear therefore to be working "behind the backs" of the human actors, pushing them in the direction of balanced power irrespective of their preferences.

Balancing

More than a few analysts have noted that a system of competitive and violence-prone states cannot be left to its own devices to produce order and guarantee the security of its members. Its tensions and conflicts are disruptive and the system has the quality of inherent instability that eventuates in the destruction of nearly all independent sources of power (Wight, 1977, p. 44; Deutsch and Singer, 1964, pp. 323–324). The realist school offers a second specification of balance of power rules that is argued to be simultaneously grounded in historical experience and logically consistent. This a system of power management rules wherein a conscientious concern for the effects of others' efforts at altering the status quo is a central assumption. A state should see its interests in blocking the actions of any others that even indirectly could place it at a disadvantage. While not relinquishing its own options to pursue actions for its own advantage, it should always block the expansive efforts of others. Such a power management style has the possibility of promoting both individual and social rewards.

In Claude's terminology, there are two versions of this nonautomatic stabilization model: the "semiautomatic" and the "manually operated." In the semiautomatic version, a limited (one or more) number of states consciously take on this special responsibility to act as the system's "balancer." Usually, such a special role is reserved to a state or states with inordinate amounts of power—states that derive special benefits from shouldering the burden of having to regulate the system (Claude, 1962; p. 48). In the manually operated version the conscious effort at seeking "equilibrium" is not limited to only a few states but is a general responsibility—and of greater effectiveness to the extent to which it is adhered to by the members of the system. Acceptance of this responsibility, while again in no way prejudicial to one's own freedom to seek aggrandizement, leads to actions that help achieve a balance and in turn preserve the multiplicity of states within the system (Claude, 1962, p. 50).

Collective Security

The third alternative, collective security, requires states (1) to renounce the unilateral use of force as a means of achieving their objectives and (2) to come to the aid of those states that have become the target of aggression by another or other states. These are the essential points of this power management style, though numerous other aspects have been grafted onto it. These additions, however, are not at the core of this conception. Rather, there are two central elements that can be described as the principle of deterrence and the principle of universality.

The principle of deterrence is the means which will achieve collective security. The key to the preservation of peace and consequent survival of states and the prevention of hegemony is the ability of states to come together in aid of another. By coalescing in support of a threatened state, the combination of power now available to it poses a fundamental problem to the would-be aggressor. The latter, confronted with a preponderance of power in opposition to itself, faces certain defeat if it presses further in its aggression. So situated, its only rational choice is to back down and cease its aggression. As A. F. K. Organski (1968, pp. 409, 417–419) points out, this logic is an "essentially correct" description of the mechanism that will preserve peace. Indeed, Iris L. Claude Jr. (1964, p. 228) notes that in this respect, that is, the invocation of the logic of deterrence, the theory of collective security is "fundamentally similar to a balance of power system involving defensive alliances." However, collective security is often considered fundamentally flawed in terms of the validity of its second major principle, universality.

The principle of universality is the necessary background condition which guarantees that the requirements for successful deterrence will be met. Underlying this are three critical assumptions. First, among all states there is a common perception as to which nation is the aggressor within an interstate dispute (Claude, 1964, p. 228; Organski, 1968, p. 409). Second, there is universal opposition to the aggression (Claude, 1964, p. 229; Organski, 1968, pp. 409, 413). Third, every state has the flexibility and latitude required to join in opposing the aggressor (Claude, 1964, p. 231; Organski, 1968, pp. 409, 415).

In the case of each assumption, analysts assert that there exist strong reasons for denying their universal validity. Organski (1968, p. 409), for example, suggests that with respect to the first assumption there is "no clear definition of aggression" to which all nations agree because of the confused character of international "squabbles." Claude (1962, p. 197) also argues that the ambiguous character of the threat or use of force within international politics makes a consensual determination of the aggressor impossible. And unless it is the case that "blame can be confidently asserted for international crises," collective security is doomed to failure (Claude, 1964, p. 228).

The second assumption envisions an interstate system wherein peace is "indivisible" (Claude, 1964, p. 229). Yet there is a fundamental contradiction to be seen in, on the one hand, assuming that "all nations are equally capable of becoming aggressors" and, on the other, maintaining that they are "all equally interested" in opposing it (Organski, 1968, pp. 413–414). For Hans J. Morgenthau and Kenneth W. Thompson (1985, p. 454), this demands that the interests of individual states be forsaken, a proposition that is contradictory of realist tenets and therefore one that has little chance of being satisfied.

The third assumption entails that all states have the flexibility to join in opposition to aggression (Organski, 1968, pp. 409, 415). Again, there is a realist basis to reject this notion. Not all states have the wherewithal to threaten to use force against an aggressor, particularly if they are in a sensitive position that might expose them to great harm should they actually become combatants (Organski, 1968, pp. 415–416). As Morgenthau and Thompson (1985, p. 454) see it, this is little more than an idealist prescription and not likely to be the basis of a realist foreign policy.

If these assumptions are incorrect, then "collective security cannot be expected to work" (Organski, 1968, p. 417). Indeed, according to Morgenthau and Thompson (1985, p. 455), there exists the "supreme paradox of collective security" in that any attempt to implement it under conditions that do not correspond to "ideal perfection," that is, without its universal principle effectively operating, will produce the "opposite effect of what it is supposed to achieve." Furthermore, the greater the distance from universalistic adherence to the three assumptions, the more likely the system is to take on aspects of the supposedly anachronistic balance of power system.

A Realpolitik Model

Overview of Basic Model

The basic model employed here is a reconstruction of the computer simulation originally developed by Stuart A. Bremer and Michael Mihalka (1977). The model is a formalization of the "automatic stabilization" image of a multistate system. In brief, the model represents a multistate system with three essential characteristics. The first characteristic is the size of the system, that is, the number of sovereign states. A maximum of 98 states can be represented. Systems of smaller size can also easily be portrayed. The second essential feature of such a system is the geopolitical character of its units. Each state unit is provided with a distinct territorial domain located in an ordered geographical space. In addition, each unit possesses some amount of a resource, military power, that is vital to its survival and is subject to growth and destruction. The third and final characteristic relates to the capacity of each of these state units to observe their environments, engage in decisionmaking, and implement their decisions. Actions take place within an iteration of the model and the consequences of these actions help to define and shape the circumstances that confront the state actors in the succeeding iterations. Within each iteration there are four major phases of activity. Three of these four processes are directly associated with war. The first phase determines whether a dispute will occur among some system members. In the second phase, the processes of dispute escalation and de-escalation are portrayed; this phase determines whether a war occurs and which states will be involved. The third phase deals with the direct consequences of war in terms of assessing costs and transferring gains. In the fourth and last phase the power capabilities of the states in the system are updated.

Model Details

Phase 1: Selection of a Potential Dispute Initiator. The objective of this phase is to identify from among the existing states that one which during the present iteration has the opportunity to choose a target for aggression. The selection procedure relies on a uniform random number generator and sets each state's probability of selection as the potential initiator equal to its relative share of the power capabilities in the system.

Phase 2: Dispute Onset and Escalation. Four stages are included within this phase which is a stylized version of interstate militarized disputes. In the first stage, the potential initiator decides whether to initiate a conflict and by selecting a neighboring state for the target of its aggression. In the second stage, the initiator is allowed to develop a countercoalition, and to determine whether to continue in its threatening mode, or to terminate the dispute. The fourth stage is contingent on the initiator pressing forward and allows the target the opportunity to widen its coalition. War occurs only if the first three stages are traversed, that is, only when the initiator has twice chosen the war option.

1. *Potential Initiator's Preliminary Actions.* The initiator state, i, compares its power capabilities with each of its neighbors. These power assessments and comparisons are based on estimates subject to error:

$$ESTPOW_i = POW_i(1.0 + ERROR_i)$$

The error term is a normally distributed proportional term with specific values determined stochastically. If no neighbor is estimated as weaker than itself, the initiator takes no action (activity in this iteration moves to the fourth and last phase, power adjustment). If more than one neighbor is perceived as weaker, the one assumed to be the weakest is selected as the target.

2. *Target's Initial Response and Associated Activities.* The target compares its own power with the estimated power of its assailant. If the comparison favors the target (it perceives itself as having more power than the initiator), it takes no further action (model moves to stage 3). An unfavorable comparison leads the target to attempt the construction of a "defensive coalition." The target considers only "minimum winning" coalitions of contiguous states. Involved here are three steps:

(a) All possible coalitions of states contiguous to opponent are assayed.
(b) The combined power of each such potential coalition is estimated.
(c) Alliance membership bids are directed toward those states in the group which are contiguous to the opponent and which have more combined power and yet are the least powerful of all such protocoalitions.

If no such coalition exists, the target state takes no action (model moves to stage 3).

The states that have received alliance bids make their decisions independently. A decision is based on the potential ally's own assessment of the estimated power of the protocoalition in comparison with its estimate of the power of the opponent. Where the protocoalition is perceived as stronger, the potential ally joins; where it is seen as weaker, the bid is rebuffed and the state stays outside the coalition.

3. *Initiator's Rejoinder to Coalition Building on the Part of Target and Associated Activities*. Depending on target's success in building a coalition, initiator acts in the following way:

(a) If target is unsuccessful in acquiring allies, the initiator opts immediately for war.

(b) Where the target has constructed an alliance, the initiator first compares its estimated power with that estimated as under control of the target's coalition. If the initiator sees itself as stronger, it opts for war; otherwise it engages in the process of attempting to build its own coalition.

The initiator seeks a coalition using the same principles as the target; that is, the members must be contiguous to the principal opponent of the coalition builder, the assumed power of the coalition is greater than the assumed power of the opponent's coalition, and the assumed power of the coalition is the minimum assumed power of those coalitions that satisfy the first two criteria. If such a coalition does not exist, the initiator withdraws from the conflict and the dispute is ended. If such a protocoalition exists, the initiator extends alliance membership bids to the potential members. As before, a state's decision to join or refrain from joining such a coalition is again contingent on its estimate of the principal success of that coalition.

If all states invited to join the coalition of the initiator accept the bids, the initiator opts for war; however, if one or more such invitations are refused, the initiator is in a position of perceived weakness vis-à-vis the target and it opts for a termination of the dispute.

4. *Target's Second Round of Coalition Building and Associated Activities*. If the initiator has opted for war in stage 3, the target compares its assumed power, or the assumed power of its alliance when such has been constructed in stage 2, against that of the initiator's side. If the target sees its side as more powerful, it refrains from attempting to acquire more allies. Conversely, if it sees its side as weaker, it attempts to expand the size of its coalition. Additional members are selected on the bases described in stage 2. States invited to join the expanded alliance act in the same independent way described in stages 2 and 3. Their actions conclude this phase of the iteration. The next phase of activity deals with the warring process and outcome.

Phase 3: War—Determining the Victor and Distributing the Benefits and Costs. There are four stages to the war phase. The first determines the victorious side in the war. In the succeeding stages, the consequences of the war, in terms of costs and benefits, are sorted out. Stage 2 of this phase deals with the determination of war costs confronted by all participants. The succeeding stage focuses on the assessment of indemnities and the fourth and final stage is given over to the processes involved in transferring territorial units.

1.   *War's Victor.* Every war has a victorious and a vanquished side. No immediately inconclusive result is represented as possible. All wars end in the period or iteration in which they began. The likelihood of victory for the initiator is a logistic function of the ratio of the initiator coalition's capabilities to the target coalition's capabilities. The exact shape of the logistic curve can be controlled by the value of one parameter. The higher the value given to the controlling parameter, the flatter is the shape of the curve in the areas where the two sides are nearly equal. That is, higher values of the parameter mean that the initiator coalition needs to have a greater margin of superiority over the target to have a good chance of victory.

2.   *Common War Participation Costs.* All participants in the war bear costs, paid in the currency of power units. All participants, regardless of whether on the victorious or vanquished side, suffer a decrease in power of equal proportion. The cost function that confronts each participant contains two principal components: (a) a parameter specifying the maximum proportional war costs and (b) the relative power of the opposing sides. The function takes the following form:

$$WARCOST = (1.0 - (LSR - 0.5)/0.5)(WARCOST_{max}),$$

where LSR is defined as the ratio of the power of the larger side to the sum of the power of both sides in the war and $WARCOST_{max}$ is the maximum proportional cost parameter.

3.   *Assessment of Spoils (Indemnities).* Each actor in the defeated coalition is assessed an indemnity equal to some constant proportion of the power units it possesses. This proportion is meant to reflect the punitiveness of the victor. The total of indemnities contributed by the defeated states is allocated across the member states of the winning coalition on the basis of each member's contribution to the total capabilities of the alliance. In addition to the direct transference of power units from the winning to the losing side, a more complicated and potentially more rewarding form of exploitation is provided for in the way of territorial transference from the principal losing state to the victorious coalition.

4.   *Assessment of Spoils (Territory).* Territorial loss occurs only to the leader of the losing coalition. The amount or size of territorial loss, that is, the distinct pieces of territory lost, is a function of the size of the loser and

the "decisiveness" of its loss. The territory taken from the loser is parceled out among the members of the winning coalition on the basis of a proportionality rule with respect to the power units of each member of the coalition. Details on the procedure whereby such transference takes place are provided later.

The "likelihood of victory" (LV) function is used to determine the proportion of the loser state's territorial holdings to be transferred. If the victor is the initiating coalition, the proportion of the loser's territories to be surrendered is the LV score. If the victor is the target coalition, the proportion is equal to 1.0 minus the LV score. If, however, the loser possesses only one territorial unit, possession is transferred and the state is eliminated from the system. States with more than one territorial unit can also be eliminated if the magnitude of their defeat, as reflected in the LV score, is sufficiently large.

The territories extracted from the loser are allocated among the members of the victorious coalition. This is done on a proportional basis with each state's share of the "booty" equal to its relative power position within the victorious coalition. With these preliminary shares specified, the selection of territorial units begins. A member of the victorious coalition effectively queues for its allotment on the basis of its relative power standing. Certain related rules are iteratively applied to guide it in its selection of a territorial unit.

The first rule allows a recipient to choose only units that are contiguous to itself. If the application of this rule produces one such territory, the unit identified is transferred. Where more than one unit is identified, a second rule is invoked. Here all contiguous territories of the loser are identified and those that if removed from the loser would split the loser into two or more parts are removed from consideration. If one territorial unit of the loser still remains, that unit is transferred. If, however, a list with more than one contiguous unit exists, which would not split the loser, the third rule is invoked. This rule chooses from the list of possible acquisitions the loser's territorial unit that provides the choosing victor with the most compact shape to its overall territorial holdings and, as a secondary consideration, also aims for a compact shape for the remaining holdings of the loser.

The logic of the model does not permit the existence of states with noncontiguous elements. Should the situation arise that a victor would be denied its "rightful reward," then, and only then, is the state "broken." With this splitting, the model effectively creates a new state. The old state takes possession of the most powerful agglomeration of territorial units that remains. The new state receives title to the rump grouping.

With the leading, that is, the most powerful, state of the victorious coalition finished with its selection of new acquisitions, the selection rights devolve upon the next most powerful and in succession to the weakest in the coalition entitled to acquire "booty." The completion of the rearrangement of the map effectively ends the war phase of the iteration.

Phase 4: Power adjustment. This is the last phase of each iteration of the model. Herein, the power in each of the territorial units held by the existing states is increased by a percentage factor. The size of this factor is the same across all states. With this updating completed, the model has passed through a full iteration and moves into a new period.

Model Extension: Incorporating Power Management Styles

For this study, the model was reconfigured to allow states to use one of the three alternative power management rules described in the last section. The principal characteristics distinguishing these three types of state are outlined in Table 12.1. The laissez-faire policy is captured effectively by the decision rules implemented within the original model. Therefore, for states so designated, no modifications were required. For states following balancing and collective security policies, however, the following changes were implemented. States employing balancing strategies were assumed to behave in basically the same way as laissez-faire states with regard to initiating conflicts; however, their policies regarding the joining of coalitions are different. Such states refuse to coalesce with aggressors, that is, states that initiate conflicts. The calculus with respect to joining a defensive coalition is also different. Whenever a balancer is invited to join such a coalition, it accepts that offer. In effect, it ignores considerations with respect to the short-term gains that only motivate laissez-faire states to enter an alliance. States committed to collective security principles reject any opportunity to initiate conflict. In addition, they eschew offers to join in aggressive coalitions and always accept bids to join defensive coalitions.

Table 12.1 Specifics of Power Management Styles

Decision Rule for:	Type of State		
	Collective Security	Power Balancing	Laissez Faire
Initiating conflict	Never initiate	Initiate when victory likely	Initiate when victory likely
Joining an offensive coalition	Never join	Never join	Join when victory likely
Joining a defensive coalition	Always join	Always join	Join when victory likely

Experimental Design

As noted above, two central questions prompt the research reported here. On the one hand, there is the problem of the relative efficacy of alternative power management styles in promoting system pluralism and preventing the rise of universal empire. On the other hand, there is the practical problem that may attach itself to the use of a particular style when embedded in an environment with other states using alternative power management rules and what this portends for the individual practitioners. Indeed, it may be the case, as often asserted, that an actor behaving in a certain way, call it altruistic, does perform a beneficial social function for the collective but only at the cost of weakening itself.

We address these two problems using the model described in the previous section. In using the model we attempt to provide an extensive set of alternative background conditions. Three fundamental sets of conditions are varied. The first, the composition of the population of states within the system, is systematically altered. Three basic configurations, or panels, of initial population distributions are employed (see Table 12.2). In the first panel, all three types of power management style are present in the initial population of the system and the proportions are relatively equal. The second and third panels include only two types of state, one of a relatively selfless type (either collective security oriented, as in panel 2, or power balancing, as in panel 3) and the more self-centered laissez-faire type.[1]

A second set of conditions included parameters governing certain critical structural and policy conditions that can be manipulated within the model. Previous studies (see Cusack and Zimmer, 1986; Cusack and Stoll, 1987) have described the putative importance of these conditions and analyzed their relevance for the two general questions guiding the present research. Four of the five parameters have been varied so as to take on low, medium, and high values (see Table 12.3): (1) the relative dispersion of power at the outset of the system experiment; (2) the restraint practiced by victors when dealing with defeated states; (3) the range of error within which decisionmakers operate when estimating power capabilities; and (4) the destructiveness of war. A fifth parameter, dealing with the shape of the likelihood of victory curve, was also varied but only so as to take on either a low or a high value (the former produces a steeper curve while the latter a flatter one within the region where the relative power ratio in a war approaches parity).

The third source of variation centers on the stochastic elements of the model. Each of the experimental runs was repeated three times with each repetition varying solely on the basis of a different setting of the "seed" used by the pseudorandom number generator within the model.

To summarize, there are three panels with different initial distributions of the system population endowed with alternative power management styles.

Table 12.2 Initial Distribution of Power Management Styles Across the Three Panels

Panels	Number of States at Start		
	Collective Security	Power Balancing	Laissez Faire
I	33	32	33
II	49	0	49
III	0	49	49

Table 12.3 Alternative Values for Experimental Factors

Experimental Factor	Alternatives		
	1	2	3
Power distribution	10	25	50
Restraint	0.05	0.10	0.25
Error	5	10	25
Destructiveness of war	0.02	0.05	0.10
Likelihood of victory	1	3	NA

Within each panel, different experiments were conducted by systematically varying five model parameters and these in turn were repeated within the context of altering the "seed" value for the random number generator. In each of the three panels, 486 separate experiments were conducted. Thus, in all, 1458 experiments were undertaken with the model for this study.

Experimental Results

System Endurance

In some earlier studies with the model (e.g., Stoll, 1986, 1987; Cusack and Zimmer, 1986; Cusack and Stoll, 1987) the system exhibited a marked tendency toward breakdown and the emergence of a universal empire; this transpired in more than 90% of the experiments. These studies shared the common characteristic of representing all states in the system as employing a laissez-faire management style. Across the experiments conducted here, varying proportions of the system's population were initialized with such a style and the remainder with one or both of the other two (i.e., balancing and collective security). As a consequence, results in terms of system endurance are in distinct contrast with the earlier studies. Across all the experiments conducted for this study, a universal empire emerged with far less frequency (less than 22% of the cases). There was, additionally, significant variation across the three panels or sets of experiments in terms of this outcome (see Table 12.4).

The second panel, which initially populated the system with equal proportions of states using collective security and laissez-faire power

Table 12.4   Relative Frequencies with Which Universal Empires Emerge

Panels	Percentage of Runs that Culminated in Empire Prior to 1500th Iteration
I	8.8
II	5.6
III	51.2
All panels	21.9

management styles, achieved the highest rate of success in preserving some degree of pluralism. Less than 6% of the experimental systems within this panel degenerated into universal empire. The success rate of the first panel, which incorporated approximately equal numbers of states with the three different management styles, rivals the second with less than 9% of the systems failing to endure. The panel with the worst performance, the third, included equal-sized subpopulations of states employing balancing and laissez-faire rules; more than 50% of the experimental runs in this panel culminated in universal empire.

State Survival

Although the second panel had only marginally better performance than the first in terms of preventing the rise of hegemony, the situation with respect to the relative prospects for state survival between the two is significantly different (see Tables 12.5 and 12.6). Over the length of the average run, a gap widens in terms of the chances of survival between these two panels so that by iteration 1500 the survival chances of a state are approximately 48% within the second panel and only 37% in the first. Both panels, however, provided far and away more conducive environments than the third, that is, the one lacking any states committed to collective security principles. Here, even by iteration 100, survival chances are markedly lower than those that obtained in the other two panels (64% to about 82%) and worsen significantly by the 300th iteration where chances for survival diminish to about 23%. By the 1500th iteration they have sunk to an average of 4% in this environment.

The results at both the system and state levels tend to reinforce one another in leading to the conclusion that the selfless power management style of collective security is beneficial for the whole system. But are its practitioners merely misguided agents helping the cause of others and suffering in the process or do they also individually gain? Table 12.7 provides some information on this question. Here one can see that the survival chances of a state practicing collective security principles are generally twice as great as those of a state employing any other style. Within an environment where all three management styles were practiced, states

Table 12.5 Numbers of States Surviving

Panels	Average Number of States at Iteration					
	0	100	300	500	1000	1500
I	98	80.32	58.42	47.05	38.47	36.69
II	98	80.56	62.33	53.88	48.67	47.63
III	98	63.92	22.15	7.87	4.08	3.99

Table 12.6 Overall Survival Rates Across Panels

Panels	Survival Changes at Iteration				
	100	300	500	1000	1500
I	81.96	59.61	48.01	39.26	37.44
II	82.21	63.61	54.98	49.66	48.60
III	65.22	22.60	8.03	4.17	4.07

committed to collective security had a survival rate of nearly 58%, while power balancers achieved only 27% and laissez-faire states 28%. In the environment where collective security states were confronted with only one other type of state, laissez faire, the former's chances of survival were even greater (64%) and the relative success rate equally high (64 versus 33% for the laissez-faire states). As noted above, there was no significant difference in the survival chances of power balancers and laissez-faire states in the first panel and this similarity is repeated in panel 3. Both types of state, however, clearly benefited by being embedded within an environment shared by collective security states.

Even in terms of relative power standings, collective security oriented states appear to be at advantage (see Table 12.8). On average, within the first panel they possess about 66% of the systemwide power by the end of the runs. This compares quite favorably with the limited achievement made by the other two types, where each held approximately 17%. Per state, this translates into a relatively advantageous position for the average practitioner of collective security. It would possess about 3.5% of system power while the average state in each of the other classes would have less than 60% of that share. In the second panel where collective security oriented and laissez-faire states combine to form the entire system population, the advantage is again significantly on the side of the former. They possess, on average, 75% of the power by the end of the experiments—which means that the average collective security state held a share of 2.4% relative to the 1.5% held by the average practitioner of laissez faire. In the third panel, a marginally better position is achieved by the practitioners of power balancing. They held an individual average of 23% while the practitioners of laissez faire held 21%.

In the limited number of cases where the system evolved into a universal empire, how did the various types of state do in terms of their chances at

Table 12.7 Survival Rates for the Different Types of State

| Panels | Average Number of States at End (Survival Rates in Parentheses) | | |
	Collective Security	Power Balancing	Laissez Faire
I	18.98 (57.52)	8.69 (27.16)	9.11 (27.61)
II	31.40 (64.08)	NA	16.21 (35.08)
III	NA	2.34 (4.78)	2.16 (4.41)

Table 12.8 Power Holdings by the Different Types of State

| Panels | Average Proportion of Power at End | | |
	Collective Security	Power Balancing	Laissez Faire
I	65.70	17.43	16.88
II	75.37	NA	24.63
III	NA	54.66	45.34

achieving control of that empire? In this regard, collective security states are at a distinct disadvantage (see Table 12.9). There is not one instance where they succeeded to universal dominance. This role was reserved for power balancers and practitioners of laissez-faire policies. Between these two types of state only small differences in success at universal empire creation are evident. In the first panel, their success rates are practically equal (4.3 versus 4.5%). In the third panel the power balancers did marginally better with one

Table 12.9 Builders of Universal Empires

| Panels | Type of State Controlling Universal Empire | | | Total |
	Collective Security	Power Balancing	Laissez Faire	
I	0 (0%)	21 (4.3%)	22 (4.5%)	43
II	0 (0%)	NA	27 (5.5%)	27
III	NA	139 (28.6%)	110 (22.6%)	249
All panels	0 (0%)	160 (11.0%)	159 (10.9%)	319

Total column indicates how many runs in a panel ended in universal empire. Percentage figures given in parentheses represent the proportion of system opportunities within the panel that a state of this type managed to create a universal empire.

of their kind, creating a universal empire in about 29% of the systems while practitioners of laissez-faire policies did this in about 23% of the systems.

Conclusion

The preservation of system pluralism and the enhancement of a state's survival chances have long been a central concern to practitioners and scholars of international politics. During the 20th century, two dominant schools of thought have come to the fore in articulating radically different power management styles within international politics for dealing with both these problems. The realists have advocated policies of selfish aggrandizement in the belief that these not only ensure the survival of the state but will, as in the stylized logics of the market mechanism, also preserve the pluralist character of the system. Idealists and others have rejected these practices, arguing that they are inefficacious at best and counterproductive at worst.

Generally associated with the idealist school, an alternative scheme for power management practices on the part of states, collective security, has been advanced. Its principal elements include the standard logic of deterrence, found in realism, as well as the renunciation of aggression and the commitment to opposing aggression on the part of others. The realists have leveled a strong attack against this latter principle. They have argued that for collective security to work, a universal commitment to the latter principle is required and that this is an extraordinarily unlikely situation. In the absence of universality, they conclude that collective security must fail. Its failure will manifest itself in the inability to stop hegemonic drives and in the costs that will be inflicted on those states that misguidedly practice it in a less than ideal world.

Through the use of a computer simulation model of a stylized multistate system, an effort has been made to evaluate three different types of powermanagement style. Two of these styles have emerged from realist thought and represent alternative formulations of balance of power policies. The third derives from an alternative tradition and takes the form of collective security policies. Drawing on an extensive number of experiments with the computer simulation mode, our analysis has concentrated on the two questions of system endurance and state survival and particular attention has been given to the relative efficacy of these alternative power management styles.

What emerges from the simulation experiments is the relative vitality of the collective security power management style. The presence of states committed to collective security, even when in a distinct minority, greatly enhances the likelihood that the system will retain its pluralistic character.

Compared with the other two power management styles, collective security at the individual level is a far more rewarding strategy. It greatly enhances state survival chances and it improves the performance of states in terms of the relative power position they achieve.

All this suggests that the realist attack on collective security, particularly in terms of the criticism of the universal principle, is incorrect. Far from undermining system pluralism, collective security does better than the two styles traditionally endorsed by the realists in preserving pluralism and maximizing the size of the system over time. What is more, for the individual practitioner, the average gain in terms of both survival chances and relative power accretion is far greater. And while universal imperium seems out of the reach of the practitioners of collective security, so is it for practically all the practitioners of power-balancing and laissez-faire policies. In sum, collective security may be uncomfortable to policymakers and perhaps realists have been too eager to provide the intellectual justification needed to reject it while at the same time insufficiently attentive to the efficacy of collective security in promoting the values that realists place on the altar of international politics.

Note

1. Note that another configuration was explored. This was one where the population was divided equally between collective security and power-balancing types. All these experimental systems proved to be profoundly peaceful. Given the rules that these states employ, disputes were possible and did occur frequently but no aggressor was ever in the position of achieving a sufficiently favorable relative power position with a dispute. Thus, no disputes escalated to war and, as a consequence, no states were destroyed through the 1500th iteration, the arbitrary time limit placed on all the experiments reported on in this study.

References

Emanuel Adler. 1987. *The Power of Ideology: The Quest for Technological Autonomy in Argentina and Brazil*. University of California Press, Berkeley, CA.

Norman Z. Alcock and Alan G. Newcombe. 1970. The perception of national power. *Journal of Conflict Resolution*, 14:335-343.

Hayward R. Alker, Jr. 1973. On political capabilities in a schedule sense: measuring power, integration, and development. In Hayward R. Alker Jr., Karl W. Deutsch, and A. H. Stoetzel, eds., *Mathematical Approaches to Politics*, Elsevier, Amsterdam.

James E. Alt, Randall L. Calvert, and Brian D. Humes. 1988. Reputation and hegemonic stability: A game-theoretic analysis. *American Political Science Review*, 82:445-466.

Gabriel Ardant. 1975. Financial policy and economic infrastructure of modern states and nations. In Charles Tilly, ed., *The Formation of Nation-States in Western Europe*, Princeton University Press, Princeton, NJ.

Raymond Aron. 1966. *Peace and War: A Theory of International Relations*. Doubleday and Company, New York.

Robert Axelrod. 1984. *The Evolution of Cooperation*. Basic Books, New York.

Edward Elias Azar. 1980. The conflict and peace data bank (COPDAB) project. *Journal of Conflict Resolution*, 24:143-52.

Peter Bachrach and Morton S. Baratz. 1962. Two faces of power. *American Political Science Review*, 56:947-952.

David A. Baldwin. 1979. Power analysis and world politics: New trends and old tendencies. *International Organization*, 31:161-194.

David A. Baldwin. 1985. *Economic Statecraft*. Princeton University Press, Princeton, NJ.

Douglas C. Bennett and Kenneth E. Sharpe. 1985. *Transnational Corporations versus the State: The Political Economy of the Mexican Auto Industry*. Princeton University Press, Princeton, NJ.

Emile Benoit. 1968. Economics of arms control and disarmament: The monetary and real costs of national defense. *The American Economic Review*, 58:398-416.

Adolph A. Berle. 1967. *Power*. Harcourt, Brace & World, New York.

Robert Berman and John C. Baker. 1982. *Soviet Strategic Forces Requirement and Responses*. The Brooking Institution, Washington, D.C.

Thomas J. Biersteker. 1980. The illusion of state power: Transnational corporations and the neutralization of host country legislation. *Journal of Peace Research*, 17:207-222.

Hubert M. Blalock, Jr. 1982. *Conceptualization and Measurement in the Social Sciences*. Sage, Beverly Hills, CA.

David Bohm. 1957. *Causality and Chance in Modern Physics*. University of Pennsylvania Press, Philadelphia.

Kenneth Boulding. 1962. *Conflict and Defense*. Harper, New York.

Stuart A. Bremer. 1980. National capabilities and war proneness. In J. David Singer, ed., *The Correlates of War II: Testing Some Realpolitik Models*, Free Press, New York.

Stuart A. Bremer and Michael Mihalka. 1977. Machiavelli in machina: Or politics among hexagons. In K. W. Deutsch, et al., ed., *Problems of World Modeling*, Ballinger, Boston.

Bernard Brodie. 1946. *The Absolute Weapon*. Harcourt, Brace, New York.

Bruce Bueno de Mesquita. 1981. *The War Trap*. Yale University Press, New Haven, CT.

Bruce Bueno de Mesquita. 1985. The war trap revisited. *American Political Science Review*, 79:156-177.

Bruce Bueno de Mesquita and David Lalman. 1986. Reason and war. *American Political Science Review*, 80:1113-1129.

Bruce Bueno de Mesquita, David Neuman, and Alvin Rabushka. 1985. *Forecasting Political Events: the Future of Hong Kong*. Yale University Press, New Haven, CT.

Bruce Bueno de Mesquita and William H. Riker. 1982. An assessment of the merits of selective nuclear proliferation. *Journal of Conflict Resolution*, 26:283-306.

R. S. Burt. 1977. Power in a social topology. In R. J. Liebert and A. W. Imershein, eds., *Power, Paradigms and Community Research*, Sage, Beverly Hills, CA.

Christy Campbell. 1984. *Nuclear Facts, Italy*, The Hamlyn Publishing Group Limited, Twickenham, UK.

James A. Caporaso. 1978. Dependence, dependency, and power in the global system: A structural and behavioral analysis. *International Organization*, 32:13-43.

Fernando H. Cardoso. 1973. Associated-dependent development: theoretical and practical implications. In Alfred Stepan, ed., *Authoritarian Brazil*, Yale University Press, New Haven, CT.

Fernando H. Cardoso and Enzo Faletto. 1978. *Dependency and Development in Latin America*. University of California Press, Berkeley, CA.

Michael Carley. 1981. *Social Measurement and Social Indicators*. George Allen & Unwin, London.

Edward Hallett Carr. 1951. *The Twentieth Century Crisis, 1919-1939*. MacMillan, London.

Robert L. Carswell. 1981. Economic sanctions and the Iran experience. *Foreign Affairs*, 2:247-265.

Raymond B. Cattell, H. Bruel, and H. Parker Hartman. 1951. An attempt at more refined definition of the cultural dimensions of syntality in modern nations. *The American Sociological Review*, 17:408-421.

Central Intelligence Agency: National Foreign Assessment Center. 1979. *Handbook of Economic Statistics*. U.S. Government Printing Office, Washington, D.C.

Central Intelligence Agency. 1985. *The World Factbook*. Central Intelligence Agency, Washington, D.C.

Christopher Chase-Dunn. 1982. *Socialist States in the World System*. Sage, Beverly Hills, CA.

Nazli Choucri and Robert North. 1974. *Nations in Conflict*. W. H. Freeman, San Francisco.

Inis L. Claude, Jr. 1962. *Power and International Relations*. Random House, New York.

Inis L. Claude, Jr. 1964. *Swords into Plowshares: The Problems and Progress of International Organization, Third Edition*. Random House, New York.

Ray S. Cline. 1975. *World Power Assessment: A Calculus of Strategic Drift*. Westview, Boulder, CO.

Ray S. Cline. 1980. *World Power Trends and U.S. Foreign Policy in the 1980s*. Westview Press, Boulder, CO

William E. Connolly. 1974. *The Terms of Political Discourse*. Princeton University Press, Princeton, NJ.

Karen S. Cook. 1982. Network structures from an exchange perspective. In Peter V. Marsden and Nan Lin, eds., *Social Structure and Network Analysis*, Sage, Beverly Hills, CA.

William Cooley and Paul Lohnes. 1971. *Multivariate Data Analysis*. Wiley, New York.

Gordon A. Craig and Alexander L. George. 1983. *Force and Statecraft: Diplomatic Problems of Our Times*. Oxford University Press, Oxford.

E. G. Cross. 1981. Economic sanctions as a tool of policy against Rhodesia. *The World Economy* 4:69-78.

Thomas R. Cusack and Richard J. Stoll. 1987. Rationality's reward in a warring state system. Paper presented at Annual Conference of the International Studies Association, Washington, D.C.

Thomas R. Cusack and Uwe Zimmer. 1986. Bases of multistate system endurance. Paper presented at Annual Conference of the International Studies Association, Anaheim, CA.

Robert A. Dahl. 1957. The concept of power. *Behavioral Science*. 1:201-215.

Robert A. Dahl. 1965. Cause and effect in the study of politics. In Daniel Lerner, ed. *Cause and Effect*, The Free Press, New York.

Robert A. Dahl. 1968. Power. In David Sills, ed., *International Encyclopedia of the Social Sciences*, pp. 405-415, Macmillan & The Free Press.

Kingsley Davis. 1954. The demographic foundations of national power. In Morrow Berger, Theodore Abel, and Page Charles H., eds., *Freedom and Control in Modern Society*, pp. 206-242, Farrar, Straus & Giroux, Inc., New York.

Karl W. Deutsch. 1963. *The Nerves of Government: Models of Political Communication and Control*. The Free Press of Glencoe, New York.

Karl W. Deutsch. 1968. *The Analysis of International Relations*. Prentice-Hall, NJ.

Karl W. Deutsch and J. David Singer. 1964. Multipolar power systems and international stability. *World Politics*. 16:390-406.

Charles F. Doran and Wes Parsons. 1980. War and the cycle of relative power. *American Political Science Review*, 74:947-965.

Arghiri Emmanuel. 1972. *Unequal Exchange: A Study of Imperialism of Trade*. Monthly Review Press, New York.

James M. Enelow. 1984. A new theory of congressional compromise. *American Political Science Review*, 78:708-718.

James M. Enelow and Melvin J. Hinich. 1984. *The Spatial Theory of Voting.* Cambridge University Press, Cambridge, MA.

Robert F. Engle and Clive W. J. Granger. 1987. Co-integration and error correction: representation, estimation, and testing. *Econometrica*, 55:251-276.

Europa Yearbook. 1982. *A World Survey.* Europa Publications, London.

Peter Evans. 1979. *Dependent Development.* Princeton University Press, Princeton, NJ.

Peter Evans. 1985. Transnational linkages and the role of the state; an analysis of developing and industrialized nations in the Post-World War II period. In Peter Evans, Dietrick Rueschemeyer, and Theda Skocpol, eds., *Bringing the State Back In*, Cambridge University Press, New York.

S. Feldman. 1982. *Israeli Nuclear Deterrence: A Strategy for the 1980s.* Columbia University Press, New York.

Andre Gunder Frank. 1969. *Latin America: Underdevelopment or Revolution.* Monthly Review Press, New York.

Bruno S. Frey. 1978. *Modern Political Economy.* Martin Robertson, Oxford.

Bruno S. Frey. 1984. *International Political Economics.* Basil Blackwell, New York.

Wilhelm Fucks. 1965. *Formeln zur Macht: Prognosen über Völker, Wirtschaft Potentiale.* Verlags-Anstalt, Germany.

Johan Galtung. 1971. A structural theory of imperialism. *Journal of Peace Research*, (2):81-117.

Gary Gereffi. 1983. *The Pharmaceutical Industry and Dependency in the Third World.* Princeton University Press, Princeton, NJ.

Gary Gereffi and Richard Newfarmer. 1985. International oligopoly and uneven development: Lessons from industrial case studies. In Richard Newfarmer, ed., *Profits, Progress, and Poverty: Case Studies of International Industries in Latin America*, University of Notre Dame Press, Notre Dame, IN.

F. Clifford German. 1960. A tentative evaluation of world power. *Journal of Conflict Resolution*, 4:138-144.

Anthony Giddens. 1979. *Central Problems in Social Theory.* University of California Press, Berkeley and Los Angeles, CA.

Robert Gilpin. 1981. *War and Change in World Politics.* Cambridge University Press, New York.

R. Gilpin. 1987. The theory of hegemonic war. *Journal of Interdisciplinary History.* 18:591-614.

Charles S. Gochman and Zeev Maoz. 1984. Militarized interstate disputes. 1816-1976. *Journal of Conflict Resolution*, 28:585-616.

Terry Goldman, Richard J. Huges, and Michael M. Nieto. 1988. Gravity and antimatter. *Scientific American*, 258:48-56.

Louis W. Goodman. 1987. *Small Nations, Giant Firms.* Holmes and Meier, New York.

Joseph Grieco. 1984. *Between Autonomy and Dependency: India's Experience with the International Computer Industry.* University of California Press, Berkeley, CA.

Silviu Guiasu and Abe Shenitzer. 1985. The principle of maximum entropy. *The Mathematical Intelligencer*, 7:42-48.

E. Gulick. 1955. *Europe's Classical Balance of Power.* Cornell University Press, Ithaca, NY.

Ernst B. Haas. 1953. The balance of power: prescription, concept, or propaganda? *World Politics*, 5:446-447.

Ernst B. Haas. 1955. Types of collective security: an examination of operational concepts. *American Political Science Review*, 20:40-62.

Stephan Haggard. 1989. forthcoming, The political economy of foreign direct investment in Latin America. *Latin American Research*, 41.

Stephan Haggard and Beth A. Simmons. 1987. Theories of international regimes. *International Organization*, 41:491-517.

John C. Harsanyi. 1962. Measurement of social power, opportunity costs, and the theory of two-person bargaining games. *Behavioral Science*, VII:67-80.

John C. Harsanyi. 1969. Measurement of social power, opportunity costs, and the theory of two-person bargaining games. In Daniel Bell, ed., *Political Power: A Reader in Theory and Research*, pp. 226-238, Free Press, New York.

Jeffrey Hart. 1976. Three approaches to the measurement of power in international relations. *International Organization*, 30:289-305.

Melvin J. Hinich and Peter Ordeshook. 1970. Plurality maximization vs. vote maximization. *American Political Science Review*, 64:772-791.

Albert O. Hirschman. 1945. *National Power and the Structure of Foreign Trade*. University of California Press, Berkeley, CA.

Albert O. Hirschman. 1981. *Essays in Trespassing: Economics to Politics and Beyond*. Cambridge University Press, New York.

Charles Hitch and Ronald McKean. 1960. *The Economics of Defense in the Nuclear Age*. Harvard University Press, Cambridge, MA.

Thomas Hobbes. 1957. *Leviathan*. Basil Blackwell, Oxford. Originally published 1651.

Thomas Hobbes. 1971. Of power. In John R. Champlin, ed., *Power*, Atherton Press, New York. Originally published 1839.

Stanley Hoffmann. 1960. *Contemporary Theory in International Relations*. Prentice-Hall, Englewood Cliffs, NJ.

Kal J. Holsti. 1983. *International Politics: A Framework for Analysis*. Prentice-Hall, Englewood Cliffs, NJ.

Ole Holsti. 1962. The belief system and national images: A case study. *Journal of Conflict Resolution*, 6:244-251.

Lewis L. House and Michael D. Ward. 1988. The behavioral power of nations. *Quality and Quantity*, 22:167-188.

Hank Houweling and Jan Siccama. 1988. Power transition as a cause of war. *Journal of Conflict Resolution*, 32:87-102.

Gary Hufbauer and Jeffrey Schott. 1985. *Economic Sanctions Reconsidered: History and Current Policy*. Institute for International Economics, Washington, D.C.

Floyd Hunter. 1953. *Community Power Structure: A Study of Decision Makers*. University of North Carolina Press, Chapel Hill, NC.

Sief Hussein. 1987. Modeling war and peace. *American Political Science Review*, 81:221-227.

Paul Huth and Bruce M. Russett. 1984. What makes deterrence work? *World Politics*, 36:496-526.

Paul Huth and Bruce M. Russett. 1988. Deterrence failure and crisis escalation. *International Studies Quarterly*, 32:29-45.

Stephen Hymer. 1976. *The International Operations of National Firms: A Study of Direct Foreign Investment*. MIT Press, Cambridge, MA.

John Ikenberry, David Lake, and Michael Mastanduno. 1988. *The State and American Foreign Economic Policy*. Cornell University Press, Ithaca, NY.

International Institute for Strategic Studies. 1981. *The Military Balance 1981-1982*. International Institute for Strategic Studies, London.

International Monetary Fund. 1981. *International Financial Statistics, Supplement on Price Statistics, no. 2*. Author, Washington, D.C.

Michael Intriligator and Dagobert L. Brito. 1984. Can arms races lead to the outbreak of war? *Journal of Conflict Resolution*, 28:63-84.

Robert Jervis. 1976. *Perception and Misperception in International Politics*. Princeton University Press, Princeton, NJ.

Abraham Kaplan. 1963. *The Conduct of Inquiry: Methodology for Behavioral Science*. Harper & Row, Publishers, New York.

Morton A. Kaplan. 1957. *System and Process in International Politics*. Wiley, New York.

Kautilya. 1967. *Arthasastra*. Mysore Printing and Publishing House, Mysore, India. Translated by M. S. Srinivs.

Paul Kennedy. 1987. *The Rise and Fall of the Great Powers*. Random House, New York.

Robert O. Keohane. 1984a. *After Hegemony: Cooperation and Discord in the World Political Economy*. Princeton University Press, Princeton, NJ.

Robert O. Keohane. 1984b. Realism, neorealism and the study of world politics. In Robert O. Keohane, ed., *Neo-realism and Its Critics*, pp. 2-26, Columbia University Press, New York.

Robert O. Keohane and Joseph Nye. 1977. *Power and Interdependence*. Little Brown, Boston.

Woosang Kim. 1987. Power, alliance, and major wars: 1816-1975. Unpublished manuscript. Hoover Institution: Stanford University, Stanford, CA.

Charles Kindleberger. 1969. *American Business Abroad: Six Lectures on Direct Investment*. Yale University Press, New Haven, CT.

Gregory King. 1973. Natural and political observations and conclusions upon the state and condition in England. In Lasslet, ed., *The Earliest Classics*, Gregg International, London. Originally published 1696.

Henry Kissinger. 1957. *A World Restored - Metternich, Castlereagh and the Problems of Peace 1812-1822*. Houghton Mifflin, Boston.

Henry Kissinger. 1979. *White House Years*. Little, Brown, Boston.

Klaus Knorr. 1956. *The War Potential of Nations*. Princeton University Press, Princeton, NJ.

Klaus Knorr. 1970. *Military Power and Potential*. D.C. Heath, Lexington, MA.

Stephen J. Kobrin. 1988. Testing the bargaining hypothesis in the manufacturing sector in developing countries. *International Organization*, 41:609-638.

Jacek Kugler. 1973. *The Consequences of War: Fluctuations in National Capabilities Following Major Wars: 1880-1970*. Ph.D. Dissertation, Microfilm Service, Ann Arbor, MI.

Jacek Kugler. 1983. The utilization of residuals: An option to indirectly measure concepts. *Political Methodology*, 9:103-120.

Jacek Kugler. 1984. Terror without deterrence? Reassessing the role of nuclear weapons. *Journal of Conflict Resolution*, 28:470-506.

Jacek Kugler and William Domke. 1986. Comparing the strength of nations. *Comparative Political Studies*. 19:39-69.

Jacek Kugler and A. F. K. Organski. 1988. The end of hegemony: Says who? mimeo.

Jacek Kugler and Frank C. Zagare. 1987. *Exploring the Stability of Deterrence*. Lynne Rienner Publishers, Boulder, CO.

Imre Lakatos. 1978. *The Methodology of Scientific Research Programs*. Cambridge University Press, Cambridge.

David Lalman. 1988. Conflict resolution and peace. *American Journal of Political Science*, 32:590-615.

Russell J. Leng. 1984. Reagan and the russians: Crisis bargaining beliefs and the historical record. *American Political Science Review*, 78:338-355.

Russell J. Leng and Hugh Wheeler. 1979. Influence strategies, success, and war. *Journal of Conflict Resolution*, 23:655-684.

Arthur Lewis. 1978. *Evaluation of the International Economic Order*. Princeton University Press, Princeton, NJ.

Richard Lindeman, Peter Merenda, and Ruth Gold. 1980. *Introduction to Bivariate and Multivariate Analysis*. Scott, Foresman, Glenville, IL.

Steven Lukes. 1974. *Power: A Radical View*. Macmillan, London.

Niccolo Machiavelli. 1950. *The Prince and the Discourses*. Random House, New York. Originally published 1513.

Andrew Mack. 1975. Why big nations lose small wars: The politics of asymmetric conflict. *World Politics*, 27:175-200.

Angus Maddison. 1969. *Economic Growth in Japan and the USSR*. W. W. Norton, New York.

Angus Maddison. 1982. *Phases of Capitalist Development*. Oxford University Press, New York.

C. Maier. 1988. Wargames: 1914-1919. *Journal of Interdisciplinary History*. 18:819-850.

Zeev Maoz. 1982. *Paths to Conflict: International Dispute Initiation. 1816-1976*. Westview Press, Boulder, CO.

Zeev Maoz. 1983. Resolve, capabilities, and the outcomes of interstate disputes. *Journal of Conflict Resolution*, 27:195-230.

James G. March. 1955. An introduction to the theory and measurement of influence. *American Political Science Review*, XLIX:431-451.

James G. March. 1957. Measurement concepts in the theory of influence. *Journal of Politics*. 19:202-26.

James G. March. 1966. The power of power. In David Easton, ed., *Varieties of Political Theory*, pp. 39-70, Prentice-Hall, Englewood Cliffs, NJ.

Charles A. McClelland. 1971. Power and influence. In John R. Champlin, ed., *Power*, Atherton Press, New York.

Charles A. McClelland. 1983. Let the user beware. *International Studies Quarterly*, 27:169-177.

Richard L. Merritt and Dina A. Zinnes. 1988. Validity of power indicators. *International Interactions*. 14:141-151.

Stephen Meyer. 1984. *The Dynamics of Nuclear Proliferation*. Chicago University Press, Chicago.

George Modelski. 1972. *Principles of World Politics*. The Free Press, New York.

George Modelski. 1987 *Long Cycles in World Politics*. University of Washington Press, Seattle, WA.

George Modelski and William R. Thompson. 1987. *Seapower in Global Politics 1494-1983*. University of Washington Press, Seattle.

Theodore H. Moran. 1974. *Multinational Corporations and the Politics of Dependence: Copper in Chile*. Princeton University Press, Princeton, NJ.

T. Clifton Morgan. 1984. A spatial model of crisis bargaining. *International Studies Quarterly*, 28:407-426.

T. Clifton Morgan. 1986. *Bargaining in international crises: A spatial model.* Ph.D. Dissertation, University of Texas at Austin.

T. Clifton Morgan. 1987. Power, resolve, and bargaining in international crises. Unpublished manuscript, Rice University.

T. Clifton Morgan. 1988a. Issue linkages in international crisis bargaining. Unpublished manuscript, Rice University.

T. Clifton Morgan. 1988b. Mediators, allies, and opportunists: Third parties in international crises. Unpublished manuscript, Rice University.

Oskar Morgenstern, Klaus Knorr, and Klaus Heiss. 1973. *Long Term Projections of Political and Military Power.* Ballinger, Cambridge, MA.

Hans Morgenthau. 1948. *Politics Among Nations: The Struggle for Power and Peace.* Alfred A. Knopf, New York.

Hans Morgenthau. 1954. *Politics Among Nations: The Struggle for Power and Peace (2nd ed.).* Alfred A. Knopf, New York.

Hans Morgenthau. 1962. *Politics Among Nations: The Struggle for Power and Peace.* Alfred A. Knopf, New York.

Hans Morgenthau and Kenneth W. Thompson. 1985. *Politics Among Nations: The Struggle for Power and Peace (6th ed.).* Alfred A. Knopf, New York.

James D. Morrow. 1985. A continuous-outcome expected utility theory of war. *Journal of Conflict Resolution.* 19:473-502.

James D. Morrow. 1987. On the theoretical basis of a measure of national risk attitudes. *International Studies Quarterly*, 31:423-438.

Benjamin A. Most and Harvey Starr. 1984. International relations theory, foreign policy substitutability, and 'nice' laws. *World Politics*, 36:383-406.

Michael G. Mulhall. 1892. *Dictionary of Statistics.* Routledge and Sons, London.

R. Musgrave. 1959. *The Theory of Public Finance.* McGraw-Hill, New York.

Lynn K. Mytelka. 1978. Technological dependence in the andean group. *International Organization*, 32:101-140.

Jack H. Nagel. 1975. *The Descriptive Analysis of Power.* Yale University Press, New Haven, CT.

John F. Nash. 1950. The bargaining problem. *Econometrica.* 18:97-109.

A. F. K. Organski. 1958. *World Politics.* Knopf, New York.

A. F. K. Organski. 1965. *The Stages of Political Development.* Knopf, New York.

A. F. K. Organski. 1968. *World Politics, (2nd ed.),* Knopf, New York.

A. F. K. Organski and Jacek Kugler. 1978. Davids and Goliaths: Predicting the outcomes of international wars. *Comparative Political Studies.* 11;141-180.

A. F. K. Organski and Jacek Kugler. 1980. *The War Ledger.* University of Chicago Press, Chicago.

A. F. K. Organski and Jacek Kugler, T. Johnson, and J. Cohen. 1984. *Births, Deaths and Taxes.* Chicago University Press, Chicago.

Kun Y. Park and Michael D. Ward. 1988. A research note on the correlates of war national capability data: Some revised procedures applied to the 1950-1980 era. *International Interactions.* 14:85-93.

Jan Pen. 1952. A general theory of bargaining. *The American Economic Review*, 27:24-42.

Raul Prebisch. 1950. *The Economic Development of Latin America and Its*

Principal Problems. United Nations Department of Economic Affairs, Lake Success, NY.

Karen A. Rasler and William R. Thompson. 1983. Global wars, public debts, and the long cycle. *World Politics*, 29:513-538.

James Lee Ray. 1986. The impact of nuclear weapons on the escalation of international conflicts. Paper presented at the Annual Meeting of the International Studies Association, Anaheim, CA, March 25-29.

James Lee Ray and J. David Singer. 1973. Measuring the concentration of power in the international system. *Sociological Methods and Research.* 1:403-437.

James Lee Ray and Ayse Vural. 1986. Power disparities and paradoxical conflict outcomes. *International Interactions.* 12:315-342.

David Riban. 1982. *Introduction to Physical Science.* McGraw-Hill, New York.

William H. Riker. 1964. Some ambiguities in the notion of power. *American Political Science Review*, 58:341-349.

William H. Riker. 1986. *The Art of Political Manipulation.* Yale University Press, New Haven, CT.

Fred S. Roberts. 1976. *Discrete Mathematical Models.* Prentice-Hall, Inc., Englewood Cliffs, NJ.

Steven Rosen. 1972. War power and the willingness to suffer. In Bruce Russett, ed., *Peace, War, and Numbers*, Sage, Beverly Hills, CA.

Bertrand Russell. 1938. *Power*, Norton, New York.

Bruce M. Russett. 1967. *International Regions and the International System: A Study in Political Ecology.* Rand McNally, Chicago, IL.

Bruce M. Russett. 1968a. Components of an operational theory of alliance formation. *Journal of Conflict Resolution.* 12:258-301.

Bruce M. Russett. 1968b. Is there a long-run trend toward concentration in the international system? *Comparative Political Studies.* 1:103-122.

Bruce M. Russett. 1968c. Delineating international regions. In J. David Singer, ed., *Quantitative International Politics: Insights and Evidence*, pp. 317-352, Free Press, New York.

Erwin K. Scheuch. 1966. Cross-national comparisons using aggregate data: Some substantive and methodological difficulties. In Richard L. Merritt and Stein Rokkan, eds., *Comparing Nations: The Use of Quantitative Data in Cross-National Research*, pp. 131-167, Yale University Press.

Steven T. Seitz. 1983. Modeling cross-national inquiry: Applications to sub-saharan Africa. Unpublished manuscript, University of Illinois at Urbana-Champaign.

Claude E. Shannon. 1948. A mathematical theory in communication. *Bell System Technical Journal*, 27:379-423, 623-656.

Herbert A. Simon. 1953. Notes on the observation and measurement of political power. *Journal of Politics.* 15:500-516.

Hans W. Singer. 1950. The distribution of gains between investing and borrowing countries. *American Economic Review*, 40:473-485.

J. David Singer. 1963. Inter-nation influence: A formal model. *American Political Science Review*, 57:420-30.

J. David Singer. 1966. The behavioral science approach to international relations: Payoffs and prospects. *SAIS Review*, X:12-20.

J. David Singer, Stuart Bremer, and John Stuckey. 1972. Capability distribution, uncertainty, and major-power war. In Bruce M. Russett, ed., *Peace, War and Numbers*, pp. 19-48, Sage, Beverly Hills, CA.

J. David Singer and Melvin Small. 1972. *The Wages of War. 1816-1965: A Statistical Handbook*. Wiley, New York.

Ruth Leger Sivard. 1983. *World Military and Social Expenditures 1980–81*. World Priorities, Leesburg, VA.

Melvin Small and J. David Singer. 1969. Formal alliances. 1816-1965: An extension of the basic data. *Journal of Peace Research*, pp. 258-282.

Melvin Small and J. David Singer. 1979. Conflict in the international system 1816-1977: Historical trends and policy futures. In J. David Singer, ed., *Explaining War*, Sage, Beverly Hills, CA.

Melvin Small and J. David Singer. 1982. *Resort to Arms: International and Civil War. 1816-1980*. Sage, Beverly Hills, CA.

Duncan Snidal. 1985. The limits of hegemonic stability theory. *International Organization*, 39:580-614.

Lewis W. Snider. 1987. Identifying the elements of state power: Where do we begin? *Comparative Political Studies*, 20:314-356.

Michael Stob. 1984. A supplement to "A Mathematician's Guide to Popular Sports." *American Mathematical Monthly*, 91:277-282.

Stockholm International Peace Research Institute. 1985. *World Armaments and Disarmaments, SIPRI Yearbook 1986*. Oxford University Press, Oxford.

Richard J. Stoll. 1982. Major power interstate conflict in the Post-World War II era. *Western Political Quarterly*, 35:587-605.

Richard J. Stoll. 1984. Power capabilities; indicators and inferences. Paper presented at the 25th Annual Convention of the International Studies Association, Atlanta, GA.

Richard J. Stoll. 1986. National survival in an anarchic world: A computer simulation. Paper presented at Annual Conference of the International Studies Association, Anaheim, CA.

Richard J. Stoll. 1987. System and state in international politics: A computer simulation. mimeo, Rice University.

Richard J. Stoll. 1988. The use of force in the Post-World War II era. Unpublished manuscript, Rice University.

Susan Strange. 1975. What is economic power and who has it? *International Journal*, 30:207-224.

Charles Lewis Taylor and Michael C. Hudson. 1972. *World Handbook of Political and Social Indicators (2nd ed.)*. Yale University Press, New Haven, CT.

Charles Lewis Taylor and David A. Jodice. 1983. *World Handbook of Political and Social Indicators (3d ed.)*. Yale University Press, New Haven, CT.

Thucydides. 1951. *The Peloponneisan War*. Random House, New York. Originally published circa 450 B.C.

Edward Tufte. 1983. *The Visual Display of Quantitative Information*. Graphic Press, Hartford, CT.

Franklin Tugwell. 1975. *The Politics of Oil in Venezuela*. Stanford University Press, Stanford, CA.

Union of International Associations. 1981. *Handbook of International Organizations (19th ed.)*. Union of International Organizations, Brussels.

United Nations. 1982. *Industrial Statistics Yearbook*. United Nations, New York.

United Nations. 1982. *Yearbook of International Trade Statistics*. United Nations, New York.

United Nations. 1983. *Energy Statistics Yearbook*. United Nations, New York.

United Nations. 1983. *National Account Statistics*. United Nations, New York.

United Nations. 1984. *Statistical Yearbook*, United Nations, New York.

United States Arms Control and Disarmament Agency. 1986. *World Military Expenditures and Arms Transfers*. U.S. Government Printing Office, Washington, D.C.

Constantine Vaitsos. 1974. *Inter-Country Income Distribution and Transnational Enterprises*. Clarendon Press, Oxford.

John Vasquez. 1983. *The Power of Power Politics*. Rutgers University Press, New Brunswick, NJ.

Raymond Vernon. 1971. *Sovereignty at Bay: The Multinational Spread of U.S. Enterprises*. Basic Books, New York.

Friedrich Waismann. 1951. *Introduction to Mathematical Thinking*. Frederick Ungar, New York.

Immanuel Wallerstein. 1979. *The Capitalist World Economy*. Cambridge University Press, Cambridge.

Immanuel Wallerstein. 1974. *The Modern World System: Capitalist Agriculture and the Origins of the European World Economy in the Sixteenth Century*. Academic, New York.

Kenneth W. Waltz. 1979. *Theory of International Politics*. Addison-Wesley, Reading, MA.

Kenneth W. Waltz. 1982. *The Spread of Nuclear Weapons; More May be Better*. Adelphi paper no. 171. International Institute for Strategic Studies, London.

Michael D. Ward and Lewis L. House. 1988. A theory of the behavioral power of nations. *Journal of Conflict Resolution*, 32:3-36.

Frank Wayman, J. David Singer, and Gary Goertz. 1983. Capabilities, allocations, and success in militarized disputes and wars 1816-1976. *International Studies Quarterly*, 27:497-515.

Erich Weede. 1983, Extended deterrence by superpower alliance. *Journal of Conflict Resolution*, 27:231-254.

Martin Wight. 1946. *Power Politics*. Royal Institute of International Affairs, London.

Martin Wight. 1977. *Systems of States*. Leicester University Press, Leicester.

Arnold Wolfers. 1962. *Discord and Collaboration: Essays on International Politics*. Johns Hopkins University Press, Baltimore.

World Bank. 1980. *World Tables (2nd ed.)*. Johns Hopkins University Press, Baltimore.

World Bank. 1984. *World Development Report*. Oxford University Press, New York.

World Bank. 1984. *World Tables*. Johns Hopkins University Press, Baltimore.

David B. Yoffie. 1983. *Power and Protectionism; Strategies of the Newly Industrializing Countries*. Columbia University Press, New York.

Frederick Zeuthen. 1968. *Problems of Monopoly and Economic Warfare*. Augustus M. Kelley, New York.

Index

agenda setting, 103
aid, foreign, 53, 69. *See also* investment
analysis: choice-theoretic framework for, 101; of power as situational and relational, 101; of power as structure, 104–109; of power as success, 103
anarchy, 210
attribute: capabilities, 104; power as, 30–31, 101
attributes, national, 42

balance: of power, 6, 135, 137–138, 140, 160–161, 177–182, 186–187, 189–191, 212, 219; strategic, 17–18, 24, 53
bargaining: crisis, 193–208; theory of, 105
bargaining power, 109. *See also* less developed countries
behavioral power, 5, 121–133; per unit, 126; salience of, 125
bipolar world, 140. *See also* world view

capabilities, 17, 23, 51; applied, 89–90; combat, 17–18, 53; demographic, 16, 55; domestic political, 110; exchange, 105–107; industrial, 16, 56; material, 124–126; military, 16–17, 33, 53–54, 56, 137–138, 166, 173; national, 54–55, 79–80, 87–91, 94; power, 1–2; power as, 122.

See also attribute; resources; variables
capability: economic, 138; nuclear, 23, 33, 53. *See also* power capability
capacity: economic, 17, 53; military, 53; political, 53, 68–70, 73, 167–173. *See also* measurement; relative political capacity
center and periphery, relations between, 114, 116. *See also* world view
commitment, 17, 23; national, 54
computer simulation, 6
conflict, international, 194. *See also* outcome
confrontation test, 39–40
consumption: of energy, 14, 16, 21, 53, 56; of fuel, 14, 33, 53
conversion process, power as, 110–113, 117–118
COPDAB, 124, 128
Correlates of War: index, 56–61, 63–65, 67, 70–71, 73–74; project, 5, 24, 33, 54–55, 91, 122, 128, 141–143, 153–154, 175, 186–187
correlations, 24, 38
COW. *See* Correlates of War
critical mass, 53

data, aggregate, 12. *See also* COPDAB
decisionmaking, 6, 100–101, 103–104, 116–117

About the Book

After a period of some stasis, scholars in the field of international relations are returning to an exploration of power relationships in world politics, with a careful eye toward avoiding the "bigger is better" syndrome that characterized much prior research. In this state-of-the-art book, they focus on what power is and what it is not, on the ways in which power has been assessed, and on the major lessons for international politics that can be gleaned through an analysis of power.